Sound-Bite Saboteurs

Sound-Bite Saboteurs

Public Discourse, Education,
and the State of Democratic Deliberation

JULIE DREW
WILLIAM LYONS
LANCE SVEHLA

SUNY
PRESS

Cover photo: tv screens image by Erik Reis/iStockphoto.com

Published by
State University of New York Press, Albany

For information, contact State University of New York Press, Albany, NY
www.sunypress.edu

Production by Diane Ganeles
Marketing by Anne M. Valentine

Library of Congress Cataloging-in-Publication Data

Drew, Julie.
    Sound-bite saboteurs : public discourse, education, and the state of
democratic deliberation / Julie Drew, William Lyons, and Lance Svehla.
        p. cm.
    Includes bibliographical references and index.
    ISBN 978-1-4384-3041-6 (hardcover : alk. paper)
    ISBN 978-1-4384-3042-3 (pbk. : alk. paper)
    1. Communication in politics—United States.   2. Mass media—Political
aspects—United States.   3. Political participation—United States.
I. Lyons, William.   II. Svehla, Lance.   III. Title.

JA85.2.U6D74 2010
320.97301'4—dc22   2009021885

10 9 8 7 6 5 4 3 2 1

For our fathers

Contents

Acknowledgments

This book is a labor of love, and like all books, the work that went into it was done by many. This book is possible because of the State University of New York (SUNY) Press Editorial Board and the enthusiastic support of our editor, James Peltz. We would also like to thank Diane Ganeles at SUNY Press for her hard work and keen editorial eye. We would like to thank our students and colleagues, the Departments of English and Political Science, and the Buchtel College of Arts & Sciences at The University of Akron for their ongoing support of our research and writing and to say "nice working with you"—which we really mean—to each other. We would also like to thank *EAPSU Online: A Journal of Critical and Creative Work* and its editor, Kim Martin Long, for permission to reprint portions of the essay "The Supremacy of the Image: Urban Students and the Idea of Secondary Orality." In addition, we each have a few people to thank by name:

Julie feels more than just a little lucky in her friends and colleagues Sid Dobrin, Joe Hardin, and Raúl Sánchez. These are her go-to guys for reading drafts, discussing ideas, and brainstorming at CCCC—not everyone gets to have that much fun while working, and she knows it. She thanks her family for their interest, support, and love: Philip and Brian Anderson; Joyce and Charles Byrd; Bill and Cheryl Drew; Jim, Sue, and Katy Drew; and Bill Lyons, most of all.

Bill would like to express his appreciation to Stuart Scheingold, Michael McCann, Bill Haltom, Austin Sarat, Helena Silverstein, Michael Musheno, Diana Kingsbury, and Bob Niery. He thanks his sons Philip and Brian, his brothers Tom and Ray, his sisters Lori, Andrea, Jenny, and Amanda, his mother Maryann, and his father Bill Sr. for all the ways they have each provided him feedback on his work for years, including on work that contributed to this project.

Lance would like to thank his mentors Thomas Newkirk and Patricia Sullivan. Their intelligence, example, and compassion continue to influence his thinking, writing, and teaching. He would also like to thank Jinny Marting for diligently reading almost everything he writes and for taking a shine to him (for no apparent reason). Finally, he would like to thank his father Joseph, mother Bessie, and siblings Jeff, Scott, Lisa, and Steven. He carries their love and memory with him everywhere he goes.

———————

Sound-Bite Sabotage

Illustrative Stories and Techniques

Built on a foundation of urban legend mixed with the occasional true story, supported by selective references to academic studies, and repeated so often even the mythmakers forget the exaggeration, half truth, and outright misinformation employed in the service of their greater good, the medical malpractice myth has filled doctors, patients, legislators, and voters with the kind of fear that short circuits critical thinking.

—Thomas Baker, *The Medical Malpractice Myth*

"Blowback". . . . It's a CIA term. Blowback does not mean simply the unintended consequences of foreign operations. It means the unintended consequences of foreign operations that are deliberately kept secret from the American public. So that when the retaliation comes, the American public is not able to put it in context, to put cause and effect together, then they come up with questions like "why do they hate us?"

—Chalmers Johnson, former CIA agent, in *Why We Fight*

I. Introduction

This book is about sound-bite sabotage—the saturation of our communication channels with interested messages disguised to appear as disinterested public information—and these phenomena are growing, and of growing concern. In 2004, during an intensely fought presidential election, Dan Rather claimed on *60 Minutes II* that he had new evidence to prove that President Bush had not completed his Texas Air National Guard duties and had lied about it. An investigation resulted in the firing of four senior executives. The Republican and Democratic Party spin on the president's new prescription drug plan only adds to citizen confusion about how to fix our health care crisis. Interest groups on all sides of the aisle saturate communication channels with interested messages designed to sell branded information about policy alternatives, candidate positions, and war and peace. Fake news emerges as a major growth industry, colonizing our living rooms and schools, town hall meetings, and water cooler conversations with reconstructed conventional wisdom that is often contrary to the best available data, and yet widely accepted as simply common sense. Taken together, this amounts to a phenomena we call sound-bite sabotage, and it is poisoning democracy in America. We start our analysis with the following recent examples:

> Rather's scoop began to unravel almost instantly, thanks to intrepid bloggers. CBS posted the documents on its website the night of the *60 Minutes II* broadcast. "Buckhead," a conservative lawyer writing in the conservative FreeRepublic.com site, called the memos forgeries a few hours later. . . . CBS dug in, calling the bloggers "partisan political" operatives. . . . Talk radio started to cover Rathergate "like a blanket," says veteran radio host Mike Siegel. Fox News did, too. At last, the pressure grew so great that mainstream outlets ABC News and the *Washington Post* began to report the story. *The New York Times* held out a bit longer—it *so* wanted to believe that the story would hurt Bush that it actually ran a headline proclaiming the memos "Fake but Accurate". . . . What emerged under this new-media and old-media spotlight wasn't pretty. CBS, it turned out, had received the memos from notorious Texan Bush-hater Bill Burkett. The network's own document experts refused to authenticate the memos. (Anderson 2005, x–xiii).

> Democrats are overselling their Medicare prescription drug bill. They claim it will bring about big price cuts for medication while Medicare experts say it won't. Republicans have been equally misleading, describing the bill as a system of severe price controls, which it isn't.

The fact is that the bill would do little more than require the Secretary of Health and Human Services to talk to drug companies about granting discounts. It specifically denies him the bargaining leverage of paying only for some drugs and not others. (Factcheck.org, January 17, 2007)

MoveOn.org Political Action began airing ads attacking four Republican senators in their home states, accusing them of favoring escalation of the war in Iraq and saying all are "willing to send tens of thousands more troops to face danger in Iraq." The ads clearly misrepresent the stands of three of the targeted senators, who in fact had publicly expressed strong disapproval of sending additional U.S. troops. (Factcheck.org, February 9, 2007)

The mid-term elections of 2006 brought an unprecedented barrage of advertising containing much that is false or misleading. We found examples of disregard for facts and honesty—on both sides—that would get a reporter fired in a heartbeat from any decent news organization. Candidates, parties and independent groups have faked quotes, twisted words, misrepresented votes and positions, and engaged in rank fear-mongering and outright fabrication. In addition to a general disregard for factual accuracy, we also found systematic attempts to mislead voters about some of the most important issues of the day. [What follows are only two examples from a much longer account.] A Democratic-leaning group ran false ads accusing a few Republican senators of voting to deny modern body armor for troops in Iraq. In fact, the amendment cited by the ad didn't mention body armor, and passing it wouldn't have allowed the Pentagon to acquire a single additional armored vest: It already was buying as many as the economy could produce. A Democratic Senatorial Campaign Committee ad repeated this false claim even after we de-bunked it. Republicans repeatedly mischaracterized the Democratic position on President Bush's National Security Agency eavesdropping program, which is being conducted without court warrants or review. An ad by the pro-Bush group Progress for America falsely gave those wiretaps credit for the thwarting of a hijack plot that was actually uncovered by Scotland Yard following up an informant's tip. (Factcheck.org).[1]

In seeking to defeat the nomination of John Ashcroft as attorney general, liberals tried to do more than make Ashcroft out to be a racist. Without argument, they sought to relocate the "mainstream" leftward, in order to make any conservative seem well out of it, an extremist. Even ostensible moderate Joe Lieberman exploited this tactic: "On issues ranging from civil rights to privacy rights," Lieberman intoned in voting against his former Senate colleague, "Senator Ashcroft has repeatedly taken positions considerably outside the mainstream of American thinking." But consider Lieberman's two stated examples: civil rights (read: racial preferences) and privacy rights (read: abortion). Columnist Charles Krauthammer correctly responds, "In a country so divided on these issues, can one seriously argue that opposing abortion and racial preferences is proof of extremism?" (Anderson 2005, 28–29)

In 2007 four Republican lawmakers visited Iraq and reported that the situation was improving. One of the four, Senator John McCain, took the opportunity to repeat the Bush Administration's sound bite about the media failing to report the good news in Iraq, as he noted how safe he was simply strolling through a Bagdad market. Representative Mike Pence (R-Indiana) added that "thousands and thousands of Iraqis were moving about in regular everyday life, like a normal outdoor market in Indiana in the summertime." But his observations were challenged in the Associated Press by a textile merchant with a shop in that market who said that the politicians "sealed off the area, put themselves in flak jackets and walked in the middle of tens of American soldiers. The market has been the target of car bombs in the past and yesterday it was the scene of sniper fire." (AP, morning edition, April 3, 2007)

II. Sound-Bite Sabotage Defined

Sound-bite saboteurs on all sides of the aisle try to move the opinion of publics toward positions that are contrary to the best available data. Rather than communicating with publics to enable more informed decision making, sound-bite sabotage occurs when public and private leaders use the tools of public relations to discredit the importance of using data, engaging in scholarly inquiry, and supporting democratic deliberation.

Seeing (hearing, reading, experiencing) sound-bite sabotage draws our attention to the commodification of political discourse rather than to the political spectacles constructed, to distract citizens from the communicative strategies mobilized by public and private elites. These strategies, like sound-bite sabotage, increase citizen confusion, encourage more passive forms of citizenship, and make citizens more vulnerable to distorted information and elites more dependent on fear mongering and spin in their efforts to manage blowback. Our analysis focuses directly on the instrumental and institutional biases that distort our information systems in ways that privilege certain ways of framing news and policy debates and water cooler conversations over others.

The organizational biases of interest group activities, news media work routines, the pressure from public relations experts to govern in order to win elections (instead of winning elections in order to govern), concentration of media ownership, deliberate efforts to weaken Federal Communications Commission (FCC) oversight of political communication, and other institutional factors converge to promote the privatization of political discourse by enabling sound-bite saboteurs to more effectively saturate old and new communication channels with interested messages, what we call branded information. Before we proceed with our identification of the techniques used by sound-bite saboteurs, we offer two more detailed illustrations of sound-bite sabotage. The first is based on work done by Jeffrey Smith on the political struggles over genetically modified foods, and the second is based on Eric Schlosser's detailed analysis of the real costs of living in a fast food nation.

Planting Seeds of Deception?

Information about nutrition that we often take as common sense or basic science—information that impacts how we feed ourselves and our children—is increasingly branded information.[2] The widespread production and consumption of genetically modified (GM) foods today is a potentially very serious risk to public health, because the science, largely controlled by private corporations, has yet to demonstrate that genetically modified food is safe to produce or consume. In fact, there has yet to be a serious effort to test, measure, and publish studies needed to even begin responding to myriad concerns about cancers, damage to DNA, allergies, the propagation of new viruses, increased antibiotic resistance, and threats to sustainable agriculture. Instead of spending on published research and support for Food and Drug Administration (FDA) testing, GM manufacturers have invested in public relations efforts to persuade us that their secret processes are highly precise (when the evidence suggests they are not) and so safe that testing and labeling—widespread outside of the United States—are unnecessary. Barry Commoner, senior scientist for the Center for Biology of Natural Systems at Queens College, said,

> None of [the] essential tests are being performed, and billions of transgenic plants are now being grown with only the most rudimentary knowledge about [their changes]. . . . Without detailed, ongoing analyses, there is no way of knowing if hazardous consequences might arise. . . . The genetically engineered crops now being grown represent a massive uncontrolled experiment whose outcome is inherently unpredictable. The results could be catastrophic. (qtd. in Smith 2003, 75)

In 1986, Monsanto came to the White House in search of *more* government regulation. They were investing billions in new technologies to genetically modify food, and they were afraid that consumers would reject GM foods as unsafe, because consumers might recall earlier Monsanto falsehoods about the safety of Agent Orange and PCBs, both now linked to cancer, birth defects, and environmental degradation. In addition to Monsanto's massive public relations efforts, aimed at making public opinion an instrument of business power, "they also needed federal regulations." As Smith argues,

> With that in place, it would be the government, not Monsanto, who would be assuring the public that GM products were safe. . . . Washington insiders watched with astonishment as the company dictated policy to the Agriculture Department (USDA), Environmental Protection Agency (EPA), and ultimately the Food and Drug Administration (FDA). According to Henry Miller, who was in charge of biotechnology issues at the FDA from 1979–1994, "the U.S. government agencies have done exactly what big agribusiness has asked them to do and told them to do." (2003, 29)

Smith reports that public criticism of lax FDA regulation led the Clinton administration to propose changes that Representative Dennis Kucinich (D-Ohio) described as "meaningless changes" designed to "deflect legitimate concerns" (2003, 146). And even these meaningless changes were never implemented by the Clinton administration. With the United States standing virtually alone, President Clinton chose to distract our attention from public safety issues as he pressured British Prime Minister Tony Blair to increase United Kingdom (UK) support for GM foods and U.S. leadership in the biotechnology sector. This public-sector spin was coordinated with private-sector public relations efforts. "Many of the world's media, particularly in the United States, have been the target of an intensive pro-biotech campaign by the industry" (2003, 183). It was so intensive that two reporters for a Florida Fox television station who researched a story that challenged Monsanto safety claims discovered that the Monsanto spokesperson routinely used phrases calculated to divert attention and to misinform, and Fox News would not support the reporters' investigative work. After Monsanto, a major advertiser on Fox, raised concerns, the station manager was fired. Fox offered to buy out the contracts of the two reporters, and when they refused, Fox attorneys insisted on eighty-three rewrites over the next six months.

> Among the numerous changes, Akre and Wilson were instructed to never reveal that the FDA's approval of rbGH was based on "short-term" testing. They were allowed to include an interview with Samuel Epstein, M.D., who stated, there "are lines of evidence showing that consumption of this milk poses risks of breast and colon cancer." The reporters were instructed, however, "not to include information that details the basis for this frightening claim." They had to remove all mention of IGF-1 [Monsanto's own studies showed an increase in IGF-1 in milk from treated cows, and other studies suggest that undigested IGF-1 is a serious problem] and any relevant studies and were not to use the word cancer again in any segments—referring only to "human health implications." The reporters also had to downplay Epstein's credentials.
>
> According to a website that documents the rewrites [see http://www.foxbghsuit.com] and the dispute, despite Epstein's "three medical degrees, a professorship of Occupational and Environmental Medicine at the University of Illinois School of Public Health, his frequent Congressional testimony as an expert on public health and environmental causes of cancer, his authorship of seven books. . . . Original references to him as a 'reputable scientist' . . . later changed

> to 'respected scientist' . . . and then 'well-credentialed M.D.'
> which was okay in Versions 10–18 until, ultimately, report-
> ers were told no such reference was acceptable." The final
> reference was simply "Scientist, University of Illinois."
> Similarly, the credentials of a second scientist, William von
> Meyer, were stripped. (Smith 2003, 191)

In this case the revisions moved from: "Dr. von Meyer has spent
thirty years studying chemical products and testing their effects on
humans. He's supervised many such tests on thousands of animals
at schools such as the University of London and UCLA. He's headed
agricultural, chemical and genetic research at some of America's most
prestigious companies" to: "scientist in Wisconsin" (Smith 2003, 191).
Smith continues:

> Despite the intense scrutiny of every claim that opposed
> rbGH, Akre and Wilson "were repeatedly instructed to
> include unverified and even some outright false statements
> by Monsanto's research director." These included:
>
> • Dr. von Meyer "has no credentials in human safety
>   evaluation."
>
> • "The cancer experts don't see the health issue."
>
> • "There are no human or animal safety issues that would
>   prevent approval."
>
> Monsanto's director also repeated a popular Monsanto claim
> that "Posilac [rbGH] is the single most-tested product in
> history." According to the reporters, however, "experts
> in the field of domestic animal science say that this claim
> is demonstrably false." (Smith 2003, 191–92)

When Fox insisted on even more falsehoods and the reporters refused,
they were fired. Then they sued Fox. While the reporters won numerous prestigious awards for courage in journalism, and the initial jury
ruled in their favor, an appeals court threw it out and compelled them
to pay the legal fees Fox News had incurred, a team that included
President Clinton's former personal attorney, fees amounting to millions of dollars (Smith 2003, 193).

What Are the Real Costs of Fast Food?

Anyone who has read the magnificent investigative analysis done
by Eric Schlosser in *Fast Food Nation* knows that he debunks several

interrelated myths that both prop up the fast food industry and harm Americans. One myth is that the West was won simply by rugged individualists entirely disdainful of big government. Schlosser writes:

> The political philosophy that now prevails in so much of the West—with its demand for lower taxes, smaller government, an unbridled free market—stands in total contradiction to the region's true economic underpinnings. No other region of the United States has been so dependent on government subsidies for so long, from the nineteenth-century construction of railroads to the twentieth-century financing of its military bases and dams. One historian has described the federal government's 1950's highway-building binge as a case study in "interstate socialism"—a phrase that aptly describes how the West was really won. The fast food industry took root alongside that interstate highway system. . . . [And] the fast food industry has worked closely with its allies in Congress and the White House to oppose new worker safety, food safety, and minimum wage laws. While publicly espousing support for the free market, the fast food chains have quietly pursued and greatly benefited from a wide variety of government subsidies. Far from being inevitable, America's fast food industry in its present form is the logical outcome of certain political and economic choices. (Schlosser 2002, 7–8)

When we are misinformed about how the West was won, our energies in defense of what actually does make America strong are dissipated into trivial and counterproductive sound-bite battles. We battle over insulating corporations from public oversight instead of a reasoned debate about which of the various ways that the government might regulate the economy are the most likely to continue and enhance our long tradition of balancing support for private property rights, and for protecting public health, public education, small farmers, and small businessmen.

When we are misinformed about how the West was won, this intentionally distorted context provides no way for us to understand why groups such as the IFA (International Franchise Association) hire insider lobbyists to stop government regulation that would have protected small business owners and to pressure public officials to ensure passage of government regulations providing loans to corporate headquarters that were originally designated for small businesses.

In this case, by defining franchises as small businesses only for the purposes of securing these loans, additional pressure was applied to be sure that franchise managers would not be defined as small business owners for the purposes of securing protection from corporate policies that would be illegal if applied to small businesses (Schlosser 2002, 101).

When we are misinformed about how the West was won, we are less vigilant about preventing government regulation that amounts to corporate welfare and encouraging government regulation that helps ease the transition from sunset to sunrise industries. We are also less vigilant about punishing corporate misconduct that does more harm to Americans each year than the total number of homicides nationwide, particularly misconduct like that of Enron or LTV Steel that undermines resilient communities, weakens family values, squanders the retirement savings of others, and disrupts the ability of the free market to generate general prosperity. While public and private leaders are always ready to focus citizen attention to support Wars on Crime, they are conspicuously silent on the even greater need for a War on the Unsafe Workplace.

> American deaths from work-related injuries per day: 16
> American deaths from work-related disease per day: 137
> Total work-related deaths per day: 153
> Total American work-related deaths per year: 55,845
> (Source: http://www.ucop.edu/cprc/occuhealth.pdf)

When we are misinformed about how the West was won, we are more likely to dismiss policy positions that involve government action or tax increases, even though we know from history that it was taxpayer dollars—government subsidies—that paid for the railroads and moon launches . . . and the highways that allowed Iowa Beef Packers (IBP) to "put its new slaughterhouses in rural areas close to the feedlots and far away from the urban strongholds of the nation's labor unions" (Schlosser 2002, 154). And these new slaughterhouses paid wages that were more than 50 percent lower than what the existing, community-centered, union, and pro-family values locations in Chicago were paying. The enormous corporate profits that resulted were not, then, a result of rugged individualists shunning government but, rather, taxpayer supported and individualistic corporate leaders *seeking* government intervention and support to undermine the financial stability of ordinary working class families and their communities. Instead of a reasonable debate about how to best raise funds to accomplish shared objectives, we are misinformed into dismissing any mention of taxation as if taxes were a threat to democratic prosperity rather than an investment in American power and wealth and progress, as a sober analysis of our history demonstrates. When we allow ourselves to believe that it was a market free from government regulation that made us the most prosperous nation on earth, we accept a phony and an inaccurate portrayal of the context within which we debate tax and spend questions today. And, importantly, we cripple our efforts to achieve our shared objective for an equally prosperous future.

When we are misinformed about how the West was won, the displacement of sober analysis by branded information creates an informational context within which we cannot fully understand the self-interested hypocrisy advertised when Walt Disney and Ray Kroc tell us American prosperity depends on a market freed from government regulation even as they pressure public officials for government regulation favorable to their private interests. While both men were self-made and innovative, particularly in developing powerful ways to market to children, their own behavior contradicts their rhetorical love affair with bashing government involvement in the economy. They contributed to candidates and pressured officials to regularly secure enormous government support and favors. "Despite a passionate opposition to socialism and to any government meddling with free enterprise, Walt Disney relied on federal funds in the 1940s to keep his business afloat." Disney and Kroc used their influence to secure special legislation giving them approval to pay below the minimum wage, to raise prices during a national price freeze, and to market to young children on television (Schlosser 2002, 31–46). And despite all the bluster about individual liberty and freedom from large bureaucratic organizations, both men treated customers and employees as enemies, because customer and employee individuality threatened the uniformity required to drive these organizations' business model and to recreate America as a fast food nation. Schlosser writes:

> Franchises and chain stores strive to offer exactly the same product or service at numerous locations. Customers are drawn to familiar brands by an instinct to avoid the unknown. A brand offers a feeling of reassurance when its products are always and everywhere the same. "We have found out . . . that we cannot trust some people who are nonconformists," declared Ray Kroc, one of the founders of McDonalds, angered by some of his franchisees. "We will

make conformists out of them in a hurry. . . . The organization cannot trust the individual; the individual must trust
the organization." (2002, 5)

Only when we are misinformed about something as fundamental
as the observed relationship between public and private sectors does it
then make sense to see our choices as either (1) interest group activity
is corrupt or (2) interest group activity is democracy in action. This
is a false choice, and *Fast Food Nation* demonstrates that fact. Interest
group activity (party activity, media activity, institutional activity, social
movement activity) is complex, sometimes corrupt, and other times
democratizing, but when we approach analysis wielding a branded
and mythical view of the relationship between market and government,
we are not equipped to reject this false choice and replace it with the
analysis needed to address the actual conflicts we face.

Interest group politics is neither corrupt nor democracy in action;
it does, however, have a major influence on policy making. It *can* be
democracy in action, it *can* be conducted in more or less corrupt ways,
and the level of corruption rises and falls over time, as a function of
many factors (including the rise or decline in effective government
oversight). We need to see these complex and contingent dynamics
clearly to understand politics, and the impact of sound-bite sabotage on
public discourse and civic education. When interest groups work well,
they provide powerfully important and timely information to policy
makers, and regulations reflect the best available data, emerging from
a process where all of the key stakeholders have provided meaningful input and contributed to an open and a deliberative process that
even those on different sides of the aisle can support as legitimate.
When interest group activity corrupts decision making and distorts
information, political scientists call it "capture." Capture suggests that
the executive and congressional branch agencies set up to oversee the
free market actors in any relevant industry have been transformed.
Instead of providing public-sector oversight, they become passive
enablers or industry cheerleaders, dependent on industry funds and
information to win elections and justify policy decisions. We can see
this dynamic in *Fast Food Nation*, tort reform advocacy, medical malpractice legislation, campaign finance reform, FDA regulatory efforts,
and other areas we will discuss throughout this book.

In Scholsser's words, this view of politics sees outcomes as "far
from inevitable. America's fast food industry in its present form is the
logical outcome of certain political and economic choices," (2002, 8),
and it is our job as citizens to understand that, and to reward those

choices we approve of and punish those we disapprove of when we vote, when we choose a career, and in what we choose to consume. And with this in mind, we are now able to see, and debate, the real costs of living in a fast food culture. Costs—hidden by sound-bite sabotage—that would at least include declining public health, rising obesity costing nearly $100 billion a year (with half of this sum paid with public tax dollars), cancers, heart disease, strokes, a declining quality of life, shrinking family farms, and disappearing living-wage manufacturing jobs being replaced by service-sector jobs, real wages that peaked in 1973, more two-income families, fewer families eating together at the dining room table, 30,000 commercials a year to overwhelm 365 dinner times a year as a branded public pedagogy suffocating parental efforts to teach our children, more children who recognize the golden arches than the Christian cross, landscapes redrawn with identical, corporate-owned franchises replacing locally owned, neighborhood mom-and-pop stores, corporate-sponsored playgrounds and children's clubs designed as viral marketing tools, and conformist managers who sign away their legal rights as a new ideal for citizenship (Schlosser 2002, 3–10, 42–47).

A more sober view of how particular forms of public-sector and private-sector partnerships have, historically, accounted for American prosperity and freedom (as well as inequality) would begin with an analysis of "the centrality of government in wealth creation from ancient times . . . as well as at its continuing great importance" (xix), as done by Republican Party strategist Kevin Phillips in his detailed political history of the American rich, *Wealth and Democracy*.[3] Phillips identifies right utopianism as the Republican malady that parallels the more commonly criticized left utopianism of Democrats. He writes:

> Whereas liberal eras often fail through utopias of social justice, brotherhood, and peace, the repetitious abuses by conservatives in the United States in turn involve worship of markets (the utopianism of the Right), elevation of self-interest rather than community, and belief in Darwinian precepts such as survival of the fittest. (2002, xxi)

And Phillips concludes that right utopian thinking results in an empirically unfounded faith in sound-bite bugaboos such as big government, or platitudes such as an unconstrained free market, mobilized to obscure the fact that wealth creation and prosperity in America have always been intimately linked to strong and widespread government action in and in support of private-sector actors. His analysis of our own history reveals both a very different formula for American prosperity and ongoing efforts to miseducate citizens with branded information peddling an ahistorical and un-American perspective on democratic capitalism.

> Laissez-faire is a pretense. *Government power and preferment have been used by the rich, not shunned.* As wealth concentration grows, especially near the crest of a drawn-out boom, so has upper-bracket control of politics and its ability to shape its own preferment. The public has reason to be aroused, because the cost to ordinary Americans has been substantial—in reduced median family income, in stagnant wages, in a diminished sense of community and commonweal, in fewer private and governmental services, and sometimes in poorer physical and mental health amid money-culture values, work hours, and competitive consumption. (Phillips 2002, xiv, emphasis added)

As Phillips points out, the proportion of total U.S. income going to the top 1 percent of our population has steadily increased over the past twenty years. In 1981, it was 9.3 percent. In 1997, it had risen to 15.8 percent, bringing it back up to 1929 levels. When we examine family wealth rather than income, the data is even more telling. The top 1 percent of American families controlled 19.9 percent of total family wealth in 1976, but that has risen steadily since that time to again reach a level not seen since 1929—in 1997, the top 1 percent of American families controlled 40.1 percent of total family wealth. The land of the free and home of the brave now stands, according to World Bank data, as a nation with more extreme economic inequality than that found in any of our closest allies, a gap that has grown through Republican and Democratic presidencies. From 1977 to 1994, according to the Congressional Budget Office, the changes in income by quintile are as follows:

> Percent Change in After-Tax Income, 1977–1994
> Poorest quintile of Americans: −16%
> Lower-middle-class quintile: −8%
> Middle-class quintile: −1%
> Upper-middle-class quintile: +4%
> Wealthiest 1 percent of Americans: +72%
> (Source: Phillips 2002, 121–37)

But U.S. income inequality is not only extreme relative to our allies, but it is extreme relative to our own history. When compared to the income distribution that prevailed in the four decades following World War II, we get a more accurate sense of what nostalgia for the fifties ought to really mean. In 1950, corporations paid 26.5 percent of total taxes collected, and payroll taxes were only 6.9 percent of the total. In 2000, corporations paid 10.2 percent (*before* the Bush administration's enormous tax cuts for the wealthiest individuals and corporations), and payroll taxes made up 31.1 percent of total taxes collected (Phillips 2002, 149). In this context, it is not difficult to imagine a political utility in sound-bite sabotage at the policy level and at the meta-conflict level of seeding public opinion with interested and favorable perspectives on democratic governance that serve to distract our attention from fears that point to the powerful, with fears that target tree-hugging liberals, teachers' unions, frivolous litigation, stranger predators, and political correctness.

Understanding how sound-bite sabotage works focuses our attention on the instrumental and institutional factors contributing to the commodification of political discourse by public-sector and private-sector leaders willing and able to saturate our communication channels with interested messages—about a variety of topics, from political opponents, to genetically modified foods, the free market, or the nature of democratic deliberation—messages we call branded information. The privatization of the ways we talk about politics matters in at least two important ways. First, as private-sector communication techniques, developed to sell Coke in the private sector, gradually come to dominate institutional dynamics central to our political communication, we observe a learning process that is antithetical to democratic deliberations. While it may be true that our choice of Coke over Pepsi is benign, a matter of personal preferences, when this logic, this perspective on communication, this cavalier attitude toward the power of advertising on our decision making is transferred to political problem solving, we begin to treat political decisions like consumer choices. We unlearn the skills of democratic citizenship and teach ourselves that invading Iraq or not, fighting global warming or not, providing affordable health care or not are similarly just matters of personal preference.[4] Everything is just opinion, so why not stick with our own, familiar, and comfortable views, insulated from bothersome data, expertise, analysis, or deliberation? Only in this context can the culture wars' suggestion that disagreements or conflicts of interest are best understood as lifestyle differences even remotely begin to make sense, much less be taken as common sense.[5]

Here and in the next section of this chapter, we will begin our examination of the phenomena illustrated in the aforementioned narratives that we call sound-bite sabotage. Throughout the book we will use a variety of sources to support our claim that there is now a deliberate effort, or what we call a calculated and an interested effort, to privatize political communication in America. We use the term *interested* to try to denote soft intentionality, for two reasons. First, it is not that controversial to contend that people tend to act in their own self-interest, nor to argue that those with superior resources have identifiable advantages in this process. Second, our objective is to link these observations about individual agency and the unequal distribution of power to the ways that organizational and institutional structures (treating culture, along with politics and economics, as a structure for analysis) amplify the advantages and agency of public and private leaders willing to distort our information systems to advance their private interests. Some of this distortion is clearly deliberate, while some is made possible by existing organizational frameworks and communicative dynamics that privilege consumerist narratives even in political, cultural, and economic arenas.

We use the word "interested" for its ordinary meaning (to be interested in this or that) and because it captures a deeper, analytical point as well: sound-bite saboteurs peddle interested messages, *designed* to exploit (and recreate) relatively independent, institutional conditions that contribute in powerful ways to the ability of some and not other agents to control their image and message—and set the agenda for deliberation—in the news. Once we mention the news, many readers are likely to imagine we are taking a position on the question of media bias. We are, and we are not, so a word of explanation is in order.

The media bias question, when framed as a liberal or conservative bias, is an analytical black hole, a perennial question better designed to keep philosophers employed than to guide productive thinking toward addressing real problems. Our strategy has been to avoid mention of "media bias" for two reasons. First, research shows that different audiences (readers, listeners, viewers) experience the same news sources as containing a liberal or conservative bias, providing powerful evidence that media bias is often in the eyes of the beholder. Second, we instead choose to use "interested" or "distorted" because our argument hopes to move beyond what we see as a tired and circular framework, instead focusing beyond just the media and arguing that sound-bite sabotage distorts our information system from a variety of directions, not just through the news media, and it is driven by the interested actions of both public and private leaders.

Therefore, while we do not directly address the liberal bias question, were we to address it, we would suggest that we are in a period of potentially significant transition from news dominated by an *official bias* (where the more objective journalists become, the more official bias they inject into the news)[6] to an information system where more explicitly partisan and commercially biased information, what we call branded information, begins to dominate news, entertainment, classroom materials, and advertising—to sell Coke, candidates, laissez-faire, or a conceptualization of limited government where public power is limited to national defense and punishing street crime. Finally, while the current period analyzed here has been dominated by conservative leadership, resulting in more illustrations of conservative sound-bite sabotage, our analytical framework is not primarily aimed at the Right, but at the powerful, and, more specifically in the next section, at the techniques they use their resource advantages to employ.

III. Sound-Bite Sabotage Techniques

First, sound-bite saboteurs try to move the opinion of publics toward positions that are contrary to the best available data. The interested messages of insurance industry lobbyists, tort reform advocates, and the genetically modified foods industry described earlier, while inconsistent with the best available data, have succeeded in colonizing conventional wisdom today. Like these, the "Southern Strategy" displaced concerns about demonstrated racial discrimination with law and order rhetoric to amplify moderate racist attitudes and awaken latent racist attitudes in voters driven to reframe black victims as a threat to white power.[7] Similarly, the Democratic Party has insisted that there is no Social Security crisis in response to President Bush's partial privatization plan, even though Democrats were themselves arguing the system was in crisis while they controlled the White House.[8]

Our interest is in understanding this approach to political and civic communication, an approach we call sound-bite sabotage. We will examine in detail throughout this book the techniques and tactics mobilized by sound-bite saboteurs, including saturating communication channels by repeating calculated messages through multiple sources to create an appearance of independent confirmation, consciously constructing prepackaged stories, amplified through old and new media, to be accepted by reporters as newsworthy (and as designed to be newsworthy), broadening the scope of the misinformation efforts, and more rapidly encouraging passive and more cynical forms of citizenship, both in our classrooms and in the larger public square.[9]

Sound-bite saboteurs construct language and issue frames to divert public attention without increasing public awareness.[10] While sound-bite saboteurs are effective leaders who learn how to *use* conflicts, they count on and aggravate citizen confusion about the fundamentally strategic nature of political conflicts.[11] Sound-bite saboteurs, recognizing conflicts as opportunities, divert public attention from leadership failures and concentrate that attention on their interested messages, cognitive schema designed by public relations experts to reconstruct common sense and reassure citizens, as subjects without agency. And the distortion constitutive of sound-bite sabotage is not random but systematic and loosely coordinated; the stories with which saboteurs saturate our communication channels are designed to carry advertisements that advance a private interest, representing it as the public interest.

Second, when sound-bite saboteurs move the opinion of publics toward positions that are contrary to the best available data, they also discredit the importance of using data to address the conflicts we face, attacking a central pillar of communication and argumentation.[12] They displace scholarly debate with public relations as a primary knowledge production mechanism—a mechanism that may be more culturally resonant because it can present an image of itself as less ambiguous and more action oriented. Public relations work is less constrained by data or peer review, meaning these experts can use their resource advantage to construct messages that are, as William Haltom and Michael McCann note in their analysis of the tort reform movement that we discuss in chapter 3, more "available, accessible, adaptable, and affirmatively actionable" (2004, 70). To the degree that argumentation is displaced by sound-bite sabotage, we undermine our capacity to come to agreements and achieve the shared values constitutive of resilient community life. This political and cultural dynamic discredits data makers and the data making process itself, as can be seen clearly in the intelligent design controversy, the stem cell controversy, Rathergate, the proliferation of PR knowledge production in sponsored think tanks, and other high-profile, elite-driven efforts to distract our attention from leadership failures and other elite-citizen conflicts. Such attempts to distract us rely on an anti-intellectualism designed to turn all positions into merely equivalent, if different, opinions and replace data analysis and serious deliberation with familiarity as the criteria for weighing one opinion or position against another.[13]

We know from our own experiences, and from J. S. Mill (1975) in *On Liberty*, that facts do not speak for themselves. To become useful knowledge, ideas must be subjected to vigorous and ongoing contestation, bringing together people who disagree yet value the open-mindedness and hope of achieving (even provisional) agreements that link individual freedom to collective prosperity.

> Wrong opinions and practices gradually yield to fact and argument: but facts and arguments, to produce any effect on the mind, must be brought before it. Very few facts are able to tell their own story, without comments to bring out their meaning. The whole strength and value, then, of human judgment, depending on the one property, that it can be set right when it is wrong, reliance can be placed on it only when the means of setting it right are kept constantly at hand. (Mill 1975, 27)

And the means of setting it right is not a naïve objectivity but the vigorous contestation of ideas, focusing us on the political and cultural preconditions for democratic deliberation. Sound-bite sabotage both undermines this dynamic and dissipates our energies to make us afraid of conflict and politics as we slowly *unlearn* the foundations of our own beliefs in individual freedom or the free market, thus remaking us without the intellectual and rhetorical skills needed to be free and prosperous. Sound-bite saboteurs short-circuit debate by truncating our thought processes with familiar sounding, but deceptively inaccurate, reassurance that silencing anyone who opposes the familiar and comfortable can only be right.

> There is the greatest difference between presuming an opinion to be true, because, with every opportunity for contesting it, it has not been refuted, and assuming its truth for the purpose of not permitting its refutation. Complete liberty of contradicting and disproving our opinion, is the very condition which justifies us in assuming its truth for purposes of action; and on no other terms can a being with human faculties have any rational assurance of being right. (Mill 1975, 26–27)

Third, we argue that, as a consequence, sound-bite saboteurs are responsible for a widespread and growing assault on the possibility and the desirability of democratic decision making. Sound-bite saboteurs, it turns out, are driving a political and cultural process that is eroding the preconditions for democratic deliberation.[14] They use public relations tools to redivide key publics along cultural lines expected to be favorable to the saboteurs own narrow, private interest and to privatize conflict management in general. This process is clearest in the stridently partisan and extremist debates animating politics in Washington, D.C., and in state capitals across the country, but it is also manifest in the ways that these debates have turned moderate leaders on both sides of the aisle into endangered species. Cooperation, as a result, is now seen by many as a sign of weakness to be overcome by remaining resolute despite the best available data (and this approach is seen as just common sense). Instead of understanding that to be free and prosperous we must "fully, frequently, and fearlessly" debate ideas directly with those who disagree with us, sound-bite sabotage encourages a cultural preference for holding our own isolated views "as a dead dogma, not a living truth" (Mill 1975, 44). Mill explains:

> There is a class of persons . . . who think it enough if a person assents undoubtingly to what they think true, though he has no knowledge whatever of the grounds of the opinion, and could not make a tenable defense of it against the most superficial objections. Such persons, if they can once get their creed taught from authority, naturally think that no good, and some harm, comes of its being allowed to be questioned. Where their influence prevails, they make it nearly impossible for the received opinion to be rejected wisely and considerately, though it may still be rejected rashly and ignorantly; for to shut out discussion entirely is seldom possible, and when it once gets in, beliefs not grounded on conviction are apt to give way before the slightest semblance of an argument. Waiving, however, this possibility—assuming that the true opinion abides in the mind, but abides as a prejudice, a belief independent of, and proof against, argument—this is not the way in which truth ought to be held by a rational being. This is not knowing the truth. Truth, thus held, is but one superstition the more, accidentally clinging to the words which enunciate a truth. (Mill 1975, 45)

Fourth, sound-bite saboteurs make it nearly impossible for us to understand the grounds of even our correctly held positions, let alone manage conflicts where we remain uncertain how to best proceed. They reframe conflicts to reconstruct common sense as an implicit background consensus to amplify fear of collective action that silences opposing views and truncates the processes that achieve political understanding. For instance, we disapprove of lying, yet we are regularly distracted from lies at the highest levels, in part, because even that truth (lying is bad) is wrapped in confusions and held more like a superstition "accidentally clinging to words that enunciate a truth." Many of us cheer for our favored leaders when they wiggle out of a tight spot with a well-placed lie; and most top political communications advisors regularly recommend all sorts of truth bending, spinning, and outright lying whenever expedient. It has become such a standard operating procedure that we hardly even notice the violations anymore, other than those of our opponents.

It is now commonplace for our leaders, public and private, Democrat and Republican, to repeatedly misled the American public, over extended periods of time, with the clear intention of impacting public policy, only to have this enormous betrayal of democracy reduced in elite public discourse to trivial questions about the meaning of "is" or, "just sixteen words," or the meaning of "mission accomplished." While leaders lying to citizens or subjects is certainly not new, we argue that there has been a quantitative and qualitative expansion of its scope beyond just lying, and this expansion is amplified by old and new media. As *Washington Post* columnist Marie Cocco put it in a recent editorial, we can all "pretty much bet the public corruption issue, in and of itself, will wither in the sun. That is, unless we come to understand that corruption involves more than bribe-taking and jet-setting junkets. It is also a hijacking of the legislative process for narrow partisan purposes rather than the public good." As Cocco outlines, the legacy of public and private leaders willing to spin without concern for democracy means that charges of a culture of corruption are met with legislation to ban flag burning or outlaw gay marriage. In our view, this confusion-generating, public-relations-driven legacy is an ongoing demonstration of a profound, elite disrespect for the rule of law, democratic deliberation, and the importance of serious intellectual inquiry.

"A major source of instability in American politics is the shifting attention of the media" (Baumgartner and Jones 1993, 103). Sound-bite saboteurs exploit this structural characteristic because their tools are more effective in contexts where there are increasingly rapid, confusing, and orchestrated shifts in media, elite, and public attentions. To ignore this threat on the basis of an expectation that new media deliver diversity to support pluralism is, according to Edelman, a mistake, because while media outlets have increased in number and scope, audience self-selection means that these each construct their own insulated political spectacle. Consequently, Edelman argues that "the chief result is a reinforcement of established ideologies that is all the more potent because it takes place in a context that highlights diverse stimuli" (1988, 122), increasing, rather than mitigating, obstacles to citizen deliberation and problem solving. We observe a widespread network of agents loosely linked as an alternative knowledge production system that finances pseudo-scientific studies and saturates communication channels with the resulting sound bites to misrepresent the nature of the conflicts we face. Such agents try to fake the context and create a phony expectation that anyone with common sense already knows that the answers are easy and analysis is a waste of time.

Fifth, sound-bite saboteurs displace efforts to make the implicit explicit or the invisible visible with brilliantly orchestrated public relations campaigns that saturate communication channels with designer images made familiar through repetition as a common-sense position where there is no discomfort, nothing worth considering beyond the immediate, most proximate, and superficially apparent. Sound-bite saboteurs understand the subjective experiences of many—frustration and anger over declining standards of living and control over our own lives—and mobilize these to confuse citizens about the nature of political conflict and increase the likelihood that private actors will have an advantage in the struggle to resolve these routine conflicts and set public policy agendas in private. If we want a color-blind society, for instance, then we reject any uncomfortable or unfamiliar data in order to insulate us from anything but the familiar sound bites, indicating that we already have a color-blind society; this delusion is threatened by data suggesting otherwise (and by those producing this data). But from 1932 to 1964, the U.S. government, in partnership with private-sector business leaders, underwrote $120 billion in mortgage loans, originally for returning GIs, that became the foundation upon which suburbanization and white flight were built. Because the Federal Housing Authority (FHA) (and partner banks) developed what is now still widely practiced, redlining, nearly none of these loans were made to the equally heroic and patriotic African American GIs. At the same time, urban renewal bulldozed inner-city neighborhoods, but 90 percent of this housing was never rebuilt, and two thirds of those displaced for shopping malls or football stadiums were non-white. What was left were high-density public housing projects and a legacy that, today, leaves black families with only one eighth the accumulated family wealth of white families (Conley 2000, 530). While sound-bite sabotage has been used to oppose policies to respond to this legacy, such as affirmative action, by advancing familiar sound bites about reverse discrimination, Tali Mendelberg finds that this is less popular naiveté and more leadership failure. When leaders make explicit the race-coded messages in law and order campaigns, such as the infamous Willie Horton ads, for instance, average Americans are empowered to see the contradiction between the sound bite and other American values, such as equality, and less likely to have our racial prejudices amplified.

In "Executing Hortons: Racial Crime in the 1988 Presidential Campaign," Mendelberg analyzed the Willie Horton ads to argue persuasively that "racial campaigns affect far more than voters' behavior at the ballot box" (1997, 134). In a controlled experiment, Mendelberg found that "exposure to Horton coverage increases the effect of prejudice, activates prejudice where it was nearly dormant, inclines prejudiced whites to reject the legitimacy of welfare programs and endorse the idea that African Americans can do without them" (145–47). Further, "without Horton exposure, prejudiced individuals are 25 percentage points more likely than unprejudiced people to oppose racially egalitarian policies; with exposure to Horton, preju-diced individuals are 40 percentage points more likely to do so than unprejudiced people" (145). Testing the alternative hypothesis, that Horton activated people's concerns about crime, the author found that "Horton did not bring out the power of crime salience [and] did not move perceptions of the importance of crime as a problem" (151). The Horton advertisements were about race and not about law and order, the mobilization of which increased resistance to policies focusing on redressing racial inequalities and "heightened perceptions of racial conflict" (151).

Sixth, sound-bite saboteurs today mobilize superior resources, access to powerful public and private institutions and organizations, and a loosely linked network of information professionals supported by right utopian corporate funding to gradually and incessantly saturate multiple political and cultural discourses—from talk radio to news to popular publishing—with the rhetoric, anecdotes, and familiar framing devices needed to reinforce their particular vision of limited government, a government limited to national defense and punish-ing criminals. Leadership investments in branded information, which infiltrate childhood and undermine family life, blur the lines between public and private by mobilizing powerful PR techniques designed to represent interested information as disinterested. Advertisements are represented as news, and normal doubts and disagreements among scholars are reframed as just another set of opinions to be dismissed. This approach to leadership and political communication supports a public pedagogy that justifies a virulently anti-democratic and anti-prosperity anti-intellectualism. "The corruption of news is an open secret. So advertisers are looking for new frontiers. . . . In the children's market, the last frontier may well be academia" (Schor 2004, 82). This is a frightening assessment of the nature of our information system and suggests that we are already raising kids trained to trust no one and no institutions: constructing an unhealthy form of cynicism as a rational response to an information system that represents carefully designed messages advertising narrow, private interests as disinterested public information and dismissing those forms of cynical performance that may serve democratic citizenship.

"Anti-intellectualism is one of the grand unifying themes," according to Frank, of the elite decision to make cultural conflicts salient as a "mutant strain of class war" that helps us make sense of the otherwise random-seeming menu of conflicts we face today (2004, 191). We see this as one part of a growing, elite-led assault on the preconditions for a democratic public sphere. By undermining the possibility and desirability of expertise and reasoning—a move with roots in extremists on both sides and made most virulent in the current alliance of leaders from the extreme evangelical community and the right utopian business community who have joined forces to reject the American social contract—sound-bite saboteurs are ultimately undermining democracy, education, and American prosperity.

IV. The Rest of the Book

In this introductory chapter we started with illustrative narratives to identify the techniques and practices constitutive of sound-bite sabotage to argue that an interest group driven, branded information system threatens to weaken meaningful notions of democratic citizenship, and in doing so, it undermines the communicative connection between individual liberty and collective prosperity that has, to date, contributed so greatly to ensuring domestic tranquility and providing for our common defense. The remaining chapters constitute our more detailed effort to unpack this larger argument.

Chapter 2 traces the roots of the techniques outlined here to private-sector leadership and argues that these techniques are designed to reduce the visibility of the speaker, attempting to erase any sense of agency beyond purchasing power, obscuring the competing interests at stake in routine political conflicts and weakening our capacity to hold powerful agents—public and private—accountable. We deepen our understanding through Harry Frankfurt's (2005) analysis of bullshitting as something significantly more important than simply lying, a strategy that seeks to systematically fake text and context, arguing that sound-bite saboteurs embrace a systematic phoniness that challenges the foundations for effective communicative action. While repeating calculated messages through multiple sources to create an appearance of independent confirmation is not a new rhetorical strategy, sound-bite sabotage amplifies this strategy by using the tools available in the new media, consciously constructing prepackaged stories to be accepted by reporters as newsworthy as designed, broadening the scope of the misinformation efforts, and more rapidly encouraging passive and more cynical forms of citizenship.

We argue that the distortion constitutive of sound-bite sabotage is not random but systematic and loosely coordinated. Further, the advertising messages saturating our communication channels and overwhelming our children contain interested information—that is, these messages are designed to carry advertisements that advance a private interest as if it were a public interest. This is what we mean by branded information. As branded information makes us more cynical, the imperative that branded information carry advertising also drives the expanding reach of these techniques from the billboards to the newsrooms, classrooms, chat rooms, and playgrounds. Well-funded and professionally mixed combinations of visible and viral branded information are, as a consequence, steadily seeping into our most intimate personal space and relationships, with the objective of driving citizen behavior by making these interested messages our operative cognitive schema, the departure points for how we see and analyze and talk about our world.

At the end of chapter 2 and the beginning of chapter 3 we connect these private-sector marketing techniques to our analysis of public-sector efforts to expand or contract the scope of political conflicts. We build on the recent work by Haltom and McCann (2004) to closely examine the case of tort reform advocacy and the putative litigation explosion as another illustration of sound-bite sabotage. We argue that this and other illustrations demonstrate that the systematic fakery of sound-bite sabotage is designed to spread doubt, to discourage active individual agency by retarding our confidence in our own judgments and our ability to understand politics and effectively manage conflict. Designed to displace more serious with more trivial conflicts to divert our attentions and exhaust our energies, information selected by virtue of its ability to carry advertisement casts aspersions on serious analysis itself in order to confuse us about what is already confusing enough: political conflict. Thus sound-bite sabotage is designed to spread doubt in a second sense as well. It is information branding designed to exploit the inescapable ambiguities embedded in an ongoing and a contingent political struggle and scientific debate, thus sowing doubts about the possibility and desirability of democratic governance itself, doubts that undermine our abilities to achieve and mobilize a common language for problem solving or deliberation.

Taken together, we argue that chapters 2 and 3 demonstrate that conflicts are opportunities for private and public-sector leaders, and we all need to see these as opportunities and choices, just as elite leaders see them, in order to understand the strategic and communicative dimensions of political conflict that are so cleverly exploited by sound-bite saboteurs. Without this sober understanding, we are more vulnerable to public and private leaders willing to amplify our fear of terrorism or drugs or sexuality or big government to justify legislative "solutions" that could not be passed absent the amplification of current conflicts as moral panics. Conflicts are, similarly, opportunities to reward key constituencies and mobilize supportive publics by directing public resources toward policies favorable to these more narrow private interests.

Chapter 4 examines the role of new media and the influence of a postmodern ethos in enabling sound-bite sabotage. New media create tremendous challenges for academics, challenges not only for our classroom pedagogy but, more viscerally, for our professional identity. When these challenges exacerbate academics' preexisting fears of declining literacy, lessening agency, and weakening modernist values, fears can turn into impediments that prevent critical engagement. New media's impact on our culture (both academic and popular) requires a refiguring of our roles as scholars and of our relationships to students, knowledge production, and information systems. We must be willing to get ourselves ideologically and professionally dirty, to engage the pop culture mediums and electronic diaspora that are forming and reforming academic and democratic life. If we are not so willing, then we risk abandoning the power of these new mediums to the manipulations of the sound-bite saboteurs.

Indeed, in this chapter we are ultimately more concerned with the *exploitation* of new media by sound-bite saboteurs than with new media themselves, exploitation designed to advance narrow private interests. While new media cause problems for public discourse, academic culture, and democratic deliberation, they also open up new sites for creative and political expression, new avenues for research, and new formats for education: blogs, podcasts, talk radio, streaming video, YouTube, and other interactive communication systems. To be sure, the new media and the tactics of the sound-bite saboteurs are intertwined, but they are not the same phenomenon, we argue, and to make them so harms not only our understanding of each component but, more importantly, their current and potential interactions. We must understand both the separate and combined influences of new media and sound-bite sabotage if we are to productively engage the first and effectively resist the second.

Finally, drawing on the work of John Dewey, especially his work to nest supposed dualisms, we hope to use this chapter to (1) respond to potential postmodern criticisms of our argument, and (2) offer an alternative to the dead end of the foundational versus anti-foundational debate. Like Dewey, we believe the process of continually seeking and testing answers is more important than any particular and necessarily contingent answers to which we come.

Chapter 5 connects our discussion of the new media to specific, popular multimedia performances and performers widely criticized as rude, outrageous, and worse, harmful to democracy in their unabashed cynicism. As we are increasingly bombarded by sound bites from multiple media, we experience ever-higher levels of anxiety about what is true, who can be believed, and what we can count on; cynicism thus has become the repository of that anxiety, as we perceive its lack of loyalty, its indiscriminate skewering of anyone and anything revealed as false, contradictory, hypocritical. If only we could stop all this cynicism, we imagine we would be on solid ground. This chapter explores the historical roots of the Western cynical movement through the work of scholars in rhetoric, philosophy, and political theory, focusing on the figure of Diogenes of Sinope, in order to demonstrate that the foundation for this movement is found in rhetorical acts or performances that "assert freedom in some particular context," and that these acts require "outsider status of the rhetor" (Branham 1996, 98). Cynicism was and is decried primarily for its lack of belief in institutional norms, and for its at-times horrifying incivility, but this chapter, citing multiple news and entertainment programs found in the new media, insists that the performance of the inappropriate by cynics may be one of our most effective tools against the branded information promulgated by sound-bite saboteurs.

Building on Murray Edelman's contention that culture is the antidote, we argue that the more we insist on belief and civility at the expense of evidence, reason, and expertise, the more narrow and rarified becomes the space from which critique might flow, and the more important outrageous, cynical, discursive performance becomes. We suggest that cynicism is a necessary component of democratic practice, in the mutually interrogative relationship between ideals or beliefs, and provisional, best practice. As teachers, we are especially interested in the pedagogical effects of sound-bite sabotage for civic communication and effective argumentation, and we contend that it is in cynicism—the cynicism produced and observed in both the classroom and the larger public square—where some measure of utility against sound-bite sabotage may be cultivated. In Dewey's distinction between and nesting of democratic ideals and democratic practices we find the possibility for powerful rhetorical engagement with sound-bite saboteurs because this framework does not end in cynicism but rather insists on an interdependent relationship between belief and evidence. And it is here, within this analytical framework, where cynicism may prove invaluable to democracy, which requires, at its heart, the knowing citizen.

We introduce chapter 6 with a brief discussion of Frank Capra's classic 1939 film *Mr. Smith Goes to Washington*, because we find in it an example of a popular cultural text that offers a map for bringing together communication systems, language games, and rhetorical techniques that are indispensable for democracy, even while they complicate it. Capra's film, we argue, views both media and rhetoric as necessary and productive, and the corruption of either as detrimental to the public good—a message that is central to our book. And, importantly, sound-bite sabotage, as both technique and political dynamic, is portrayed in the film as neither a simple Right/Left, Republican/Democrat, red state/blue state phenomenon; sound-bite sabotage is a multilayered, multifaceted, media-savvy attempt from competing ideological bases not to win an argument but to destroy the grounds on which argument can occur. The question remains, then, to what extent and in what contexts those rhetorical strategies and new media utilized by sound-bite saboteurs are value-free skills, tools, and technologies that *may* be put to good use within a strong, participatory democracy; and, conversely, to what extent, and in what contexts, are those skills, tools, and technologies always already constituted and defined by the uses to which they are put?

In this ongoing struggle, since cultural texts often operate as antidotes to political spectacle, we start with a cultural example that demonstrates the possibility of using the tools of modern advertising and public relations to construct familiar and authoritative slogans, saturate our communications channels, and persuade citizens to understand and support those changes that mark a particular path toward a particular set of agreed upon goals. We argue, however, that this is not *simply* true, nor is it always true, because the contexts in which we use such tools are always changing, and, consequently, so are the tools themselves. The traces of previous, overlapping contexts remain—in us and in the tools themselves. We argue, therefore, that this question of tools—of rhetoric and media—must be understood as a complex and an ongoing problem that resists final solutions, that the work of evaluation and analysis within ever-changing social and political contexts and articulations does not, can not, end.

We conclude with the pedagogical implications of sound-bite sabotage, arguing that an expanded notion of teaching and learning extends well beyond the classroom (despite the increasing presence of media technology and popular culture texts in classrooms), and also expands the figure of *teacher* to include both public and private leaders in an acknowledgment that teaching and learning happen in extra-classroom settings in arguably more powerful and less visible ways that, if unremarked and unattended to, harm our ability to address the challenges we face within the framework of democratic citizenship.

2

Roots of Sound-Bite Sabotage

Private-Sector Leadership

Companies spend billions of dollars to create positive brand associations for their products. ... Corporations have infiltrated the core activities and institutions of childhood, with virtually no resistance from government or parents. Advertising is widespread in schools. Electronic media are replacing conventional play. We have become a nation that places a lower priority on teaching its children how to thrive socially, intellectually, even spiritually, than it does on training them to consume.

—Juliet Schor, *Born to Buy*

I. Introduction

In this chapter we will advance our argument in five steps. First, we will trace the roots of the techniques outlined in chapter 1 to private-sector leadership and further clarify what we mean by "sound-bite sabotage" and "branded information." Second, we will argue that these sabotage techniques are designed to (1) reduce the visibility of the speaker (writer, designer, agent); (2) erase any sense of agency in the consumer of branded information beyond purchasing power; (3) obscure the competing interests at stake; and (4) reduce our capacity to hold powerful agents accountable. We further argue that these techniques are applied not just to the selling of particular products but to selling brand loyalty and a consumer culture in general, meaning that these techniques are used to create interested political messages

31

selling a worldview that serves as a foundation for citizenship-as-consumption. As such, these techniques can be seen spreading like a contagion into other arenas of popular and political discourse, reconstructing common sense by saturating multiple communication channels with interested messages, first to sell consumer culture and then to sell a particular vision of American democracy expected to support a consumer culture that is, quite literally, driving us insane.

Third, we argue that sound-bite sabotage, though a close relative, is significantly more insidious and injurious than what has popularly, though superficially, been referred to as "spin." More like Harry Frankfurt's concept of bullshitting, sound-bite sabotage is not simply lying but a strategy that fakes context as well. Sound-bite saboteurs embrace a systematic phoniness that undermines the foundations for effective communicative action. While repeating calculated messages through multiple sources to create an appearance of independent confirmation is not a new rhetorical strategy, the number, speed, nature, and interconnectedness of these sources, not to mention the ease with which they can be manipulated, are new and powerful. Sound-bite sabotage amplifies the strategy of confirmation through repetition by exploiting the tools available in both old and new media, consciously constructing prepackaged stories to be accepted by reporters as newsworthy as designed, broadening the scope of misinformation efforts and more rapidly encouraging passive and more cynical forms of citizenship. These are often highly paid experts willing to repeatedly fake text and context, to mobilize falsehoods, partial truths, or accurate but misleading statements with the intention of miseducating citizens. They do this by misrepresenting both the relative harms of the challenges we face, as well as their own leadership intentions and capacities.

Sound-bite saboteurs enthusiastically produce free-floating signifiers, repeatedly releasing these into loosely linked echo chambers to, as Barack Obama notes, "metastasize throughout the body politic, as an entire industry of insult" (2006, 16) *designed* to make rational, data-driven, and consensus-building democratic deliberations more difficult and more frustrating. Our fourth section in this chapter will focus on examining one current illustration—our ongoing culture wars—of how these techniques can be mobilized through expensive repetition, saturating multiple communication channels, to displace competing conflicts on the public agenda in order to redivide key constituencies and advance a set of political and cultural conditions that increase the political utility of sound-bite sabotage. Finally, we will transition, connecting these private-sector marketing techniques to our analysis of interrelated public-sector efforts to expand or contract the scope of political conflicts in the next chapter, where we closely examine the case of tort reform advocacy and the putative litigation explosion as another illustration of sound-bite sabotage.

We will demonstrate, first with reference to private-sector leadership, that the distortion constitutive of sound-bite sabotage is not random but calculated and loosely coordinated. Further, the advertising messages saturating our communication channels and overwhelming our children contain *interested information*—that is, these messages are designed to carry advertisements that advance a private interest in selling consumer culture as if it were a public interest. As branded information makes us more cynical, the imperative that branded information carry advertising also drives the expanding reach of these techniques from the billboards to the news, classrooms, chat rooms, and playgrounds. Well-funded and professionally mixed combinations of visible and viral branded information are, as a consequence, steadily seeping into our most intimate personal space and relationships, with the objective of driving citizen behavior by making these interested messages our operative socio-cognitive schema, the departure points for how we see and analyze and talk about our world.

Private-sector investments in branded information, infiltrating childhood and undermining family life, blur the lines between the public and the private by creating powerful PR techniques designed to represent interested information as disinterested. Businesses spend hundreds of billions of dollars in these efforts, and research shows that these include using the techniques outlined here in efforts to systematically reconstruct public opinion as "an instrument of business power." As John Bogle, lifelong Republican and founder of Vanguard, observes, our private-sector corporate leadership routinely misinforms the public, marking our private-sector evolution from sloganeering to BS and spin. A bullshitter, like a sound-bite saboteur, may sell snake oil, but the more serious damage is that done to our shared understandings of communication, deliberation, and those foundational institutions that depend on communicative action, like the rule of law and resilient communities.[1]

In our concluding chapter we will begin a conversation to identify both existing countertrends and potential antidotes to sound-bite sabotage. We start in these first three chapters by identifying the techniques—used by public and private leaders—constitutive of sound-bite sabotage to argue that an interest-group driven, branded-information system threatens to weaken meaningful notions of democratic citizenship, and in doing so, to undermine the communicative connection between individual liberty and collective prosperity that has, to date, contributed so greatly to ensuring domestic tranquility and providing for our common defense.[2] This chapter begins our more detailed effort to unpack this larger argument.

The Private-Sector Roots of Sound-Bite Sabotage: Consumer Culture Is Driving Us Insane

Our focus in this and the following chapter is on the role of public and private leadership in the production of sound-bite sabotage. The role of elected officials is examined at various points throughout the book, and perhaps most powerfully in Mendelberg's experimental analysis of the Willie Horton ad. While we see public and private leaders working on parallel tracks in this regard, here we will attempt to focus our analysis on private-sector leadership. Sound-bite sabotage has deep roots in private-sector advertising, the rise of public relations consultants, and techniques developed in the private sector that now have a strong presence in public-sector political campaigns.

The United States is the most consumer-oriented society in the world. . . . The architects of this culture—the companies that make, market, and advertise consumer products—have now set their sights on children. . . . The sheer extent of children's immersion in consumer culture is unprecedented. In the past, consuming was modest in comparison to other activities, such as work, play, school, and religious involvement. Now, marketed leisure has replaced unstructured socializing, and most of what kids do revolves around commodities. . . . These developments have not been beneficial for children. My research shows that those who are more involved in consumer culture fare far worse in psychological and social terms. What's more, my findings reverse the conventional wisdom that dysfunctional kids are drawn to consumer culture; in fact, the reverse is true. Involvement in consumer culture causes dysfunction. (Schor 2004, 9–17)[3]

When conventional wisdom is contrary to the best available data, we wonder how it came to be accepted as common sense, and whose interests are served by treating it as given, natural, taken for granted. Juliet Schor focuses her analysis on the ways we market to children to help us understand the larger dynamics at work here, arguing that we harm our children in a variety of ways. We want to suggest that this harm is not limited to children and contributes mightily to our vulnerability to sound-bite saboteurs. According to Schor, advertising, and the information system built around attaching advertising to everything we do, teaches all of us "that wealth and aspiration to wealth are cool," while learning to live simply and "modestly means living like a loser" (2004, 48).

> Public relations has become a standard feature of children's marketing campaigns, and advertising agencies offer PR divisions as part of their basic services. New products get press releases, with tie-ins to general trends or news, if possible. When a new academic study is published, PR firms rush to tie it to their client's products, producing not only print releases but also video news releases. VNRs, as they are known, include the product in a subtle way and without identifying the sponsor. VNRs are provided free of charge to cash-strapped local stations, which air them as news rather than the advertising that they are. . . . These stories become opportunities to solicit more paid advertising. . . . You might imagine the information comes from an enterprising reporter pounding the playground pavement, but the more likely scene is coffee with the agency's public relations representative. Public relations has become attractive to advertisers because it bypasses consumers' cynicism about ads. (Schor 2004, 81–82)

We argue that the techniques identified in chapter 1 are powerful tools for reproducing and disseminating socio-cognitive schema—ready-made and interested blueprints for making sense of our complex and interdependent world. These are also techniques for managing public perceptions of institutions and processes, and in the current period, we will argue that these have been used to create a virtually shared, anti-intellectual and anti-government political culture.[4] For Schor, these techniques operate in contexts constructed to be independent of traditional countervailing forces and constraints rooted in a competitive and an open political culture. Returning to what we can learn by observing the impact of these on childhood, Schor argues the following:

> Marketing was fundamentally altering the experience of childhood. Corporations have infiltrated the core activities and institutions of childhood, with virtually no resistance from government or parents. Advertising is widespread in schools. Electronic media are replacing conventional play. We have become a nation that places a lower priority on teaching its children how to thrive socially, intellectually,

even spiritually, than it does on training them to consume.
The long-term consequences of this development are omi-
nous. (2004, 13)

Some of the most likely consequences of this commercialization of
childhood include the fact that current U.S. teens "have emerged as
the most brand-oriented, consumer-involved, materialistic generation in history" (Schor 2004, 13). A survey of fifteen countries found
75 percent of U.S. youth want to be rich as a life goal, higher than
anywhere else except India. "More children here than anywhere else
believe that their clothes and brands describe who they are and define
their social status" (13). And Schor links these elite-provided beliefs
to rising obesity, ADD, drug use, electronic addictions, and bullying.
"Today's average (i.e., normal) young person between the ages of
nine and seventeen scores as high on anxiety scales as children who
were admitted to clinics for psychiatric disorders in 1957" (13). Our
consumer culture is literally driving us insane, but most discussions
of these threats to family and community focus on welfare mothers,
deadbeat dads, permissive courts, or opposition to prayer in public
schools rather than leadership and elite agency driving distorted
political and cultural communication.[5]

Schor points out that even most research into these disorders
focuses on proximate causes (working mothers, income, divorce), but
that "these explanations are insufficient" and often misleading. Research
does not support popularized claims about negative impacts on children putatively associated with working mothers. Poverty does have
strong negative effects, but middle-class suburban youth and kids from
two-parent families are showing the same afflictions. "Conservatives
have blamed liberal values and the decline of patriarchal authority.
But the research shows that children with authoritarian parents tend
to have more, not fewer, behavioral problems" (14). Is it possible that
our comparatively underregulated free-market system is an important
cause of the decline in family values and the atrophy of community,
and our failure to see this—indeed, our distorted perspective that
seems designed to prevent us from seeing this—might be an illustration of sound-bite sabotage?

Schor argues that "the ills . . . range from the physical to the psychological, to the social" (14). In our view, the data support the claim
that the illness has infected our political culture, depriving us of the
conflict management skills, deliberation skills, media literacy skills,
and intellectual skills necessary for meaningful democratic citizenship.

"Social pathologies are promoted by the materialistic and exclusionary messages of ads and marketing. Indeed, Martin Lindstrom reports that 'fear and pressure are the two most common elements characterizing the daily lives of tweens' and that the exploitation of anxiety in ads has steadily increased in the past few years" (14).

Selling Branded Information

"By three or three and a half, experts say, children start to believe that brands communicate their personal qualities" (Schor 2004, 19). At the start of first grade a typical kid can identify 200 brands. "American children view an estimated 40,000 commercials annually. They also make approximately 3,000 requests for products or services each year" (20). For American teenagers, the picture is just as bleak. Those aspects of teen consumer culture designed and marketed by adult leaders are "saturated with violence, alcohol, drugs, and guns" (20) as well as gratuitous sexuality. Yet instead of calling for government regulation of the free market, our leaders focus citizen attention on charter schools, extreme punishment, abstinence, and single moms as either solutions or culprits. The political culture born in this communicative context is "rife with materialism and preaches that if you're not rich, you're a loser" (20), if you are poor you belong in jail, and if you do not look like me, I am right to be afraid of you. In this profit-driven, sound-bite culture, private-sector elites spend billions on experts in various fields to exploit adolescent and class conflicts with branded information that further subjects our children to "unremitting pressure to conform to the market's definition of cool" (20).

The distortion constitutive of this sound-bite sabotage is not random but calculated and loosely coordinated. In the private sector it is coordinated by public relations and marketing experts seeking to erase the traces of their agency, including the degree to which agency has been disproportionately available to them—and both the calculation and the coordination of sound-bite sabotage promote consumerist worldviews that are effectively anti-parent and anti-family, because sound-bite saboteurs expect that their distorted messages will increase sales. Advertising saturating our communication channels overwhelms our children with interested information—that is, these messages are designed to carry advertisements that advance a private interest in selling consumer culture as if it were a public interest. This branded information, as we saw earlier, is violent in at least two ways. First, the messages themselves are "saturated with violence, alcohol, drugs,

and guns." Second, these well-funded, omnipresent, designer messages are professionally calibrated to miseducate our children and
misinform us all: they package consumer culture to encourage citizen
identities that are derived from product branding, encouraging us all
to see consumer culture as something natural, given, and unchange-
able—and entirely good for us too.

This abuse is driven by private-sector elites who operate "a
marketing juggernaut characterized by growing reach, effectiveness,
and audacity," spending $15 billion on ads to kids in 2004, up from
$100 million in 1983 (21). Enormous amounts of industry research are
conducted to craft messages of "kid-friendly worlds free of annoy-
ing parents and teachers," (22) relying on "attitude" and shock value
and sexuality delivered by stealth, guerilla, or peer-to-peer tactics in
schools, during Boy Scout meetings, or on PBS. Surveys show that
kids see the problem, do not like saturation ads or feeling they need
to buy things to be cool, but how can we expect kids to defend themselves against a $15 billion a year industry when enormous profits
and adult careers are at stake? Yet sound-bite saboteurs frame these
conflicts as a permissive parents problem, or a soft criminal justice
system, or greedy teachers unions rather than the more profound and
far-reaching failure of public and private leadership suggested by our
examination of the data here.

"Companies spend billions to create positive brand associations
for their products, attempting to connect them with culturally valued images, feelings, and sensibilities" (26). Branding is a decision-
making shortcut, like party affiliation, that reduces the need to analyze
when the "products are hardly differentiable without the labels" (26).
While this is a winning strategy "and youth have eagerly embraced
an ethic of labels and logos," (26), it is also a sign of an information system that has come untethered and is more purely symbolic,
free-floating image making, designed not to educate but to carry
advertising. Private-sector leaders routinely invest enormous amounts
to both brand information and to prevent legislative action that seeks
to protect children from the threat of a public square where only
information designed to effectively carry advertising can find a place.[6]
These leadership efforts extend beyond traditional advertisement: as
"corporations infiltrate childhood" by driving a wedge between children and parents, "daily life" comes to be increasingly "structured
by commercial and consumer activities" (13, 29). To understand the
roots of sound-bite sabotage, in short, Schor recommends "a stroll
down Madison Avenue" (37).

Private-Sector Elites Marketing Cool Undermine Family Values

"Marketers have defined cool as the key to social success," and the "genius of cool is its versatility." It is an untethered, detached, free-floating signifier, though "one theme is that cool is socially exclusive, that is, expensive," and that the marketing of cool encourages kids to want to be older, to seek out the taboo, the dangerous, and the sensual (Schor 2004, 47–48). At the same time, "marketers have perverted our venerable history of generational conflict to create a sophisticated and powerful 'antiadultism' within the commercial world" (51) that commercializes declining respect for authority (the often healthy democratic challenges to insulated authority, including those of the cynical performer undercutting mindless and undeserved respect for authority, which we will discuss at length in chapter 5) and reframes it in ways that undermine both family (as Schor argues) and respect for the intergenerational conflicts that are our first lessons in problem solving, deliberation, and intellectual inquiry. "Advertisers have kicked the parents out. They make fun of parents" (54), creating conditions for what Dyson refers to as a juvenocracy (2001, 36). And as Schor, summarizing George Gerbner, argues, these messages in ads are not benign. The "heavy TV watchers have their views of the real world shaped by what they see on the screen," exaggerating the threat of crime, fear of strangers, adopting inaccurate views on government, how wealthy Americans are, and on the relationship between spending and saving, while encouraging "age-inappropriate behavior and desires" that increase confusion, erode self-esteem (by setting kids up for failure), and drive "a wedge between children and their parents or teachers" (Schor 2004, 64–65).

Because "products need buzz" and kids are quickly made cynical about commercials, marketers expand the scope of saturation to encircle and constantly bombard kids with an infinite number of "consumer touchpoints" that are carefully constructed combinations of "visibility and virality . . . overt and covert actions" (75). As a result, news becomes a key element of this public relations assault, because it is experienced (at least for now) as more credible. "But as the ties between the news and advertising divisions of media have gotten closer, consumers catch on and become more skeptical about the news media as well" (81–83). And, not surprisingly, this direct assault on news content is now accepted practice for the White House, as we will examine in chapter 3, regardless of the political party of the president.[7] As branded information makes us more cynical, it also expands the scope of this conflict from the billboards—places where products have traditionally been advertised—to the news, our classrooms, and playgrounds. Well-funded and professionally mixed combinations of visible and viral branded information are colonizing what Harry Boyte calls the "free social spaces" required for democratic deliberation, with the objective of displacing more active forms of citizenship by making these systematically phony socio-cognitive schemas the departure points for how we see and analyze and talk about our world.[8]

Private-sector investments in branded information, which infiltrates childhood and undermines family life, blur the lines between public and private by creating powerful PR techniques designed to represent interested information as disinterested, advertisements as news, normal disagreements among decent people as reasons to fear conflict itself (which, we argue, constructs common sense to support a background consensus that justifies anti-intellectualism, since the kind of ongoing and vigorous contestation of ideas necessary to bring democracy and prosperity together is easily suffocated when we are afraid of conflict itself and fail to learn the intellectual and interpersonal skills needed to understand and productively address the conflicts that threaten our families and communities). "The corruption of news is an open secret. So advertisers are looking for new frontiers. . . . In the children's market, the last frontier may well be academia" (Schor 2004, 82). This is a frightening assessment of the nature of our information system and suggests we are distorting public discourse in ways that may be breeding disengaged cynics—frustrated, marginalized, and disempowered by design.

Corporations proactively write curriculum, now more than ever, as sponsored educational materials (SEM) that saturate even elementary school classrooms with a very interested, consumerist, corporate message (91–96). One study found that 80 percent of these materials was blatantly biased, "expensive propaganda" designed to "obscure the nature of" the challenges we face. Remember the four basic food groups? We wonder what future research might reveal as the true cost, in terms of obesity and other nutrition-related health problems, of these free "science" materials provided by the dairy and beef lobbies. "Businesses are willing to spend millions of dollars on crummy classroom materials, but have proven unwilling to pay taxes to support high-quality, serious curricula for the nation's children" (96). Companies, like big tobacco, selectively release data to misinform—and seriously harm—relevant publics. They develop sophisticated public relations campaigns to focus our analysis on consumer choice and individual responsibility (to blame parents, even as their propaganda campaigns make a focus on consumer choice a diversion) and to deflect attention from leadership decisions on product development and advertising. They then contribute enormous sums of money to ensure that legislators vote to perpetuate this process and frame their votes as democratic responsiveness, because they were responding to the initial misinformation being reflected back to them by constituents mobilized by elite-led public relations campaigns (126–28).

Private Leadership: Branding Public Opinion as an Instrument of Corporate Power

Mark Smith examines the "widespread assumption" among critics and business-friendly scholars that business unity leads to increased business political power and "a diminished capacity for average citizens to affect policies" (2000, 8). He argues that this assumption is wrong. "Policies match the collective desires of business only when citizens, through their policy preferences and voting choices, embrace ideas and candidates supportive of what business wants. To bolster its odds of winning in politics, business needs to seek backing from the broader public" (8). Smith's findings indicate that "overt mechanisms of power are only mildly useful," and he concludes, therefore, like Lewis Powell,[9] that business must seek to manage public opinion directly:

> Based upon the findings of this study, *the most effective political strategy for a unified business community involves influencing public opinion.* . . . The evidence suggests that in the last two decades, corporate America has helped cause, at least to some extent, changes in public desires regarding what government should and should not do. . . . [Business wins by] instigating favorable changes in public opinion and election outcomes. (Smith 2000, 10–11, 167, emphasis added)

The mechanisms for this private-sector public relations assault include funding conservative think tanks that train scores of conservative talking heads who now dominate the commentariat, building powerful media outlets owned by right-utopian[10] business leaders willing and able to run these explicitly partisan information enterprises often operated at enormous losses (the *Washington Times*, for instance). It also includes endowed professorships, sponsored research, lobbying for FCC changes that made possible the explosion in conservative talk radio and religious broadcasting, Internet blogs, and, of course, the links between these and the public information initiatives of elected officials. We will examine these mechanisms is more detail in chapter 3, since these are clearly public-sector applications of the tools developed in the private sector that we are identifying in this chapter. Smith's research focuses on several areas where the superior resources available to the business community provide it with unmistakable advantages in the battle over public opinion, the arguments about what we ought to be arguing about, and what we take to be common sense.

Smith focuses his analysis on privately funded think tanks that now (anticipating the line of argument we develop with Veyne, below) challenge universities in a struggle to produce knowledge. Right utopian business leaders fund think tanks to produce interested, quasischolarly studies that can then be widely circulated to influence politicians and public opinion. We say quasischolarly[11] because the studies produced have rarely survived the blind peer review process associated with university scholarship. The analysts hired for think tanks, though very skilled, specialize in the public relations skills useful for shaping public opinion. Think tank analysts are not independent researchers (their paychecks and career paths are explicitly linked to corporate sponsorship), yet they "maintain an air of detachment and impartiality unavailable to corporate leaders or officials of business-related interest groups," and, through the conferences and connections made available by their corporate sponsors, they have unusual access to policy makers and the media (170).

Think tanks are not new, but their explosive growth is, and they "only recently became conspicuous political actors in Washington" (171). Measuring their impact through participation in congressional hearings we see a rapid and recent rise. From 1953 to 1969, their total yearly appearances before congressional committees was only just above zero, but since about 1970 they have become the dominant private presence at these hearings. According to Smith, and as argued in the Powell memo, businesses believed that their values were "being undermined by political elites in academia and the media, creating a political system incapable of appreciating the virtues of free markets and limited government" (172). They sought to counter this bias by funding their own research.[12] President Nixon's treasury secretary, William Simon, was one of the first, after the 1971 Powell memo, to call for corporations to subsidize research in *A Time for the Truth* and, like Powell, to represent this clear effort to advance private, corporate interests as the public interest. But, according to Smith, a "financial campaign to articulate and publicize pro-business principles and policies was already under way when Simon penned his exhortations and it continued thereafter. Thanks to funding from many corporations, trade associations, and foundations, the number and reach of conservative think tanks mushroomed" (2000, 173).[13]

Increasing conservative corporate support for the creation and operation of think tanks is well documented (see Alterman 2003; Anderson 2005; Brock 2004; Chomsky 2002), and we will come back to this trend in our discussion of public-sector leadership in chapter 3, and cynicism in chapter 5, as well as in our concluding chapter. The question Smith investigates is the impact on public opinion, the degree to which these investments have succeeded "making public mood an instrument of business power" (2000, 174). To impact public opinion "the news media must amplify the primary themes" from these think tanks and those themes must be shown to help citizens determine their positions. Smith analyzed the *Washington Post* from 1977 to 1994 and found that over 10,000 stories refer to think tanks and 70 percent of these refer to one of eight think tanks (181). Smith counted the number of stories linking either conservative or liberal think tanks to public opinion (with various controls explained, including controlling for degree of anti-government rhetoric generally, making this measured link to public opinion a conservative estimate). He found that of the think tanks taking partisan positions, there was a clear advantage to conservative think tanks in the number of stories where they were cited, and this advantage has been growing larger since 1980 (184). "Among those that exhibit clear points of view as organizations, the conservative institutes dominate their liberal counterparts" (185).

The links Smith found between the themes articulated by conservative think tanks and public opinion demonstrate that "the ability of business as a collective to embed its interests in government policy appears to change according to the relative effectiveness of competing think tanks in publicizing their messages . . . *[shaping] people's broad preferences on the proper role of government*" (195–96, emphasis added). We can see in Smith's findings an intentional leadership trajectory from Powell to Simon to talk radio, Fox News and the network of conservative think tanks, commentators, news outlets, and other institutions supporting new information production experts. This section makes it clear that this was *designed* to exploit the resource superiority of the business community to create a well-funded, wide-ranging, and loosely coordinated public relations effort constructed to make public opinion an instrument of corporate power. David Brock, a journalist whose career was launched as a prominent voice within this network, has called this a *Republican Noise Machine*, but we are more interested in the larger communicative trend, observable in the behavior of Democratic and Republican, private and public leaders today—a willingness to mobilize visible and viral, overt and covert propaganda techniques to displace public information and deliberation with interested, branded information.

II. Sound-Bite Sabotage: Faking Text and Context

We live in an information culture increasingly dominated by sound bites—short and familiar slogans constructed to condense larger arguments into memorable phrases, saturating communication channels in the hope that these will become the starting points for public deliberations. Political sound bites are public-sector advertisements designed to secure electoral support by mobilizing some publics and muting others.[14] Studies show that the average length of a television sound bite has been shrinking over time, from more than fifteen seconds in 1980 to less than seven seconds today. While this clearly demonstrates one of the ways that sound bites sabotage information, operating as condensation symbols within an information system that truncates political deliberation, another angle on this dynamic involves examining the ways that sound-bite saboteurs displace debate about how to best address the most harm-filled conflicts we face with fear-driven, anti-government sentiments that short-circuit problem solving. They present a phony perspective on the art of political compromise by insulating us from disagreement—from disagreeable others—and insulating all of us from evidence, deliberation, and critical public scrutiny.[15]

As J. S. Mill and others have argued, the pragmatic case (that is, beyond the clearly strong normative case) for individual liberty and social democracy depends on an ongoing, vigorous, widespread, data-based contestation among competing perspectives and policy positions that constitutes the provisionally universal communicative preconditions for what Habermas famously called a bourgeois public sphere. As a public pedagogy, sound-bite sabotage threatens this pragmatic justification by encouraging forms of cynicism that are antithetical to meaningful democratic citizenship, as we will discuss in chapter 5. Following Mill, we *learn* the meaning of fundamental shared values such as liberty by observing the consequences of our actions and remaining perpetually prepared to participate in the open and informed mediation of disagreements over how to best interpret these observations. It is this context, this ongoing process of bringing together people who disagree to collaborate toward achieving agreements and achieving shared values through deliberative practices, which concretely expresses our democratic aspirations by linking individual rights to collective responsibilities and a reasonable expectation of social justice and general prosperity. And this context of ongoing and open contestation that makes democratic deliberation work is not only the foundation of freedom and prosperity, but it also reflects a deep-seated cultural commitment to decision-making processes that recognize the inescapable disorder created by the ambiguity and contingency of knowledge claims—a commitment that is systematically distorted by sound-bite sabotage.

Material and cultural prosperity emerges, in fits and starts, without guarantees, from the deliberative interactions of free individuals embedded in resilient deliberative communities: where we use, rather than fear, our conflicts. And these interactions—the contextual foundation of both the possibility and the desirability of living in a democratic society—are systematically undermined by an information system that displaces political conflicts (over power and resources) with cultural conflicts (political spectacles that dissipate the power of citizens by focusing them on divisive, narrowcast conflicts—constructing disagreement itself as a marker of the underclass), exploiting and amplifying trends in the mass media that dramatize, personalize, and fragment communication in general, including trends in the mass marketing of political candidates through image control and argumentation by sound bite.

According to political scientist and media expert W. Lance Bennett, when public or private leaders fail to control their image in the news this often results in political failure (1996, 81). Not surprisingly, we observe public and private leaders spending very large sums of money *trying* to control images in the news. The analysis of the rising role of image control efforts in politics highlights a dynamic that draws from the power of Madison Avenue advertisers to package candidates and coalitions, insulated from critique not only by billions of dollars invested in smothering communication channels to enforce brand loyalty but also by the very nature and speed of electronic communication, which encourages overload and segmentation. The spreading of sophisticated, often viral, image-making techniques from the private sector into the public sector has also expanded the cultural role of political sound bites from slogans that explicitly summarize larger arguments about the role of government into "free-floating signifiers," what Harry Frankfurt (2005) calls "bullshit," and what talking heads today might call "spin." The distinction—from transparent summary slogans to BS to spin—is captured well by Frankfurt in his description

of bluffing to highlight the differences between simply lying and systematically bullshitting. And the distinction hinges on understanding
the meaning-giving *context* within which utterances are shared.

> The concept most central to the distinctive nature of a lie is
> that of falsity. . . . Unlike plain lying, however, it [bluffing] is
> more especially a matter not of falsity but of fakery. This is
> what accounts for its nearness to bullshit. For the essence of
> bullshit is not that it is false but that it is phony. . . . [Just as
> what] is wrong with a counterfeit is not what it is like, but
> how it was made. This points to a similar and fundamental
> aspect of the essential nature of bullshit: although it is pro-
> duced without concern for the truth, it need not be false.
> The bullshitter is faking things. But this does not mean he
> necessarily gets it wrong. (Frankfurt 2005, 46–48)

It is by focusing on how knowledge and shared values are produced
through observation and communication—the processes, preconditions,
and procedures—that Frankfurt differentiates individual instances of
just plain falsehoods (generally remedied through open and informed
debate) from systematic phoniness—a far more devastating cancer
eating away at the trust that enables communication capable of coordinating social action. Bullshitting one's way through a situation does
not just spread falsehoods, it disrupts communication at a structural,
preconditional, contextual level.

> It involves a program of producing bullshit to whatever
> extent the circumstances require. . . . [When one bullshits his
> way through, his] focus is panoramic, rather than particular.
> He does not limit himself to inserting a certain falsehood
> at a specific point, and thus he is not constrained by the
> truths surrounding that point or intersecting it. *He is pre-*
> *pared, so far as required, to fake the context as well.* (Frankfurt
> 2005, 51–53, emphasis added)[16]

Consider, for instance, Schattschneider's insight that the core of politics is the struggle over meta-conflicts, that is, our fights over which
problems will be *made* salient and placed on the public agenda and
which will be displaced. The heart of politics, then, is our ongoing
argument over context at two levels: *what* we ought to be arguing about
(partially explaining how image and common sense so often become
particularly important and powerful political tools and themselves

the subject of significant struggle) and *where* is the most appropriate place for that argument. This second part highlights the importance of venue or jurisdiction, of choosing between more privatized approaches to conflict (such as mediation, direct negotiation, or various forms of informal justice seeking to empower the disputants to resolve the conflict themselves) or more publicized approaches that rely more heavily on formal court processes, legal advocacy, or criminal justice agencies in order to prevent private conflicts from escalating into vigilante justice or family feuds. When this struggle is driven directly by public relations experts and marketing imperatives, we see various venues overwhelmed by spin control, image making, and bullshitting that may sell a candidate like a Coke, but that also confuse us and systematically disrupt a central mechanism for political communication and problem solving. And it is not only ivory-tower academics who are alarmed.

Successful business leader, mutual fund manager, and lifelong Republican John Bogle argues that a major threat to American prosperity is "the remarkable erosion that has taken place over the past two decades in the conduct and values of our business leaders, our investment bankers, and our money managers . . . [and] a political system corrupted by the staggering infusion of money that is, to be blunt about it, rarely given by disinterested citizens who expect no return on their investment" (2005, xvi–xvii). Bogle, a pioneer in the mutual fund industry as founder of Vanguard, concludes that corporate leadership has shifted "from stewardship to salesmanship," and this has meant astronomical compensation packages linked to unchecked executive power,[17] ineffective managerialism[18] that suffocates innovation and destroys shareholder value, *and the routine reporting of misinformation by private-sector leaders* that constrains data-based decision making (xxii, 177).[19]

In a sound-bite culture our already atrophied ability to trust elite discourse about policy or law or democracy is further attenuated, damaging the communication mechanisms and democratic processes—public and private—generally relied upon to remedy bad policy or replace failed leadership, as increasingly cynical citizens are trained to distrust leaders in general, to dismiss evidence as merely someone else's opinion, and to live as if deliberation were an impossible ideal.

This highlights an often overlooked dialectical relationship between the anti-intellectual and anti-progress elements of an information system that rejects evidence and data, treats positions shared by nearly all biologists as mere opinions on a par with the creationist preferences of home-school advocates and religious ideologues, diminishes the complex challenge of decision making in contexts of uncertainty and contingency, and obscures the productive disorderliness inherent in the ongoing contestation of views constitutive of both freedom and prosperity. Sound-bite saboteurs, and the zero-tolerance culture they feed off of and nourish, impoverish public debate in ways that undermine the entrepreneurial, participatory, and progressive culture that has been the engine of both our rising standards of living and our (more slowly) expanding democratic inclusiveness—an engine that we are training ourselves to misunderstand.

Myths, Knowledge Production, and Liberty

Historian Richard Hofstadter argues that since the America mind was shaped through evangelical Protestantism, and the role of intellectuals is constrained by both this starting point and the strength of American business leaders insisting that even the scholarly professions "aped businessmen and adapted the standards of their own crafts to those of business," we have developed a culture where to be masculine means to be unconcerned with the intellectual or cultural world (1963, 50). This tradition of anti-intellectualism suffocates thought, even to the point of creating a public school system controlled by "people who joyfully and militantly proclaim their hostility to intellect" (51).[20]

> The truth is that much of American education aims, simply and brazenly, to turn out experts who are not intellectuals or men of culture at all. ... One of the major virtues of liberal society in the past was that it made possible such a variety of styles of intellectual life—one can find men notable for being passionate and rebellious ... clever and complex. ... What matters is the openness and generosity needed to comprehend the varieties of excellence that could be found even in a single and rather parochial society. (Hofstadter 1963, 428–32)

While our tradition of anti-intellectualism (and the anti-intellectualism of our public schools) waxes and wanes, it nonetheless has a long history. And this tradition is amplified by the move from news to instant news, from elite-controlled analysis to instant analysis and consumption that can avoid traditional filters to reach attentive publics and circulate widely in the form of sound bites masquerading as common sense. As Paul Veyne argues, truths are not simply common

sense or realistic, they are historical. When ancient poets and historians created entire royal dynasties "they were not forgers, nor were
they acting in bad faith. They were simply following what was, at
that time, the normal way of arriving at truth" (1988, xii). When a
position emerges as conventional wisdom—like the world is flat, or
black-skinned humans are property, or evolution happens, or the atom
is the smallest particle of matter—we may hold these truths to be self-
evident, but that does not erase the particular contexts grounding these
as *provisional* truths; they remain "products of the imagination" (xii),
emerging from historically specific processes for achieving agreement
within scholarly or political or cultural communities.

According to Veyne, truths are "products of the imagination"
and always have been. Not imagination as a dream state that widens
our vision, but one that creates what Kuhn called paradigms, what
others have called hegemonic discourses, or metanarratives, and what
Veyne calls, simply, "boundaries." He contends that outside of these
is nothing, "not even future truths," because "we cannot make them
speak. Religions and literatures, as well as politics, modes of conduct,
and sciences are formed within these containers. This imagination is
a faculty, but in the Kantian sense of the word. It is transcendental;
it creates our world. . . . However—and this would make any Kantian
worthy of the name faint in horror—this transcendence is historical;
for cultures succeed on another, and each one is different. Men do not
find truth; they create it, as they create their history" (xii).[21]

As Mill notes, each era, sect, party, nation, or community believes
its truths to be the self-evident culmination of a linear process of
knowledge acquisition leading up to our age or demonstrating the
superiority of our sect, even as history continuously shows future
generations revealing the profoundly ordinary hubris driving such
self-affirmation. Our point draws from this analysis to remind us
that each era or sect or community constructs prevailing—normalized—approaches to arriving at what is taken to be common sense,
level-headedness, conventional wisdom. Sound-bite saboteurs are
important in part because they are not only impacting policy decisions, remaking common sense in their own image, but they are also
contributing to the reconstitution of our normal ways of deliberating,
thinking, arguing, and achieving agreements—through which any
future problem solving and policy making decisions must pass.

If our decision-making processes are based on powerfully self-
interested distortions, public information controlled to advance private
interests, and myths that make already complicated conflicts more
confusing, then sound-bite saboteurs are a threat to the possibility and

desirability of a democratic society. Since meta-conflicts are an ongoing struggle to define the problem itself, we cannot simply contrast *myths* with some predigested, preferred but unscrutinized version of *reality*. Fortunately, we can access a richer understanding of the role that myths play in our evolving and contested knowledge production systems by seeing how they have worked in the past.

Common Sense, Branded Information, and Socio-Cognitive Landscapes

We create our own stories, but not always as we choose.[22] And in the particular historical transition that Veyne analyzes (from Greek myths to more modern forms of recording history) we see changes homologous to the move from news to instant news today. Ancient historians, according to Veyne, did not cite their sources for the same reasons modern historians do (1988, 5). For ancients, historical truth as the received text, the successful passing on of traditions, was just copied and "authenticated by consensus over time." Then, authentication came to be specialized in scholarly communities and the time frame shortened from the consensus of centuries to the use of footnotes authoritative enough to, rather quickly by comparison, persuade relevant publics, thus warranting scholarly publication. Veyne identifies these as "indiscreetly seeking to force consensus," much "like jurists do," professionalizing and legalizing the transmission mechanisms for tradition and belief making (6). Veyne argues that citations emerged as the normal way of arriving at provisional truths in response to "theological controversy and juridical practice" (11), transforming historical truths from "truths of anonymous reason without an author" to either revelation or law.

This change coincided with the rise of universities, and efforts to establish and preserve an intellectual monopoly over this newly normalized process of knowledge production. Historians who were dependents of lords and wrote for their masters and for the common reader were replaced by scholars writing for scholars.[23] While this process is complex, our point here is that dramatically shortening the time-testedness of knowledge production opens a door to confusing the short-term salience of fashionable fables, whether under the cover of science or sponsored scholarship, with provisional truths tested over time by relevant expert communities in near-constant dialogue with ordinary citizens about observations based on lived experiences. As persuasion and deliberation increasingly came to operate as exclusive spectator sports, "objectivity" emerges as a more commonplace tool of persuasion, and the patient elapsing of time to test the power of this or that idea or policy or perspective is eclipsed by (relatively) instant footnoting, a conversation among experts that increasingly excludes ordinary folk and the political-cultural discourses that animate their lives and communities.

"In its own genre," according to Veyne, "ancient history was as complete a means of creating beliefs as our journalism today, which it resembles a great deal" (5). If we focus on this connection between Veyne's work and today's information system, we come to see earlier changes in the speed of producing knowledge—of *achieving* shared values—and the ways that earlier articulations of provisional truths similarly combined kernels of truth with packaging that distorted a good portion of their truth content, similarly transforming these into dead dogmas with diminished normative and communicative utility as a basis for (potentially) shared language or values. And, then as now, it is the packaging that is a key source of confusion.

> Mythical tradition transmits an authentic kernel that over the ages has been overgrown with legends. These legends, not the kernel itself, are the source of the difficulty. . . . In legend we see history magnified by the "spirit of the people." . . . But for a Greek the same myth is a truth that has been altered by popular naiveté. (Veyne 1988, 14)

This packaging may manifest itself as "popular naiveté," or distortions in the ways average citizens speak and think about politics, but to the degree that this is widespread and calculated we argue that culpability ought to be more closely tied to the most relevant and proximate forms of agency—that is, to public and private leaders. Different schema, or framings, or cognitive landscapes, or prevailing notions of common sense, or conventional wisdom will make different conflicts or aspects of conflicts salient. And the power to direct this process, while not monopolized by any individual, group, or class, is disproportionately managed by public officials and the private leaders of our information system. Sound-bite sabotage highlights the fact that in our current situation, leaders more often than not choose to manage this process with techniques that involve systematic phoniness, fakery, spin, and bullshit to place their preferred conflicts on the policy agenda by embedding them at the front of the public imagination as branded information, displacing other conflicts arguably more important to ordinary citizens.

III. Displacing Conflicts to Redivide Publics: Culture Wars

One image, competing to frame our collective imaginations today, is the "imagined" world of two Americas as red state and blue state, a ready-made culturally resonant explanation for the elections since 2000 that obscures the two Americas divided by widening racial and economic inequalities by instead dramatizing multilateralist, urban, secular lifestyle differences designed to rub unilateralist, down-waged, religious people the wrong way. It also obscures what connects us as a people, culture, and nation. The ready-madeness of this macro-framing device is a key aspect of how sound-bite sabotage works. According to Thomas Frank, Gertrude Himmelfarb's 1999 book, *One Nation, Two Cultures*, among other cultural artifacts, contributed to creating a ready-made and already familiar narrative designed to make it easier to see Democrats as the party of the elite. Using the (Volvo-driving, tax-hiking, government-expanding, sushi-eating, body-piercing, Hollywood-loving) latte label to suggest "that liberals are identifiable by their tastes and consumer preferences, and that their tastes and preferences reveal the essential arrogance and for-eignness of liberalism" in blue state America, the book obscures the elitist nature of both the Democratic Party and the Republican Party leadership (Frank 2004, 16–17).

This currently prevailing myth of two Americas is premised on a thin, advertisement-driven, lifestyle conflict (that ought to be as politi-cally irrelevant as it is intellectually inert). It is driven by and reinforces a zero-tolerance political culture that thrives on communication by sound bite. And, even on its own cultural terms, it makes no sense. While the Democratic Party has its own leadership elites (who are no more out of touch with ordinary Americans then Republican Party elites) and Democratic elites certainly court support from corporate elites,[24] the cultural identification of Democrats as *the* elites, suggesting, for instance, that ordinary yellow dog Democrats are essentially arrogant foreign influences, distracts public attention from the powerful elite coalitions actually undermining ordinary communities.[25]

As Frank demonstrates with reference to Kansas—the home of Hallmark cards—blue states are, like the federal government, also being devoured from the inside by local Enrons who secure enormous tax breaks that undermine public schools, public security, and the public health, only to leave town anyway, trying to "socialize the risk and privatize the profits" (2004, 39). But this "epidemic of white-collar crime" that is the "silent partner of the suburb's contentment" escapes the culpability that the behavior of these elites warrants. These Democratic and Republican, public and private leaders are never identified as a corrupt elite, separated from working families and responsible for the atrophy of American community life (46).

Even while these leaders savage our communities, many Americans continue to praise their leadership and vision, directing their resentment and frustration instead toward other average American families: blue state Democrats somehow irrationally captured, with sound and fury, under the latte label, or red state Republicans insultingly caricatured as gun-toting, bible-thumping, poorly educated, uncultured, xenophobic hicks. The most troublesome manifestation of this is the fact that while these private leaders have plundered our communities by seeking and securing multiple forms of government favor, they continue to insist, contrary to their own behavior, that American prosperity depends on shrinking the government that their enormous preferential treatment enlarges, arguing that privatization is always more efficient, while their private charter schools run on public tax dollars without oversight or accountability, and they shamelessly assert over and over again, in various media, that the private sector is always superior to the public sector as a mechanism for sober and realistic decision making.

We saw earlier that Bogle sees current corporate leadership quite differently. Kevin Phillips, the chief strategist for the national Republican Party during the Nixon years, argues persuasively in *Wealth and Democracy* that this laissez-faire image has not been accurate at any time in American history. Eric Schlosser, in *Fast Food Nation*, and Jeffrey Smith, in *Seeds of Deception*, both provide detailed case studies to document elite-driven interest group activity as elite-led, extra-legal violence against our information system. Paul Krugman, in a series of editorials in the *New York Times*, made the same case with regard to our current health care crisis, a case subsequently expanded upon in Tom Baker's (2005) brilliant new book *The Medical Malpractice Myth*.

Reflecting on 200 years of American history, Phillips concludes that when the American private-sector elites periodically become so greedy that they threaten the goose that lays the golden eggs, it has been other elites—as trust-busters or Progressive era reformers, for instance—who have emerged to remind us that our free market produces the most prosperity when government regulations temper its tendency to undermine American values such as prudence, community, and equality (2002, xiv). His history of the American rich makes it clear that despite the public claims of some corporate leaders, we have a long and proud tradition of public-private collaboration and that, in fact, a sober examination of our own historical record reveals that far from shunning government involvement in the economy, the wealthy have repeatedly sought it out and profited from it.[26]

Frank recognizes that current efforts to displace political-economic conflicts over living wage jobs, affordable health care, a safe food supply, and clean air and water with divisive and distracting cultural conflicts over flag burning, gay marriage, or protecting the life of stem cells manifest this two-edged assault on American democracy: pillaging our tax dollars and polluting our understanding of how public-private partnerships produce collective prosperity.[27] Frank describes the cultural cleavage component of this bait and switch, where citizen-consumers are persuaded to support the faction of leadership elites most hostile to their own working-class communities and the forms of democratic citizenship that are more likely to link individual freedom with community prosperity. We are seduced by a government-enabled, private-sector driven rush to suburbia, a culture distinct for its failure to nurture independent thinking individuals, innovative entrepreneurial problem solvers, or the resilient communities that produce future democratic leaders. Instead, it is a cultural *milieu* devoid of spirit, what Richard Rhodes calls "cupcake land." And cupcake land is not only justifiably criticized in *Pleasantville* or *South Park* or *Weeds* for being without soul, it is often a place of mean-spirited soul-lessness.

Beginning after World War II with subsidized federal loans for (white only) returning GIs, continuing as public- and private-sector redlining in the aftermath of desegregation orders and white flight, and concluding with government-sponsored corporate flight in the 1980s and 1990s, the escape to suburbia encourages sprawl and its associated environmental hazards, concentrated disadvantage, and exaggerated racial and economic inequalities.[28] Frank uses Rhodes's term *cupcake land* to describe the larger political and cultural significance of displacing attention to serious political and economic conflicts with this cultural cleavage.

> Cupcake Land encourages no culture but that which increases property values; supports no learning but that which burnishes the brand; hears no opinions but those that will further fatten the cupcake elite; tolerates no rebellion but that expressed in haircuts and piercings and alternative rock. (Frank 2004, 49)

Thus the experience of living in cupcake land prepares citizens for the suggestion that the key conflicts in America surround lifestyle choices, making the red state versus blue state culturally familiar as a foundation for exploiting a commonsense form of background knowledge with political utility. Kansas, however, is in "free fall" and, according to Frank, cannot blame an increasingly conservative Supreme Court, the missing-in-action liberal media bias, or successful public policies such as Social Security, Medicare, or Medicaid, though many still try. "The culprit is the conservatives' beloved free-market capitalism, a system that, at its most unrestrained, has little use for small town merchants or the agricultural system that supported the small towns in the first place. Deregulated capitalism is what has allowed Wal-Mart to crush local businesses across Kansas and, even more important, what has driven agriculture . . . to a state of near collapse" (59–62).[29] Frank, in other words, focuses on the more proximate cause: an ideological frenzy for privatization and merger mania. Reagan-Clinton deregulation was "crafted to strengthen the conglomerates while weakening farmers" (63), undermining family values, and destroying many traditional communities such as those that surround us as we write.[30]

The political and rhetorical goal of these culture warriors and sound-bite saboteurs has been to make divisive cultural and lifestyle conflicts salient in order to displace difficult enough conflicts over rising family-level material insecurities. Reframing this frustration and concern as red state-blue state conflicts redivides key publics to insulate leaders from responsibility, culpability, and critical public scrutiny and makes possible the category "Reagan Democrat," the realignment of Catholic voters, and the wholesale collapse of the New Deal coalition in the Southeast.

Making lifestyle conflicts—over who the government will allow to marry, for instance—more salient redivides publics in ways that make public debate less productive and more of a spectacle (passionate but fragmented and dramatized to divert public energies) for at least three reasons. First, given the inescapable fact that political and economic conflicts are causing more material harm to American families, the proxy status of these replacement conflicts confuses policy debates, frustrates attentive publics, and encourages that toxic combination of self-righteous hysteria and dependent powerlessness often seen in elite-driven moral panics or in its more routine form: governing through crime.[31] Second, these proxy conflicts are often framed as perennial questions or narrowcast to the same end, constructing them as nearly irresolvable (by fiat), as festering flesh wounds distracting attention from the cancers within.[32] Third, once leaders have mobilized our most extreme cultural warriors they can wait for the foreseeably hor-rified reaction (even from moderate allies) inevitable in a competitive, private, commercial media that prefers to dramatize, personalize, and fragment the news (Bennett 1996). This *market-driven* media response is then used by right utopian freemarketeers as evidence of a *government*-encouraged persecution of religion and an unjustifiable denial of equal time for conservative views, all made familiar in the context of a now decades-long, continuous drumbeat about "liberal media bias" (Frank 2004, 98).

Frank argues that the key to repackaging political and economic conflicts as cultural and lifestyle conflicts is a very thin notion of a liberal elite that only makes sense on the basis of misunderstood and exaggerated differences in consumer preferences, mapped onto a tendency for those with less education to experience watching the news or discussing educational reform as a personal slight (as being scolded), and familiar geographical cues to divert attention from economic conflicts and the behavior of those leading both dominant political coalitions. "The idea of a liberal elite is not intellectually robust. It's never been enunciated with anything approaching scholarly rigor, it has been refuted countless times, and it falls apart under any sort of systematic scrutiny. Yet the idea persists" (115), in part because there are powerful agents willing and able, with the assistance of tools made possible through the old and new media, to make it so. And it persists along with the notion that conservatives are the persecuted victims (making their rants justified) to support "a crusade in which one's material interests are suspended in favor of vague cultural grievances that are all-important and yet incapable of ever being assuaged" (121). Sound-bite saboteurs highlight real "feelings of powerlessness" and indignation by cataloguing (123) stories and long lists of "minor protocol infractions" that only make sense as a frame through one rhetorical move encouraged by the leadership of both parties: "the systematic erasure of the economic" (127).

Frank argues that this is an Old-Left vision of the world with economics drained out (129) so it can be turned on liberals as an "intensely personal politics," where "its proponents might get the facts wrong, [but] they get the subjective experience right" (137). We argue that this is a right-utopian vision of American democracy—amplified by new media—with our everyday economic and political conflicts displaced by cultural conflicts that not only obscure class and racial conflict but also undermine our efforts to learn the arts of argumentation and political compromise in order to become informed citizens participating in ongoing, meaningful democratic deliberations.

Frank argues that those selling cultural conflicts are also imposing "a theory of how the political world works . . . [and] a ready-made identity" (157). While Frank highlights the culpability of conservative leaders at this time, we would widen the scope to all of us, noting that this ready-made citizen identity imposed by sound-bite saboteurs encourages us to understand ourselves as "victims besieged by a hateful world," even as it obscures the more serious harms. Instead, we are all victims—the more so, the more angrily we scream—and this status absolves us of responsibility for what goes on around us (159). "It excuses [us] for [our] failures; it justifies the most irresponsible rages; and it allows [us], both in politics and private life, to resolve disputes by pointing [our] fingers at the outside world and blaming it all" on others (159). When Democrats and Republicans agree on the North American Free Trade Agreement (NAFTA), the savings and loan bailout, the Omnibus Crime Bill, and most other core political positions, this invites a focus on cultural and lifestyle conflicts to differentiate them—guns and God, protecting the life of the fetus and the stem cell, flag burning and intelligent design—and the implied role of government that is highlighted by making these conflicts salient (177): limit government to national defense, crime control, and defending the most extreme, right-utopian views of a narrow elite faction, even when these are manifestly contrary to our best available science and most considered scholarly judgments.[33]

"Anti-intellectualism is one of the grand unifying themes," according to Frank, of the elite decision to make cultural conflicts salient as a "mutant strain of class war that underpins so many of Kansas's otherwise random-seeming grievances" (191). We see this as one part of a growing, elite-led assault on the preconditions for a democratic public sphere. By undermining the possibility and desirability of expertise and reasoning—a move with roots in extremists on both sides and made most virulent in the current alliance of leaders from the evangelical and right-utopian business communities, who have joined forces to reject the American social contract with about as much integrity as Joseph McCarthy demonstrated in rejecting Cold War Sinologists—sound-bite saboteurs are ultimately undermining democracy, education, and American prosperity.

Before we proceed with our larger argument in this chapter, it is incumbent that we examine the connection of sound-bite sabotage to religious activism, a connection that we have, up until this point, only briefly noted. The contamination of religious discourse and religious activism with and by sound-bite sabotage is one of the most disturbing victories of the sound-bite saboteurs. Whereas much of religious activism (the abolitionist movement, Martin Luther King Jr., Catholic social theory) was, at one time, a powerful voice for the public interest, the common good, and the disenfranchised—and, no doubt, to some degree still is—many of today's religious activists seem more interested in being apologists for the wealthy, the powerful, and the ultra-conservative. We believe that resisting sound-bite saboteurs means, to some degree, working to disconnect religious activism from the political utility of sound-bite sabotage.

IV. Fundamentalist-Business Right Utopian Coalition

Our product is doubt.

—Quoted from a tobacco company's internal memo
by Al Gore in *An Inconvenient Truth*

According to Steven Weissman, if we are simply attentive to what many of the most prominent private leaders of the evangelical Christian Right actually say themselves, then it is immediately clear that they are radical revolutionaries intent on dramatically changing the nature of Democracy in America.[34] For instance, Randall Terry, the founder of Operation Rescue, is quoted by Weissman as saying, "Our goal is a Christian Nation. . . . We have a Biblical duty, we are called by God to conquer this country. We don't want equal time. We don't want Pluralism. We want theocracy." And this vision of an American theocracy is candidly identified, over and over, as without constraints, above the rule of law, and seemingly outside of commonplace understandings of Christian living. Terry came to Operation Rescue in 1987, after a failed effort to become a rock star, "organizing violent blockades at abortion clinics around the country and openly applauding vandalism, arson, and the murder of doctors and clinic workers." Terry repeatedly called on Governor Jeb Bush to violate a court order—bolstered by Senator Frist's now infamous long-distance medical diagnosis on the basis of a short videotape—in the Terry Schiavo case. The party of less government and state's rights, here as in *Gore v. US*, actively sought out federal government intervention to overrule state court actions.

Branded Information Undermines Spirituality

Frank Rich argues that these religious leaders willingly transform spirituality into just another cluster of sound bites available for public relations experts intent on confusing citizen-consumers.

Whatever your religious denomination, or lack of same, it was hard not to be swept up in last week's televised pageantry from Rome: the grandeur of St. Peter's Square, the panoply of the cardinals, the continuity of history embodied by the joyous emergence of the 265th pope. As a show of faith, it's a tough act to follow. But that has not stopped some ingenious American hucksters from trying. Tonight is the much-awaited "Justice Sunday," the judge-bashing rally being disseminated nationwide by cable, satellite and Internet from a megachurch in Louisville. It may not boast a plume of smoke emerging from above the Sistine Chapel, but it will feature its share of smoke and mirrors as well as traditions that, while not dating back a couple of millenniums, do at least recall the 1920's immortalized in "Elmer Gantry." These traditions have less to do with the earnest practice of religion by an actual church, as we witnessed from Rome, than with the exploitation of religion by political operatives and other cynics with worldly ends. While Sinclair Lewis wrote that Gantry, his hypocritical evangelical preacher, "was born to be a senator," we now have senators who are born to be Gantrys. One of them, the Senate majority leader, Bill Frist, hatched plans to be beamed into tonight's festivities by videotape, a stunt that in itself imbues "Justice Sunday" with a touch of all-American spectacle worthy of "The Wizard of Oz." (Rich 2005a)

Rich is concerned about both the immediate incoherence of "Justice Sunday" and the larger threat presented by such calculated, well-funded, and fundamentally fraudulent campaigns to conquer common sense. He points out that the fakery here involves "sham claims" to victimhood and "solidarity with the civil rights movement" (2005a). These private leaders turn history on its head to suggest that those who used the filibuster in the past to prevent the passage of civil rights legislation—despite the fact that these current leaders are their political and ideological descendants—would somehow stand tall on principle today against using that same tool. Despite a Supreme Court with seven out of nine justices appointed by increasingly conservative Republican presidents, "Justice Sunday" speakers simply repeat Tom Delay's doubly groundless (since it also distorts the complex question of judicial independence), but infuriating, sound bite that the courts are the "left's last legislative body."

Rich continues, noting that "the 'Justice Sunday' mob is also lying when it claims to despise activist judges as a matter of principle. Only weeks ago it was desperately seeking activist judges who might intervene in the Terri Schiavo case as boldly as Scalia & Co. had in *Bush v. Gore*" (2005a). When religious leaders act like elected public officials, we need to hold them to the same standards. In this case, they go a step further.

> Tonight's megachurch setting and pseudoreligious accouterments notwithstanding, the actual organizer of "Justice Sunday" isn't a clergyman at all but a former state legislator and candidate for insurance commissioner in Louisiana, Tony Perkins. He now runs the *Family Research Council*, a Washington propaganda machine devoted to debunking "myths" like "People are born gay" and "Homosexuals are no more likely to molest children than heterosexuals are." It will give you an idea of the level of Mr. Perkins's hysteria that, as reported by *The American Prospect*, he told a gathering in Washington this month that the judiciary poses "a greater threat to representative government" than "terrorist groups." (Rich 2005a)

One of the characteristics of the new-media amplified, interest-group driven phenomena we call sound-bite sabotage is that public and private leaders who might have recently been shunned as marginal demagogues are suddenly embraced, brought to the bosom of the establishment and delivered to living rooms across America in prime time by prominent members of Congress, including former Senate Majority Leader Bill Frist. This story reveals a dynamic larger than lying; it reveals a more wholesale and loosely coordinated misrepresentation that, as a public pedagogy, can only weaken the social and cultural foundations for even our limited democratic public square.

This alliance between private- and public-sector extremists intent on systematically misinforming Americans also extends beyond troublesome and divisive mobilizations of religious rhetoric, organizations, and voters. It extends directly to the production of prepackaged news stories. Barstow and Stein remind us that the Bush administration secretly hired journalist Armstrong Williams (at a cost to taxpayers of $240,000) to pose as an independent voice in support of the president's No Child Left Behind Act, legislation that appeals to religious conservatives. They also document the extensive use of video news releases (VNR), a common practice in the Clinton administration, by the Bush White House.[35] This is branded information leeching into the structures themselves, becoming a branded information *system*. Our students intuitively understand this, of course, and thus many of them approach their academic work with the cynical belief that "you can prove anything with statistics," thereby dismissing argument itself. According to Barstow and Stein, our students' cynicism is not without warrant:

> "Thank you, Bush. Thank you, U.S.A.," a jubilant Iraqi-American told a camera crew in Kansas City for a segment about reaction to the fall of Baghdad. A second report told of "another success" in the Bush administration's "drive to strengthen aviation security"; the reporter called it "one of the most remarkable campaigns in aviation history." A third segment, broadcast in January, described the administration's determination to open markets for American farmers. To a viewer, each report looked like any other 90-second segment on the local news. In fact, the federal government produced all three. The report from Kansas City was made by the State Department. The "reporter" covering airport safety was actually a public relations professional working under a false name for the Transportation Security Administration. The farming segment was done by the Agriculture Department's office of communications. . . .
>
> Under the Bush administration, the federal government has aggressively used a well-established tool of public relations: the prepackaged, ready-to-serve news report that major corporations have long distributed to TV stations to pitch everything from headache remedies to auto insurance. In all, at least 20 federal agencies, including the Defense Department and the Census Bureau, have made and distributed hundreds of television news segments in the past four years, records and interviews show. Many were subsequently broadcast on local stations across the country without any acknowledgement of the government's role in their production. (Barstow and Stein 2005)

Barstow and Stein note that this past year, the Government Accountability Office (GAO), an institution controlled by a Republican Congress, ruled three times that these "news" segments "may constitute 'covert propaganda' even if their origin is made clear to the television stations." A study by congressional Democrats estimated that the Bush administration has spent $254 million tax dollars in its first term on public relations contracts—using taxpayer funds to purchase private-sector products designed to persuade those same taxpayers that the administration is doing a good job, rather than simply using the funds toward actually doing a good job. And such PR expenditures are not simply one White House gone off the deep end; this is widespread practice among public leaders, already supported by a large and growing set of private-sector firms producing thousands of video news releases a year, around the globe. It is an industry that already gives an annual award, the Bronze Anvil, for the best privately produced news release. And, according to Barstow and Stein (2005), the industry's powerful connections are not only in the White House.

> Fox, for example, has an arrangement with Medialink to distribute video news releases to 130 affiliates through its video feed service, Fox News Edge. CNN distributes releases to 750 stations in the United States and Canada through a similar feed service, CNN Newsource. Associated Press Television News does the same thing worldwide with its Global Video Wire.

And Barstow and Stein make it clear that the growing use of VNRs impacts the quality of the information citizens get. In a story produced by the White House on the president's Medicare Drug Bill, the secretary of Health and Human Services knew the questions ahead of time, the segment was distributed according to an election cycle schedule, and the GAO found that the piece "was 'not strictly factual,' that it contained 'notable omissions,' and that it amounted to 'a favorable report' about a controversial program." Despite this finding, this video news release "reached an audience of millions."[36]

The Political Significance of Private-Sector Contributions to Sound-Bite Sabotage

First, the techniques detailed earlier directly impact citizens and our political culture. The intentional, professionally constructed, generously funded combinations of visible and viral, overt and covert designer messages that advertise interested information as public information create demonstrable, though largely ignored, harm to our children and body politic. We observe coordinated efforts to use the powerful tools of public relations and marketing to make public opinion an instrument of business power, making citizens more cynical and news more confusing. In our view, these techniques allow private-sector leaders to utilize their superior resources and exploit the opportunities within the conflicts we face by intentionally seeking to redistribute interpretive frames and socio-cognitive schema in ways that advertise the commonsense status of anti-intellectual, anti-government, and anti-progress sentiments embedded into public deliberations as a background consensus upon which our policy debates are played out.

Second, these techniques have spread into political campaigns as analyzed in the next chapter. We really begin to see this contagion at work, however, in our analysis of the mobilization of culture wars to displace conflicts over living wage jobs, affordable health care, or saving the planet with more trivial conflicts over posting the Ten Commandments, stopping the nearly nonexistent surge in flag burning, or preventing loving couples from committing as life partners.[37] Culture wars are fueled by the steady drumbeat from at least two sources over the past decades: from the Religious Right, whose suddenly unrestricted TV access to our living rooms and wallets, following FCC rule changes that have mobilized an old-media driven, fundamentalist revival, has enabled private-sector leaders such as Reverend Pat Robertson not simply to interpret the *New Testament* message to sell a prosperity gospel but, more insidiously, to pedal an ultra-conservative social agenda. And, from the political operatives running a wide range of interest groups, think tanks, and media outlets (funded by ultra-conservative right-utopian business leaders, family foundations, and cult leaders such as Reverend Moon, who owns the extremely conservative *Washington Times*), we have other powerful analytical tools, such as the red state-blue state schema discussed, sending messages that reinforce these efforts to reconstruct common sense around the self-evident truths—coincidentally advancing the private priorities of these interested groups—advertised by encouraging us to argue about cultural conflicts.

Third, on a more abstract level, the information control techniques developed in the private sector highlight the various ways that current leadership attempts to control images in the news—to win the battle over determining what we will argue about—by mobilizing their superior financial and marketing resources to saturate communication channels, from schoolyards to the evening news, textbooks to talking heads, with branded information. Branded information is made up of interested, designer messages constructed to carry advertisements for products, consumer culture, and the particularly distorted view of limited government that right-utopian business and religious leaders believe will best advance their private interests. As we have noted, this means they try to represent private and interested messages as if they were simply public information provided as a public service, most clearly demonstrated in the form of video news releases and sponsored educational materials.

We have seen in Schor's analysis of private-sector advertising to children, Smith's analysis of business efforts to make public opinion an instrument of corporate power, and Bogle's observation that corporate leaders routinely disseminate propaganda an illustration of the growing presence and power of information that is directly produced by interested parties and designed to direct or manipulate public opinion to the benefit of these private parties. Like the invasion of our children's classrooms by Channel One, or the widespread use of video news releases and sponsored educational materials encouraging us to eat ourselves to death, this is an interest-group driven problem we call branded information—messages that are cynically designed to advertise rather than inform, with that advertising deliberately cloaked to mislead the public. We will see in the tort reform case in the next chapter that branded information emerges from a wide range of loosely coordinated interest group activities, where private agents try to represent their narrow private interests as the public interest, focusing on reframing our conversations about key conflicts according to themes favorable to their private interests.

Conflicts as Opportunities

Public-Sector Leadership

I saw that people, not just in California, but across the nation, were hungry for a new kind of politics, a politics that looks beyond the old labels, the old ways, the old arguments. . . . People are disgusted with the mind-set that would rather get nothing done than accomplish something through compromise.

—Governor Arnold Schwarzenegger, Republican, California

With the rest of the public, I had watched campaign culture metastasize throughout the body politic, as an entire industry of insult—both perpetual and somehow profitable—emerged to dominate cable television, talk radio, and the *New York Times* best-seller list. . . . What's troubling is the gap between the magnitude of our challenges and the smallness of our politics—the ease with which we are distracted by the petty and trivial, our chronic avoidance of tough decisions, our seeming inability to build a working consensus to tackle any big problem.

—Senator Barack Obama, Democrat, Illinois

I. The Power to Brand Information and Construct Common Sense

In February 1992, seventy-nine-year-old Stella Liebeck was admitted to the hospital for third-degree burns suffered while in a parked car.[1] She would spend a week in the hospital, leaving earlier than doctors recommended because she could not afford to stay longer.

This recently retired salesclerk from a longtime Republican family had never filed a lawsuit before, but after treatment by a vascular surgeon, which included painful skin grafts for injuries so serious she was left permanently disfigured (and partially disabled for two years), she did write a letter to McDonalds. In that letter, she accepted responsibility for her role in the harm caused, but asked McDonalds to cover $20,000 of her medical expenses and to check their coffee machines and reevaluate temperature standards to prevent future injuries. McDonalds refused to reevaluate its policies and offered her $800. As her bills continued to mount, Liebeck sought a lawyer who requested $90,000 to cover expenses, pain, and suffering. McDonalds again rejected her request to settle this privately.

Two rejections, for very reasonable amounts of compensation, given the severity of her injuries and the financial burden of treating them, resulted in her lawyer filing a formal complaint in court. In that complaint, she charged that policy decisions by corporate leaders, over many years, demonstrated an ongoing and a reckless indifference to customer safety and resulted in the selling of a dangerous product with inadequate warnings (a violation of the Uniform Commercial Code, by which all businesses must abide). A court date was set, and an offer to settle for $300,000 was again rejected by McDonalds. A court-ordered mediator recommended a $225,000 settlement, and McDonalds again refused. When the trial started in August 1994, both parties agreed that Liebeck spilled the coffee. The disagreement centered on whether or not McDonalds shared blame on the basis of recklessly serving a product known to cause harm to customers. Prior to Liebeck's injuries, McDonalds had received over 700 similar complaints about serious injuries and still refused to alter its coffee production processes.

We are all familiar with the McDonalds' version of the story—the harm caused was solely Liebeck's fault—because this is the version that dominated the news for months and continues to dominate conversations about greedy lawyers and irresponsible plaintiffs looking to cash in on the litigation lottery. Liebeck's version of the story focused on product liability. It is a violation of the law to knowingly serve a harmful product, and her lawyers argued that McDonalds knowingly and recklessly served a harmfully hot product that was defectively and negligently designed and delivered in violation of Uniform Commercial Code. But, for our purposes, the real story here is the fact that we are all only familiar with the McDonalds' version of the story. "Media coverage," according to Haltom and McCann, systematically misrepresented Liebeck's story, consistently stating "that

Liebeck contended that the spill was McDonalds' fault. In fact, she claimed instead that McDonalds had failed to abide by standards that many or most businesses must meet" (2004, 188), standards designed to protect customer safety.

If the coffee we brew at home is about 150 degrees and McDonald's coffee was served at 180 to 190 degrees, even higher than other fast food restaurants, then it is not reasonable to expect a customer to anticipate that the simple act of spilling coffee purchased from McDonalds would be so severely harmful. Further, previous complaints showed that McDonalds knew their customers were unaware of the danger. According to the jurors who heard all the evidence on both sides, McDonalds' refusal to respond demonstrated reckless indifference to customer safety. Jurors, who studies show come to cases like this very skeptical of plaintiff claims, were nevertheless persuaded by Liebeck's story and decided that she was 20 percent responsible and McDonalds was 80 percent responsible for knowingly and recklessly causing such severe harm. They awarded Liebeck $160,000 in compensatory damages plus $2.7 million in punitive damages (double the $1.35 million of profit per day that McDonalds earns on coffee sales alone).[2] Nevertheless, punitive damages were reduced on appeal to $480,000. This was appealed again, and the judge ordered a settlement conference, where a lower figure was agreed to, but that agreement remains confidential.

These, in brief, were the competing stories in court, but it looked much different in the news. How is it that the popularized version of this story, told and retold, came to be so widespread and so unrelated to the facts of the case itself? In *Distorting the Law*, Haltom and McCann analyze this now infamous coffee case by contrasting the facts of the case as presented in trial with the stages of its reconstitution in the media, highlighting four conclusions relevant to our analysis of soundbite sabotage. First, the details of these competing legal arguments, the less familiar story lines (about product liability), the reasonableness of the plaintiff's initial requests and McDonalds' refusal at several stages to either resolve the conflict in response to these reasonable requests or to change its harm causing policies, as well as the severity of the harm caused that persuaded jurors to agree with the plaintiff, were selected out of popular accounts as less newsworthy. Journalistic preferences for personalized, dramatized, fragmented, and normalized news (Bennett 1996) resulted in no coverage of the trial before the verdict, denying even attentive readers any context for making sense out of a verdict packaged as a sensationalized illustration of declining individual responsibility and the explosion of frivolous litigation, rather than as an example of corporate negligence causing serious and lifelong injury to an unsuspecting customer.

Second, the stories in these selected media accounts reflected the impact of interest group activity by "selecting and neglecting" the same aspects of the story as those highlighted in the interested messages of tort reform advocates, whose decades-long public relations campaign had "conditioned the context of media reporting, elite discourse, and public understanding so that the McDonalds' coffee case attained symbolic significance so quickly (rather than being regarded as an aberration)" (Haltom and McCann 2004, 223). Media accounts dramatized the story by highlighting the high initial dollar award and the false claim that Liebeck contended that the spill was McDonalds' fault, while ignoring details about the severity of the injuries caused. Media accounts demonstrably favored the branded story frames that were mass marketed by interest groups trying to pressure public officials for public policy favorable to their private interests; in this case, pressuring for their preferred approach to tort reform.

Third, these media accounts made it difficult for attentive readers to put the verdict into any meaningful context, other than the phony context provided by tort reform advocates and encapsulated in decontextualized, but politically calculated, sound bites such as "litigation lottery" or "litigation explosion." One consequence, according to Haltom and McCann, is that carefully constructed "gaps in public knowledge about the specifics of the case simply made it easier to impute greater moral blame to Liebeck, the injured victim" (207). The erasure of the complex legal context that resulted in no coverage of the trial and amplified coverage of post-trial public relations statements miseducated citizens about this particular conflict and invited the commentariat to repackage these fragmented and dramatized factoids into stories about personal irresponsibility and greed, transforming an aberration into an illustration of a nonexistent trend that tort reform advocates are interested in making salient.[3]

Finally, these interested media accounts were simplified, *selected* (that is, these were not random distortions, but the data show that they were driven by interested messages to frame the story around the branded themes being marketed by tort reform advocates), and recycled to saturate multiple communication channels with branded information. Even when the *Wall Street Journal* published a detailed story demonstrating the inaccuracies of these interested "tort tales," after the appeals court reduced the punitive award by more than 80 percent, and after a final settlement was reached, the opportunity to correct the widespread and distorted media account was never taken.

The same misleading stories—using the same now-known-to-be inaccurate figures (like $2.7 million)—continued to circulate as both news and jokes, appearing in speeches, editorials, and beyond, as if they were just common sense.

Leibeck's personal injury story highlights the specific techniques used by sound-bite saboteurs to design branded information, messages that are presented—and repeatedly represented—as disinterested public information, but, as we will see more clearly in this chapter, they actually mobilize powerfully sculpted and unambiguously interested positions. Branded information is driven by loose coalitions of interest groups, that is, persons who share a narrow private interest and pressure—directly and indirectly—for public policies favorable to those private interests. In the last chapter we dug into the roots of sound-bite sabotage in private-sector marketing techniques constitutive of branded information. Here we advance our argument by examining the role that public-sector leadership plays in sound-bite sabotage.

In his classic analysis of political conflict, Schattschneider (1975) emphasizes that a core element in any political struggle is the contest over mobilizing particular publics by making some conflicts (or aspects of conflicts) salient in order to displace other, competing conflicts on the public policy agenda. More powerful agents will often try to narrow the scope of any conflict to encourage privatized approaches to managing it, approaches that generally strengthen their hand. Weaker parties will tend to favor broadening the scope, publicizing conflicts in order to mobilize government agency and relocate conflict resolution from private forums into public forums where negotiations are open, reasonably fair procedures are already established, and decisions are, at least potentially, subject to critical public scrutiny. While there are no guarantees in politics, publicizing (or socializing, as Schattschneider calls it) conflicts is one strategy that can strengthen the hand of the weaker disputant.[4]

We saw in movies such as *Erin Brokovich* and recent tobacco litigation that courts can transform isolated, cancer-stricken families into class action claimants able to secure compensation from powerful corporations, securing remedies for serious harm done that would have been unimaginable had the conflicts remained private disputes. Citizen pressure for seatbelts or clean air and water or to close abortion clinics mobilizes government agency by publicizing these conflicts to reject privatized approaches. This strategy—reframing conflicts to displace competing frames—can overcome the odds and result, for instance, in President Nixon signing legislation to create OSHA, auto emission standards, and the Environmental Protection Agency (EPA).

Using these analytical tools, however, does not mean that privatized conflict management cannot be a public good. It does mean that we need to understand our options and how the choices we make (and the choices we are precluded from considering because they have been displaced from the agenda by elites) often implicitly and sometimes explicitly impact the political power of various agents, because expanding or contracting the scope of any conflict is at the heart of political strategy. And it is a critical tool needed to understand how politics—the art of compromise amidst ongoing struggle—really works, or sometimes does not work so well. And these intellectual, social, and pragmatic tools, gained through understanding our own experiences with conflict and through thoughtfully observing how larger conflicts around us are managed, are essential for combating sound-bite sabotage, working toward media literacy, and learning the skills of democratic citizenship—how to participate in political conversations. Everyday lawmaking, implementation, and judicial interpretation, as well as restorative justice, contract law, and plea bargaining, remind us that effective conflict management is often a fluid and contingent combination of public and private approaches, and the strong connection between democracy and a thriving civil society, analyzed famously by Robert Putnam, Alexis de Tocqueville, and others, makes it clear that there are certainly times when privatized approaches or frames are superior, both instrumentally and normatively.

> Frames are mental structures that shape the way we see the world. As a result, they shape the goals we seek, the plans we make, the way we act, and what counts as a good or bad outcome of our actions. In politics our frames shape our social policies and the institutions we form to carry out policies. To change our frames is to change all of this. Reframing is social change. . . . Reframing is changing the way the public sees the world. *It is changing what counts as common sense.* Because language activates frames, new language is required for new frames. Thinking differently requires speaking differently. (Lakoff 2004, xv, emphasis added)

We need to understand the choices we make in addressing our everyday conflicts as choices we make in how we frame larger conflicts. Do we call 911 or knock on our neighbor's door to manage a barking dog? Do we bemoan a tort litigation explosion to compound the harm done to injured parties in these disputes, or do we recognize that the data indicate there is no such explosion? As in the case of tort reform, reframing the larger conflict reveals that these are well-funded efforts to persuade us that insulating particular and narrow *private* business interests from legal liability is actually in the *public* interest—even if business negligence causes severe harm.

These interested messages are a political form of branded information, sound bites constructed to carry advertisements, designed to justify insulation from litigation that might hold business leaders accountable when their negligence causes harm to others. Taking advantage of the opportunity presented by conflict, an opportunity amplified for those with the resources and access to best exploit conflicts (that is, the affluent, particularly corporate leaders and their affiliated think tanks and talking heads, private leaders of media organizations, and allied public officials), leaders reframe conflicts to advance narrower private interests. In the illustration considered in this chapter, tort reform advocates also deny redress to those seriously harmed by corporate negligence.

These are the choices we all make when we elect public leaders articulating a privatized vision of American democracy, a vision we argue is often designed to carry advertisements that insulate private-sector leaders from critical public scrutiny. The popularized version of the conflict, which is nonrandomly in alignment with the McDonalds' version, highlights the greedy litigiousness of Stella Liebeck. The meta-conflict involves choosing to publicize or privatize the management of this conflict, choosing how to frame it, and how to think and talk about it, and in doing so to choose between two visions of American government, both visions of limited government with competing notions of how and where to apply those limitations. One view aspires to a government limited to crime and punishment and national defense.[5] Another view aspires to a government with constitutionally limited powers (limited by the scope of our individual freedoms, as in "Congress shall make no law abridging our freedom of speech") and a constitutional obligation, in the commerce clause power, to regulate the free market in the public interest. But branded information advertising tort reform obscures this meta-conflict, trivializing the choices we are actually making—the combination of choices we might make if we instead saw these competing visions as interrelated and overlapping—by focusing public attention on the most superficial and least important aspects of the political spectacle.[6]

This distinction, between conflicts framed as private or public matters, turns out to be but one dimension of a larger analytical point: the way we choose to frame our conflicts matters. Schattschneider highlights the important political differences between choosing privatized or publicized approaches to conflict. His analysis uses this analytical lens to demonstrate the democratic superiority of national political parties to more narrow interest groups as mechanisms for addressing the conflicts we face. We accept this and build on the general insight to argue that, to the degree that sound-bite sabotage is driven by interested parties peddling branded information, sound-bite saboteurs seek to exploit our confusion about the choices we make and the strategic communication at the heart of political struggle. Today, ongoing decisions regarding privatized and publicized approaches to conflict are drowning in a rhetoric of false choice, in images saturating old and new media that suggest only the virtues of privatization (including privatizing the military) and the apparently self-evident truth that publicizing conflict management, that public agency itself, is always the problem (always less efficient, less effective, than privatization).

But our point is larger than Schattschneider's illustration about the relative capacities of political parties or interest groups to strengthen democratic mechanisms of decision making—the systematic fakery of sound-bite sabotage is designed to spread doubt, to discourage active individual agency by retarding our confidence in our own judgments and our ability to understand politics and effectively manage conflict. For us, Schattschneider highlights the fact that when powerful agents frame any conflict as private or public in ways that confuse citizens and dissipate public energies, they obscure our understanding of this meta-conflict, and meta-choice. As we will argue in greater detail in chapter 4, they destroy an interactive, co-constituting binary in favor of either-or thinking. Further, when they present us with an agenda that masks these meta-choices to obscure the competing interests struggling over how to frame this conflict, citizen confusion about political conflict increases. For instance, the information, provided to classrooms as curricula, to TV stations as video news releases, and to consumers as product information and lifestyle choices, is branded to obscure meta-conflicts such as privatized versus publicized approaches to conflict. Designed to displace more serious with more trivial conflicts to divert our attention and exhaust our energies, information selected by virtue of its ability to carry advertising casts aspersions on serious analysis itself in order to confuse us about what is already confusing enough: politics, which is, according to Hanna Arendt, the only real alternative to violence.[7] Thus sound-bite sabotage is designed to spread doubt in a second sense as well. It is information branding designed to exploit the inescapable ambiguities embedded in political struggle and scientific debate, to sow doubts in our language and cognitive

schema about the possibility and desirability of democratic deliberation (e.g., evolution and creationism are just theories).[8]

Sound-bite saboteurs depend on the confusion that often predictably follows from their systematic efforts to sow doubt in order
to increase confusion and support more passive forms of citizenship
(in contrast to sowing doubt to increase clarity, expose hypocrisy,
reveal how power and politics work, base problem solving on the
best available data, and support more engaged forms of cynicism and
citizenship, as we will examine in chapter 5). Their superior resources
command a level of attention in the new and old media that gives
them a measurable advantage in controlling image and agenda, text
and context, in and through the news.[9] They succeed by representing their private interests as the public interest. Following the logic
of the Powell memo, the Republican and Democratic noise machines
see it in their private interest to cultivate citizens so confused that
they cannot act on their own and so alienated they are unwilling to
trust any form of expertise to act on their behalf, because sound-bite
saboteurs have saturated our imaginations with images of leadership
whose expertise is used to sow doubts about the value of data and
deliberation, to increase confusion and disable citizen communication.
To the degree that sound-bite saboteurs succeed, they sow doubts
that divide publics in ways that threaten to undermine active citizen
agency, individually or in solidarity with others.

"What happens in politics," according to Schattschneider,
"depends on the way in which people are divided. . . . The outcome
of the game of politics depends on which of a multitude of possible conflicts gains the dominant position" (1975, 60). Framing and
reframing—from private to public, individual to neighborhood, place
to race,[10] local to national, crime control to due process, volitional to
structural, political to cultural—changes the scope and salience of
various, competing conflicts. In doing so, it alters the division of key
publics taking an active interest in any particular conflict *made* salient
and put on the public agenda, and accomplished more swiftly and
with greater sweep by new media. If the conflict we are focusing on
is stranger-predator pedophilia, admittedly a frightening crime, then
concerned parents are more likely to gravitate toward a zero-tolerance
electoral coalition, favoring the extremely punitive approaches we
often hear about today and opposing efforts to treat or prevent or
reintegrate offenders who appear so entirely unlike us. Whereas if the
conflict is reframed to name those most likely to harm our children in
this way—heterosexual family members—concerned parents are more

likely to gravitate toward a more balanced approach to this troubling conflict, one likely to include punishment along with treatment, prevention, and reintegrative shaming.

A war against irrational cowards is likely to result in imprudent preemptive invasion and consistently inept, wasteful, and frustrating postwar nation building. A war against our actual enemies, who mobilize a rational worldview that we reject because it requires our destruction, might lead to more productive, if less expressively satisfying in the short term, approaches to this conflict. Highlighting the everyday political struggles over conflict salience—the meta-struggles over image, venue, procedure, and due process—emphasizes inescapably strategic elements that political insiders understand and accept as the way that politics works. Leaders fight meta-conflicts over how we should talk about any particular conflict, because this choice will highlight one set of factors, variables, and conditions that is important to some concerned publics—and determine which agents have responsibility or jurisdiction over managing the conflict in question—and displace competing frames that highlight alternative venues, conditions, and the publics concerned about these alternatives (Baumgartner and Jones 1993; Lyons and Drew 2006).

Displacing conflicts means *amplifying* one subset of conflicts, fears, issues, and agendas (and the publics whose interests and concerns intersect with these)—making these salient to mobilize these publics—and *subordinating* or obscuring others. Since conflicts compete for public attention and resources, the key battleground shifts to this struggle over meta-conflicts: which conflicts to amplify and which to subordinate, a dilemma that may often seem confusing to citizens because it plays out as relatively obscure procedural battles over venue. But this confusion also serves, largely, to insulate these meta-conflicts from public scrutiny, creating conditions for an insertion by interested parties—sound-bite saboteurs—of distracting mudslinging over image alone, or culture wars to displace a focus on more important political and economic struggles. This generally satisfies interests shared by both political parties, because this "basic pattern of all politics," as Schattschneider calls it, only makes sense once one appreciates the counter-intuitive insight that effective leaders try to *use* conflicts even more often than they try to resolve them (see Christie 1977; Galanter 1975; Simon 2007; Lyons and Drew 2006).

In this sense, then, conflicts are opportunities for private- and public-sector leaders. As we have noted, we need to see these as opportunities and choices, just as elite leaders see them, in order to understand politics. Without this sober understanding, we are more vulnerable to public and private leaders willing to amplify our fear of terrorism or drugs or pedophilia or big government to justify legislative "solutions" they could not pass absent this particular amplification of current conflicts as moral panics. Conflicts are at the same time opportunities to reward key constituencies and mobilize supportive publics by directing public resources toward policies favorable to these more narrow private interests. The New Deal coalition strengthened its supporters when it directed massive amounts of federal funding to its constituencies managing various safety net programs in large inner-city neighborhoods, or enormous new bureaucracies charged with running Social Security.[11]

II. Opportunities to Divert Attention:
Scripting Doubtful Citizenship

If conflicts are opportunities, which are more readily exploited by elite agents with resource and access advantages, then the next question is: Opportunities to do what? We will argue that since the key difference in American politics is not between Democrats and Republicans but between public and private elites and the rest of us conflicts create two distinct types of opportunities for those with superior resources to exploit. First, in this section we will build on the previous chapter to examine how leaders exploit these strategic advantages to win narrow policy conflicts, often by representing their preferred private interests as a public interest. Here we will focus on one particular technique taken from the public relations field: framing, as used by sound-bite saboteurs. We argue that, while powerful, framing remains a tool for diverting attention by seeding citizen doubts about the efficacy of our own political agency. Second, in section III we will analyze how leaders exploit conflicts as opportunities to try to saturate communication channels with larger, interested, and professionally framed messages they believe will advance their particular vision of American democracy.

Amplifying Some Conflicts and Muting Others:
The Power of Issue Framing

George Lakoff, a frequent adviser to Democratic Party candidates, argues that research in the cognitive sciences shows that "people think in frames and metaphors," and that these frames operate in such a way that "when facts don't fit the frames, the frames are kept and the facts are ignored" (2004, 73). Lakoff's work highlights the movement of marketing techniques from the private selling of consumer culture to the public struggle over issue salience that is central to political conflict. Like advertisers, Lakoff and his Republican Party counterparts, most prominently the legendary Karl Rove, focus on language and images, arguing that "when you control the language you control the message" (xii). This struggle centers on establishing the prominence of your frame in people's minds and on the tips of their tongues—your language, your interpretive stories and metaphors, your movie, your background consensus. The techniques developed to sell tobacco are now the dominant techniques used in these meta-conflicts over how to frame public deliberation as well. Issue framing by highly trained spin doctors is a public-sector form of information branding. Visible and viral techniques designed to advance private interests as public information are hidden, embedded within the structure of the debates themselves, as an effort to insulate these meta-conflict strategies from critical public scrutiny. One consequence of this is that citizens begin to behave like consumers, with policy debates driven by brand loyalty, resulting in a consumer culture designed to make public opinion an instrument of business power. We should not be surprised that, in this context, cynicism about the possibility of cooperation grows. "Attacking your opponents' frame reinforces their message," so Lakoff's advice is to avoid engaging in policy debates with those who hold opposing views (xiii). Better to ignore your opponent, avoid challenging political conversations about the future of American democracy, and work on reframing the entire debate over what is and what is not just plain common sense to advance your own competing interest.

For Lakoff, frames change what we see and "the way we reason and what counts as common sense" (xv). For this reason, the Lakoff-Rove public relations approach to policy deliberation makes the profoundly undemocratic suggestion that the winning strategy is to construct an information system modeled on the Tower of Babel, where we intentionally speak in mutually unintelligible languages and spread forms of social autism through viral marketing. As Lakoff puts it, "When you are arguing against the other side: Do not use their language" (3). While a serious challenge to democratic deliberation, this strategy cannot be dismissed for simply normative reasons. If their words draw you into their frames, their worldview, their movie, their trap, then we must be attentive to the ways that language and images can be professionally designed to filter out inconvenient facts, uncomfortable contradictions, and even the possibility of reasonable positions contrary to our own.

In our view, this is a prescription for sound-bite sabotage, unless we move beyond a narrow and an interested focus on framing alone to develop a language (with text and images) that invites open and informed deliberation, as we see in Barack Obama's *Audacity of Hope* or John Danforth's *Faith and Politics*, for instance. While we are not contending that there is an entirely neutral or value-free language waiting to be constructed, we are arguing that it is manifestly preferable that we continue to work toward the ideal or aspiration captured here rather than simply develop competing scripts for alternate movies, with the same biases as the language developed by our opponents. This pattern favors insulating the elite strategies we highlight here from scrutiny, makes understanding politics more difficult, and increases the capacity of those with resources to divert public attention in ways that decrease public awareness.[12]

We certainly do need to recognize and understand the power behind language and issue framing, but not in order to *avoid* the difficult conversations we need to engage in with those who hold opposing views. Language and framing designed to avoid communication are at the heart of sound-bite sabotage. We need to deconstruct those frames that move us toward positions contrary to our best available data, that discredit data gathering, serious analysis, and deliberation itself, but not to silence our opponents by exploiting our superior resources to saturate them with our own favored sound bites. We need leaders to speak in ways that we expect will advance partisan positions *and* strengthen the political and cultural preconditions for democratic deliberation—what we call "nesting" in chapter 4. Such leadership would be more democratic, and we address this question further in our concluding chapter.

As Brock, Frank, Lakoff, and others have argued, we need to make explicit the implicit links between interested positions articulated through privately funded think tanks, media outlets, and interest group activities funded by anti-intellectual extremists.[13] "They are not stupid. They are winning because they are smart." They win, because "they say what they idealistically believe," unconstrained by data or propriety. They make complex arguments popular. "This kind of language use is a science. . . . When you think you just lack words, what you really lack are ideas. Ideas come in the form of frames. When the frames are there, the words come readily." For instance, why not link progressive ideas around the frame "taxes are a wise investment in the future" (Lakoff 2004, 17–25) instead of either running from any mention of taxes (and contributing to the impoverishment of the public sector) or just repeating the same tired rhetoric about this or that policy without addressing the powerfully popularized notions associated with irresponsible "tax and spend" leadership. Without reframing at the meta-conflict level, any policy idea that will cost money is at risk of defeat at the hands of forces unrelated to the merits of that policy. With only reframing, we simply replace one ready-made and interested position with another, skipping the thinking and deliberation required to make democracy both possible and desirable.

According to Lakoff, we need to understand all of this in order to avoid being typecast, avoid being trapped in another's movie, avoid being dismissed without being heard. "In an ongoing conversation, your job is to establish a position of respect and dignity, and then keep it." Avoid the usual mistakes: do not negate their claims; reframe the debate. *"Once your frame is accepted into the discourse, everything you say is just common sense.* Why? Because that's what common sense is: reasoning within a common-place, accepted frame" (Lakoff 2004, 115–16, emphasis in original). We see the power in Lakoff's analysis of the importance of language and framing but want to avoid simply using his insights to replicate and compound distortions through a better use of sabotage. Instead, more democratic forms of discourse that take the power of language and framing seriously also need to be sure not to simply replicate divisiveness, amplified by old or new media, further encouraging passive and dependent forms of misinformed and doubtful citizenship supporting democracy limited to a cynical spectator sport.

Private Ownership and Public Spectacles: Mutually
Reinforcing Propagandizing

According to Noam Chomsky, the transformation of democracy into a spectator sport began with public-sector efforts by the Wilson administration's Creel Commission to mobilize a pacifist population to fight the Germans in 1916. They developed the PR techniques that were then applied to a long series of "crises," from the Red scare to Kennedy's missile gap or Johnson's Gulf of Tonkin incident to the Vietnam syndrome and beyond. "Propaganda is to democracy what a bludgeon is to a totalitarian state" (Chomsky 2002, 20–21). Quoting political scientist Harold Lasswell, Chomsky identifies several public and private and progressive and conservative leaders, advocating that America "not succumb to 'democratic dogmatisms about men being the best judges of their own interests.' " Instead, Chomsky, quoting Kennedy administration favorite Reinhold Niebuhr, explains that these public and private leaders thought we ought to "create 'necessary illusions' and emotionally potent 'oversimplifications' to keep the naïve simpletons more or less on course" (20).

Chomsky concludes that this is "one reason why people have found it so easy over the years to drift from one position to another without any particular sense of change. It's just a matter of assessing where power is. Maybe there will be a popular revolution, and that will put us into state power; or maybe there won't be, in which case we'll just work for the people with real power: the business community. *But we'll do the same thing.* We'll drive the stupid masses toward a world that they're too dumb to understand for themselves" (15–16, emphasis added). Since Chomsky argues that the techniques we have focused on have long been used by leaders on both sides, he provides a nonpartisan long-term perspective on tactics central to sound-bite sabotage, linking public and private leadership.

"The leading figure in the public relations industry, Edward Bernays, actually came out of the Creel Commission. He was part of it, learned his lessons there and went on to develop what he called the 'engineering of consent,' which he described as 'the essence of democracy' " (29). Bernays was also the architect of the public relations campaign for the United Fruit Company in 1954 (when they mobilized the United States to overthrow the democratically elected government of Guatemala). His legacy can still be seen in Reagan-era programs that were wildly unpopular (rearmament, cutting social programs) before the administration's propaganda redirected public concerns (31), as well as in the work of Karl Rove and George Lakoff. The public relations industry became the enormous force it is today at the same time the Creel Commission and Red scare were in full swing. And these techniques were applied against unions in the 1930s as the Wagner Act prohibited private use of force against strikers, and leaders turned to public relations efforts to reframe entire communities of steel or rubber workers as "disruptive" and "anti-American." While these labels had no coherent empirical referent, the ability to saturate communication channels with them gave them real power. And this gets us to the conclusion we want to take from Chomsky:

> The point of public relations slogans like "Support our troops" is that they don't mean anything. . . . That's the whole point of good propaganda. You want to create a slogan that nobody is going to be against, and everybody's going to be for. Nobody knows what it means, because it doesn't mean anything. Its crucial value is that it diverts

> your attention from a question that *does* mean something: Do
> you support our policy? That's the one you're not allowed
> to talk about. (Chomsky 2002, 26, emphasis in original)

While we do not agree that sound bites mean *nothing*, we agree that
they are a diversionary tool that works by obscuring the more important questions about power that democratic citizens need to ask and
relentlessly pursue. Robert McChesney similarly traces the roots of
current information system biases to historical trends that culminate
in private-sector control over the mass media and, in particular, the
ways that a privatized media invite exploitation "by politicians and
public figures, who learned how to take advantage of their roles as
legitimate news sources by carefully manipulating their coverage. More
importantly, the emergence of professional journalism was quickly followed by the establishment of public relations as an industry whose
primary function is to generate favorable coverage in the press without
public awareness of its activities" (1997, 15). *Diverting public attention*
without increasing public awareness is at the heart of sound-bite sabotage.
"With fewer journalists, limited budgets, low salaries and lower
morale, the balance of power has shifted dramatically to the public
relations industry, which seeks to fill the news media with coverage
sympathetic to its clients" (25).

    This analysis supports work done separately by the formerly
extreme Right journalist David Brock and Progressive journalist Eric
Alterman, emphasizing that big business has initiated and lavishly
funded wide-ranging public relations campaigns that seek to divert both
public attention from policy questions that matter and to confuse publics
about the challenges we face and how politics works (or sometimes does
not work) in order to "weaken opposition to the business position [or]
at least make it easier for powerful interests to ignore popular opinion"
(McChesney 1997, 26).[14] Lakoff demonstrates the power of framing, and
these other scholars connect this technique to sound-bite sabotage, but
our analysis suggests that while a focus on framing alone may win an
election or sell a Coke, it remains premised on disempowering forms of
seeding citizen doubt, avoiding serious communication, and weakening
the possibility of democratic deliberation.

    So, while framing is important, we need a richer analytical tool
box to continue unpacking sound-bite sabotage. We will do this by
moving from the ways sound-bite saboteurs, recognizing conflict as
opportunity, frame and divert citizen attention to win policy debates
or discrete electoral contests. In the next section we will examine the
ways in which these same techniques are used with larger interests

in mind to saturate communication channels with branded information designed not just to mobilize citizens on policy questions but to reconstruct common sense, undermine citizen communication and deliberation skills, and seed doubts about the possibility and desirability of democratic governance itself.

III. Opportunities to Concentrate Attention: Reassuring Citizen Subjects

Conflicts are opportunities for leaders. Choosing among the conflicts we face, which of the many conflicts ought to be prioritized by putting it on the public agenda, is the heart and soul of politics. We participate in our own de-skilling and disempowerment when we allow leaders, public or private, to persuade us that conflicts are problems for leaders, or even that conflict is unusual or abnormal, or that only deviants or kids on the prison track or third world countries struggle with conflicts, or that we ought to fear conflict itself. Conflict is normal and routine and *effective leaders learn how to use conflicts*—by amplifying some and muting others—as one of their most powerful tools of governance.[15] Certainly the most thoughtful and persuasive articulation of this essential political insight today can be found in the work of Jonathan Simon, most particularly his *Governing through Crime*. But this insight is also rooted in Schattschneider's classic work as well:

> Conflict is so powerful an instrument of politics that all regimes are of necessity concerned with its management, with its use in governing, and with its effectiveness as an instrument of change, growth, and unity. The grand strategy of politics deals with public policy concerning conflict. This is the ultimate policy. The most powerful instrument for the control of conflict is conflict itself. . . . Political conflict is not like an intercollegiate debate in which the opponents agree in advance on a definition of the issues. As a matter of fact, *the definition of the alternatives is the supreme instrument of power;* the antagonists can rarely agree on what the issues are because power is involved in the definition. He who determines what politics is about runs the country, because the definition of the alternatives is the choice of conflicts, and the choice of conflicts allocates power. It follows that all conflict is confusing. (Schattschneider 1975, 65–66, emphasis in original)

All politics is confusing because we are fighting two wars at the same time. We want to get a stop sign put up on a dangerous street corner, and we want either the mayor's office or our city councilwoman to be able to do this without interference. As the battle over who has the legal authority becomes increasingly arcane, involving complicated uses of Robert's Rules of Order, decisions about which subcommittee has jurisdiction, and ending up both in the papers and in the courts, we soon discover—in practice—that politics is confusing. Politics is confusing, in part, because one common strategy, conflict displacement, has the added benefit for leadership of making politics even more confusing for the rest of us. By its very nature conflict plays out on multiple levels, and we fight to try to define and fix the particular level. It is often the more obscure procedural levels that matter the most, that is, that play the largest role in determining substantive outcomes.

Procedural complexity can certainly create confusion for citizens denied a stop sign because a state court ruled that city managers do not have the same statutory authority as an elected mayor, which sends the question back to a different subcommittee for another hearing. What do such maneuvers have to do with my stop sign, citizens wonder? Understanding the importance of meta-conflicts and conflict displacement is, therefore, central to understanding the structural preconditions for sound-bite sabotage. If conflict displacement is already an established elite political strategy, and we add (1) the growth of an alternative and interested knowledge production system, and (2) the powerful tools available in old and new media to reframe and amplify, then this time-honored strategy can result in adding more confusion, which advances the private interests of sound-bite saboteurs and their affluent sponsors.

Analyzing conflict displacement as a central aspect of political struggle is not new. Schattschneider's work comparing political parties with interest groups is only the most famous. Baumgartner and Jones have written the most authoritative analysis of interest group politics available today, and it builds on Schattschneider's insight here to highlight, again, the centrality of the struggle over image and venue in our efforts to displace competing conflicts (or competing ways of framing a particular conflict) from the public agenda and direct attention to our preferred framing of our preferred conflicts. While certainly complex, this perspective highlights the strategic heart of politics, the importance of often obscure meta-conflicts over framing and venue, and the central role of elite leadership in a democratic society if we are to be able to navigate these waters.

The most important thing about any democratic regime is the way in which it *uses* and exploits popular sovereignty, what questions it refers to the public for decision or guidance, how it refers them to the public, how the alternatives are defined, and how it respects the limitations of the public. A good democratic system protects the public against the demand that it do impossible things. *The unforgivable sin of democratic politics is to dissipate the power of the public by putting it to trivial uses.* (Schattschneider 1975, 137, emphases added)

Schattschneider's point is that one opportunity created by conflicts and meta-conflicts is that leaders can choose to dissipate public energies by focusing on those more trivial conflicts that cause less harm, or the publicized aspects of conflicts that divert attention from real decision makers, thereby displacing a focus on conflicts causing greater harm and preventing a better understanding of the distribution of agency. Such conflicts also create an opportunity to focus citizen anger and frustration on harm caused by individual citizens and away from the much larger harm caused by leadership failures (see Glassner 1999). Sound-bite saboteurs, recognizing conflicts as opportunities, make the unforgivable sin their bread-and-butter mechanism for diverting public attention from leadership failures and *concentrating that attention on their interested messages,* the socio-cognitive schema designed by public relations experts to reconstruct common sense and reassure citizens as subjects without agency.

Conflict as an Opportunity to Construct Common Sense

But their interested messages are not only about "Coke is It." They are also efforts, as we saw in the previous chapter, to sell brand loyalty by constructing the imperatives of consumer culture, culture wars, and a right-utopian perspective on the free market as common sense. David Engel argues that understanding the complex and contingent ways that we manage ordinary conflicts over the meaning of law and community points to the importance of parallel struggles over what ought to be taken to be common sense. His analysis reveals a framing struggle over a perceived litigation explosion that turns out to be "less about the quantity of litigation at any given time than about the interests being asserted or protected through litigation and the kinds of individuals or groups involved in cases that the courts are asked to resolve" (1984, 551).

It turns out that the conflicts in the communities he observed focused on the complex political and cultural construction of competing attitudes regarding the meaning of tort (personal injury) and contract litigation. Engel finds that area farmers had developed a local culture where insiders looked down upon personal injury claims but valued contract claims. Longtime residents amplified and *made* salient their perception of a problem of litigiousness driven by personal injury claims brought by more recent immigrant factory workers, despite data to the contrary, to mute and reduce the political and economic power of these claims and the communities concerned about these.

Engel finds that the conflicts are rooted in two competing and culturally conditioned ideas of what an injury is and how (different kinds of) conflicts ought to be normatively evaluated, that is, how these conflicts should be framed: as narrow and private conflicts (where informal networks only available to longtime insiders are used to resolve conflicts) or broadly publicized in court (where tort law provided a modest resource to level the playing field for more recent arrivals). Further, these competing notions about the nature of injury, community, and law were themselves reflections of how these two communities understood *individualism*—as individual rights or individual self-sufficiency. Engel demonstrated how each understanding, while consistent with competing but interwoven threads within American political thought, grew out of the particular socioeconomic structure those holding that view lived and worked within, one agrarian and the other commercial, one rooted in place for generations and another grounded in a more modern and mobile labor force, one tied to tradition and the other to a vision of the future.

Most important for our work here, the leaders of each community designed a way of framing their conflicts that depended significantly on competing images of what "level-headed" and "realistic" meant, and each image differed according to what made sense in their own particular circumstances and what advanced their private interests, their preferred way of framing the core conflicts, as just plain old common sense and self-evidently in the public interest. This meta-conflict over the construction of common sense made the displacement of one framing of this conflict over the meaning of law and community with a preferred alternative—just a matter of common sense. Since the payoff is enormous when leaders can rely on images as powerful as common sense in their efforts to concentrate attention on their interested messages, sound-bite saboteurs take advantage of any opportunity to fight meta-conflicts.

Like Lakoff's analysis of how language frames cognition through the images that particular frames bring to mind, Edelman argues that images, "rather than meticulous descriptions, become the currency in which we think about and mutually negotiate changes in the world we inhabit" (2001, 12). And not all images are created equal; some dominate, displacing other images, "because they flow from established power and economic relationships and, in turn, are essential for the creation and preservation of both public and private power relations" (13). When elites succeed at reconstructing the images of common sense that concentrate the attentions of the audiences they seek, they are mobilizing images with monumental political and cultural power. While average citizens are likely to experience common sense as shared and immutable, a scholarly perspective on image manipulation, like reframing strategies that simply recycle one of two interested elite positions, highlights the ways that the ambiguity and mutability of common sense work as an instrument of the powerful.

Simply reframing or re-imaging common sense, powerful as these tools clearly are, remains a form of discursive and socio-cognitive fragmentation harmful to the social and cultural foundations of democratic deliberation. An information system where powerful agents *simply* compete to reframe issues reassures citizens by treating them more like subjects, agency-poor pinballs bouncing from this bell to that whistle. Sound-bite sabotage creates this dynamic, resulting in mobilized (but often more profoundly cynical) publics with agency more concentrated among elites. At the same time, however, for normative and instrumental reasons, sound-bite saboteurs do not simply reframe or only re-imagine. They do not just divert attention from their efforts to represent private interests as public interests. They also reframe and re-imagine in order to concentrate the attention of key publics in ways that construct alternative (and at least virtually shared) languages and images about politics and agency and the free market that they expect to better enable them to advance their private interests by reassuring the agency impoverished that the system is working.

Concentrating Our Attention on Liberal Bias

One of the most powerful illustrations of sound-bite saboteurs succeeding in this cultural investment strategy is the commonplace—and arguably incorrect—reference in public debates to the self-evident truth that there is a liberal bias in the media.[16] As noted by conservative David Brock,

> From my very first days at the *Washington Times*, I was
> schooled to invoke "liberal bias" to deflect attention from
> my own biases and journalistic lapses. . . . I was delivering a
> truckload of nonfacts, half-truths, and innuendos, not "bal-
> ance" or "the other side." What I show in *The Republican
> Noise Machine* is that my experience was not the exception
> but the rule. The "liberal media" mantra aside, if one looks
> and listens closely to what the right wing says when it
> thinks others may not be paying attention, there should be
> no doubt that it has made potent political gains not despite
> the media but *through* it. Rush Limbaugh says his program
> has "redefined the media" and refers to the "Limbaugh echo
> chamber syndrome," by which messaging originating on his
> show drives the 24-hour news cycle. "The radical left," he
> says, "is furious that liberals no longer set the agenda in
> the national media." (2004, 8, emphasis in original)

According to Brock, "conservative *New York Times* columnist David
Brooks argues the new media have 'cohered to form a dazzlingly
efficient ideology delivery system that swamps liberal efforts to get
their ideas out.' . . . According to Bill O'Reilly 'For decades [liberals]
controlled the agenda on TV news. That's over.' " (2004, 9). Brock
concludes, therefore, that the noise machine was "a deliberate, well-
financed, and expressly acknowledged communications and deregula-
tory plan" developed "in close coordination with Republican Party
leadership . . . with the intention of skewing American politics sharply
to the right. The plan has succeeded spectacularly. The implications
of this right-wing media incursion extend well beyond particular
political outcomes to the heart of our democracy. . . . This conscious
effort by the right wing to misinform the American citizenry—to collapse the distinction between journalism and propaganda—is thus an
assault on democracy itself" (8–11). While we argue that the trend
Brock identifies is a less strictly partisan affair, our point here is that,
given his account of his own experience as a sound-bite saboteur and
the widespread willingness of conservative leaders to recognize their
domination of our information system, it is difficult to conclude that
there is a self-evident liberal bias in the media.

Eric Alterman further confirms this finding in *What Liberal Media?*
He quotes Rich Bond (1992 chair of the RNC), saying, "There was
some strategy to bashing the liberal media; if you watch any great
coach, what they try to do is 'work the refs' " (2003, 2). Media-savvy
Republican Party strategist James Baker noted that while individual

stories may skew one way or the other, "on balance I don't think we had anything to complain about" (2).

Why does the Right succeed so much more in "working the refs," the crowd, the audience today? It is no accident, and it is certainly not a uniquely right-wing phenomena. It is rooted in a most ordinary form of political conflict: private interest group pressure on public officials for policies favorable to their private interests directed at distorting political communication generally. Today this pressure is better funded and more coordinated on the Right, making their efforts to work the refs, to script our political spectacles, more powerful. We argue that the wealth of concrete detail provided by Brock and Alterman demonstrates the furious amount of private interest group activity and its enormous influence. The currently prevailing powerhouses at working the refs enjoy much more generous corporate, private foundation, and wealthy individual funding for papers such as the *Washington Times* (operated at losses of $100 million and counting), the *New York Post* (Murdoch has operated at heavy losses for twenty-five years), or magazines such as the *Weekly Standard* (Murdoch loses about $1 million a year), or even wire services such as UPI (now controlled by Reverend Moon).

The power of these commercial distribution networks is amplified by an allied team of think tanks that similarly enjoys more generous corporate, private foundation, and wealthy individual funding: the Hoover Institute, the American Enterprise Institute, the Competitive Enterprise Institute, the Manhattan Institute, the Heritage Foundation (created with Coors funds, also used through Heritage to support the "Conservative Lunch Club" that launched the careers of George Will, Trent Lott, Paul Weyrich, and others), the National Center for Policy Analysis, and the CATO Institute (supports *City Journal*). These and other related think tanks provide career platforms to develop and employ conservative activists as journalists writing for publications funded from the same sources, such as *The Public Interest* or *The American Spectator*. And many of these nurtured conservatives are now regular commentators for all of the television and cable networks, on talk radio, and in the blogsphere, creating an impression of a broad and spontaneous movement intersecting around conservative themes, whereas in reality they started their divergent careers from remarkably similar—and not disinterested—designer starting points.[17]

Alterman quotes two other powerful private-sector leaders who recognize the interested phoniness of the "liberal bias" refrain:

Patrick Buchanan, among the most conservative pundits and presidential candidates in the republic's history, found that he could not identify any allegedly liberal bias against him during his presidential candidacies. "I've gotten balanced coverage . . . all we could have asked. For heaven's sake, [referring to the 1996 presidential campaign] we kid about the 'liberal media,' but every Republican on earth does that." . . . And even William Kristol, without a doubt the most influential Republican/neoconservative publicist in America, has come clean on the issue. "I admit it," he told a reporter. "The liberal media were never that powerful, and the whole thing was often used as an excuse by conservatives for conservative failures." (2003, 2)

Alterman concludes that the "liberal media" refrain is as phony as it is widespread. It is an effort to systematically reshape one common-sense image that plays a powerful role as a background consensus—an asserted rather than achieved agreement over one meta-conflict—upon which other arguments are built. And this powerful sound-bite sabotages our information system as it "empowers conservatives to control debate in the United States to the point where liberals cannot even hope for a fair shake anymore" (2003, 2).[18]

For our purposes the central point here is that the taken-for-granted status of the all-purpose charge of "liberal bias" can be seen as an illustration of sound-bite saboteurs' public-sector investments in faking context to not only divert, but also concentrate, the attentions of key publics. This particular refrain, having near commonsense status today, reassures citizen subjects that their ever-decreasing number of encounters with challenging perspectives or discomforting data can be safely dismissed as a reflection of the well-known liberal bias in the media, public schools, universities, the publishing industry, Congress, and the courts.

As we will see when we examine the case of tort reform advocacy later in this chapter, sound-bite saboteurs see conflict as an opportunity to do more than win an isolated policy debate; they see it as an invitation to advance their particular vision of American democracy as common sense and use this as the cultural foundation for winning countless policy debates. Their current right-utopian perspective on the free market has roots in the interested messages embedded in branded information and articulates one fairly extreme vision of good government as if it were common sense.

Paul Krugman argues in the *New York Times*, for instance, that our current inability to think seriously about health care reform is rooted in prevailing notions of common sense about the relationship between public and private sectors, notions packaged and sold by out-of-the-mainstream right utopians, who continually assert, despite overwhelming data to the contrary in the case of health care, that privatization is always more efficient than government service delivery. This operates as a powerful ideological obstacle to sober deliberation about our current health care crisis, and in a way that favors public policy tilted toward the private interests of those designing and marketing the prevailing notions upon which the policy conclusions are based (Krugman 2005b).[19]

> Those of us who accuse the administration of inventing a Social Security crisis are often accused, in return, of do-nothingism, of refusing to face up to the nation's problems. I plead not guilty: America does face a real crisis—but it's in health care, not Social Security. Well-informed business executives agree. A recent survey of chief financial officers at major corporations found that 65 percent regard immediate action on health care costs as "very important." Only 31 percent said the same about Social Security reform. But serious health care reform isn't on the table, and in the current political climate it probably can't be. You see, the health care crisis is ideologically inconvenient. . . .
>
> To get effective reform, however, we'll need to shed some preconceptions—in particular, the ideologically driven belief that government is always the problem and market competition is always the solution. The fact is that in health care, the private sector is often bloated and bureaucratic, while some government agencies—notably the Veterans Administration system—are lean and efficient. In health care, competition and personal choice can and do lead to higher costs and lower quality. The United States has the most privatized, competitive health system in the advanced world; it also has by far the highest costs, and close to the worst results. (Krugman 2005b)

Echoing portions of Tom Baker's brilliant analysis of *The Medical Malpractice Myth*, Krugman demonstrates that we have the most privatized—but one of the lowest quality—health care systems in the industrialized world. And, even with the most privatized system, our government pays more per person for health care than the governments in countries routinely criticized for having national health care (2005d).[20] For Krugman, the obstacle to even seeing these facts is ideological. It is a policy obstacle, preventing us from more efficiently allocating tax dollars to reduce harm to over 40 million Americans, rooted in the widely shared false notion that privatized is always better than government provision. And it is not a random obstacle but an interested obstacle, because it also sows a fundamentally crippling sense of doubt about what governments can accomplish.

We see similarly powerful challenges to this interested reconstruction of common sense in *Seeds of Deception, The Medical Malpractice Myth, Culture of Fear, Crimes against Nature, Born to Buy, Wealth and Democracy*, David Brock's work, and Mark Smith's work. These works document elite exploitation of conflicts to sow doubt about particular policy positions and self-governance itself. Ambiguity and healthy debate are reframed as a frighteningly secular and relativist world where average citizens can no longer rely on experts, where all positions are just someone's opinion, and we are encouraged to choose the opinion set—along with our newest outfit—that is the most familiar and comfortable fit, because its familiarity reassures us that it is widely shared and appropriate. Each documents an attention distracting *and concentrating* noise in the news, among talking heads in the commentariat, on television, talk radio, and the blogosphere that can be traced to the interested messages of powerful corporations or wealthy individuals who, since the Powell memo in this particular period, have consciously sought to create their own alternative information, expertise, and knowledge-production industry.[21] One of their central objectives is to sell their own right-utopian, anti-government regulation, fragmented and confusing perspective on politics. And these investments have succeeded—in part on the basis of sound-bite sabotage—in distorting our information system, weakening scientific inquiry and public education, and constructing this particular perspective on governance as authoritative, by making it so familiar it feels like common sense.

Branded Information and Interest Group Activities

Baumgartner and Jones are perhaps the most respected analysts of interest group politics in America today, and their punctuated equilibrium model focuses explicitly on the struggle over issue framing through image and venue control. The two factors that account for both stasis and change are "how issues are portrayed and which institutions [as a result] have jurisdiction over them" (Baumgartner and Jones 1993, 1). Framing and image contests, individual, interest group, and institutional competition over effective agency, are the core micro-mechanisms that, over time, constitute our macro decision-making processes as "culturally reshaped mosaics" (6), where any current zeitgeist operates as a provisional background consensus—a temporary, but no less powerful, monopoly of political understanding on particular issues.

Powerful, because these contingent monopolies operate as a form of common sense about what is rational and level-headed in particular policy arenas, and for government action generally. Powerful, because these ideological mechanisms operate in conjunction with institutional structures to limit access to policy arenas and, thereby, limit debate within them. The combination of image and venue prevailing at any given moment, then, reflects the successful mobilization of particular private-interest groups in the form of a dominant paradigm, however provisional, that sets our public agenda—that constitutes what we will argue about.

> Every interest, every group, every policy entrepreneur has a primary interest in establishing a monopoly—a monopoly of political understandings concerning the policy of interest, and an institutional arrangement that reinforces that understanding. (Baumgartner and Jones 1993, 6)

In this context, and as Lakoff would recommend, political and cultural agents "need not alter the opinions of their adversaries" (Baumgartner and Jones 1993, 4) if they can persuade others to think of the issue differently enough to alter jurisdiction or reframe the conflict by controlling its image in the news. If successful, they can write a new script for enacting the relevant policy debate, enhancing their control over the terms of debate in particular areas of interest and over the institutional arrangements that reinforce that understanding. This analysis describes a fluid situation, where "political stability is contingent on the actions of political entrepreneurs" (14). That is, we see political conflict as normal and ongoing, complex and structurally vulnerable to exploitation by interest group lobbyists. And we see a conflict management dynamic that is increasingly vulnerable to those interested private parties with public relations skills, because the provisional stability observed in the temporary policy monopolies constitutive of our political system "are maintained through the allocation of attention of government elites and the apathy of those not keenly interested in the particular issue handled by the policy subsystem" (18).[22]

While Baumgartner and Jones highlight the apathy of those "not keenly interested," their point about the allocation of attention also suggests that the political dynamic they describe has the secondary consequence of encouraging apathy among others, including many who would be keenly interested, but either lack the resources needed to have a hired lobbyist at every subcommittee hearing, or have had their attentions diverted and concentrated on more trivial issues—one core technique of sound-bite sabotage, a technique that has grown more significant as traditional interest groups have come to dominate both outsider and insider approaches to pressure group politics. Diverting the public's attention to trivial issues adds to their superior insider access, and the application of their superior resources to take advantage of the tools of public relations to directly make public opinion an instrument of business power.[23]

Traditional interest groups are private citizens who share an economic or occupational interest and pressure public officials for policies favorable to that shared private interest. These include business and labor groups, and these groups constitute the overwhelming majority of interest groups (over 80 percent) and are even more dominant in terms of resources available to them to pressure public officials. Public interest groups are private citizens who share an interest in an ideal or a cause and pressure public officials for policies favorable to that shared interest. Traditional interest groups have always enjoyed an enormous lobbying advantage derived from their superior access to decision makers—access rooted in several factors: shared social class, educational pedigree, residential locations, career paths, and the fact that many of these private-sector lobbyists are recently retired public-sector leaders. Known as the "revolving door," high-level government employees who work for the FDA, for instance, retire and become paid lobbyists for the pharmaceutical industry, lobbying their former colleagues at the FDA. This is the insider game.

Over the past forty years, however, traditional interest groups have become much more active and now dominate the outsider game as well (grassroots organizing, public education campaigns, etc.). That is, in addition to the access advantages, they are also now exploiting their superior resources to try to pressure for public policies favorable to their private interests by seeking to manage public opinion more directly. When the powerfully connected create policy monopolies insulated from democratic scrutiny, these "arrangements are maintained through the allocation of attention." We can see this as a structural and an interested inattentiveness to the atrophy of democratic deliberation at the highest levels (Baumgartner and Jones 1993, 26). Since "any time political actors can introduce new dimensions of conflict, they can destabilize a previously stable situation," in an increasingly media-driven communicative context, attentiveness and apathy—and strategies to distribute these—become more important political variables, and those with expertise in public relations become more powerful political agents.

People have a limited capacity for "simultaneous attention to different information," limiting the public agenda to perhaps six issues at a time, and political entrepreneurs know journalists' work routines and try to provide prepackaged story frames that simplify complex issues in ways that "move their issues into more receptive venues" (105). Further, as issues move into the public sphere, the temptation to exaggerate claims rises, because journalist work routines favor dramatizing routine conflict. Thus public and private interested parties exploit market and professional imperatives of the mass media to amplify conflicts and distort public agendas, imposing "more intense coverage than circumstances warrant" (105), in part because the struggle over the allocation of attention has expanded the scope of meta-conflicts to include the growing importance of public relations experts willing to fake both text and context and the loosely coordinated networking of these agents in the funding patterns of private-sector leaders we have described. It is this combination that supports our claim in this section that sound-bite sabotage is not only about diverting attention but also, and perhaps more importantly, about concentrating attention on particular and interested perspectives regarding the nature of democratic governance and about the relationship between public and private leaders in democratic societies.

Because rhetorical battles over issue framing mobilize media bias, impacting institutional venues and policy outcomes, politics is, in fact, made more confusing in order to advance private interests. When public attention is drawn to divisive and largely expressive cultural conflicts that highlight only government incompetence to construct privatization as always preferred, deliberation among those with opposing views is made more difficult to achieve, because these meta-conflicts are more hidden from public view (and scrutiny), and the interested approaches to these conflicts are simply asserted, saturating our communication channels, as common sense. Even public interested leaders are then pressured to ignore rather than refute competing images, speaking to different audiences with rolling talking points, making systematic treatment of any issue difficult because there are incentives to focus on only one aspect, encouraging leadership behavior that increases political and cultural instability.

Reassuring Images That Discourage Individual Agency

When the fragmented politics and distorted information examined earlier do not sufficiently insulate any particular policy arena from meaningful citizen agency, competing positions can still make it to the table anyway. In this context, the larger cultural investments at the level of common sense and prevailing notions of American democracy, also discussed earlier, provide a readily available reservoir of resentments for elites to amplify in their ongoing efforts to divert citizen attention by displacing conflicts. "Widely held animosities similarly divert attention from the need for social change because they are far more intense as political beliefs than recognition of the need for institutional reforms and so are readily exploited" (Edelman 2001, 23). Widespread, but dubious, animosity toward liberal bias is one such reassuring image.[24] Complex and overlapping differences in income, lifestyle, family wealth, and education can also be condensed into familiar stereotypes, given the resources to access and saturate our information system. But designing interested messages about "demons to explain unfortunate conditions is a strategy for avoiding the analysis that is necessary to understand and remedy the conditions" (33), and it is a strategy for confusing individual or collective citizen efforts to self-govern.

In this context, leadership is less about policy competence and more about "skill in manipulating the spectacle of building audiences and keeping them entertained" and redividing competing publics "to legitimize conventional assumptions" that obscure the importance of analyzing interest group activity (40, 56). For Edelman, this distortion is one key reason politics can be experienced as heated and confusing, even as policy change is minimal. Information that is useful for democratic citizens must challenge our views. It is more useful when it is both news and new, rather than simply confirmative, familiar, and comfortable. But commercialized news socializes us to expect entertaining news and to fear and loathe news that contains or demands serious analysis. Private leaders (of the mass media, in particular) and public leaders (who exploit these media) encourage us to see cooperation and compromise as uncomfortable signs of weakness, ambiguity and complexity as avoidable, given the reassuring images readily available to displace these and suffocate serious analysis. Edelman argues that the only reasonable conclusion we can draw is that the language of policy agendas is more about reassurance than about problem solving (Edelman 1995, 405).

DeLuca and Buell (2005) argue in their study of demonization that sound-bite sabotage often involves "techniques of self-validation," where our own "group identity is buttressed, one's values and moral worth are demonstrated, by placing them all in stark relief against that of one's antagonists. Resentments, anger, and outrage are *cultivated*" (49, emphasis added). Stanley Fish (2001) identifies one recent leadership effort to cultivate and redirect citizen outrage through appeals to commonsense notions that, upon closer examination, prove to be phony and dangerous. In analyzing the debates over who was or was not cowardly and irrational immediately following the terrorist attacks on 9/11, he provides one of the best texts available for clarifying this point about concentrating public attention to reassure citizen subjects.[25]

Fish points out that "cowardly" fails to describe the terrorists' actions. More importantly, we do not "condone that act" when we choose to describe it more productively. "In fact, you put yourself in a better position to respond to it by taking its true measure. Making the enemy smaller than he is blinds us to the danger he presents and gives him the advantage that comes along with having been underestimated" (2001). The same is true when we label terrorists irrational. "The better course is to think of these men as bearers of a rationality we reject, because its goal is our destruction. If we take the trouble to understand that rationality, we might have a better chance of figuring out what its adherents will do next and preventing it." Taking the trouble to understand that rationality is, of course, precisely what we hope our intelligence analysts are doing. That is, we hope that they either ignore or are smart enough to discount as dangerous propaganda leadership efforts to focus our attentions on interested reconstructions of commonsense images about the evil, cowardly, and irrational nature of our enemies designed to reassure us that "they hate us because we are free."

Focusing our attention on these reassuring images encourages us to be both outraged and helpless, left with only patriotic support of elite preferred approaches to the conflict, no matter how ill advised. Fish highlights the importance of language and images in the struggle over what we will argue about. Further, just as accurately describing terrorist behavior does not mean we condone it, seeing the contingency and ambiguity at the center of politics does not reduce self-government to a morally vapid relativism—a claim that has itself seeped into popular culture as a form of commonsense sound-bite sabotage with roots in the same dynamics we are trying to unpack in this chapter. But allowing leaders to dissuade us from accurately describing and clearly seeing does confuse, even if it also superficially reassures, and both undermine effective citizen agency.

> Terrorism is the name of a style of warfare in service of a cause. It is the cause, and the passions informing it, that confront us. Focusing on something called international terrorism—detached from any specific purposeful agenda—only confuses matters. This should have been evident when President Vladimir Putin of Russia insisted that any war against international terrorism must have as one of its objectives victory against the rebels in Chechnya. (Fish 2001)

Or, when the Chinese took the opportunity created by this conflict to step up their suppression of Tibetan freedom fighters, now conveniently called terrorists. The confusion that grows from interested misnomers like these is also painfully apparent in the new film *Babel*, where childhood stupidity and a late night return from a family wedding are, in the context of a global war on terror, immediately suspect enough to mobilize the military of two powerful nations—with tragic consequences to the lives of ordinary citizens. But, Fish points out, simply recognizing the misnomer as branded information is not enough, because we also need to use this insight to better understand the very serious political struggle that this label seeks to misrepresent, a struggle that clearly implicates sound-bite saboteurs' efforts to seed within common sense a perspective on analysis that is profoundly anti-intellectual—to encourage a worldview that is a threat to both scholarly inquiry and national security. Fish writes:

> When Reuters decided to be careful about using the word "terrorism" because, according to its news director, one man's terrorist is another man's freedom fighter, Martin Kaplan, associate dean of the Annenberg School for Communication at the University of Southern California, castigated what he saw as one more instance of cultural relativism. But Reuters is simply recognizing how unhelpful the word is, because it prevents us from making distinctions that would allow us to get a better picture of where we are and what we might do. If you think of yourself as the target of terrorism with a capital T, your opponent is everywhere and nowhere. But if you think of yourself as

the target of a terrorist who comes from somewhere, even if he operates internationally, you can at least try to anticipate his future assaults.

Is this the end of relativism? If by relativism one means a cast of mind that renders you unable to prefer your own convictions to those of your adversary, then relativism could hardly end because it never began. Our convictions are by definition preferred; that's what makes them our convictions. Relativizing them is neither an option nor a danger.

But if by relativism one means the practice of putting yourself in your adversary's shoes, not in order to wear them as your own but in order to have some understanding (far short of approval) of why someone else might want to wear them, then relativism will not and should not end, because it is simply another name for serious thought. (2001)

One of our core contentions in this book is that the phenomenon we call sound-bite sabotage is fundamentally and purposefully anti-intellectual in the sense that it attacks the communicative and political-cultural preconditions for serious thought, deliberation, and collective problem solving.[26] The Powell memo makes the intention clear. Because the techniques identified here can educate as well as misinform, sound-bite sabotage is a dynamic where elites *choose* to miseducate key publics. We can use the tools of modern advertising and public relations to construct familiar and authoritative slogans, saturate our communication channels with them, and persuade citizens—by teaching them what the best available data show about these conflicts—to understand and support those steps that mark a path to a better future.[27] One might argue that the campaigns to teach us about heart disease risk factors, to prevent forest fires, or to understand (in order to avoid fear and chaos) the various ways anthrax is or is not ingested are recent illustrations of such positive use of these tools in the public sector. These same tools, however, can be used to mislead, misinform, and distract citizens, "dissipating public energies by focusing them on trivial issues," by displacing those conflicts that create the most harm in our lives from the public agenda to focus public attention on those fears our rulers determine for us.[28]

It is this aspect of sound-bite saboteurs that we want to highlight in this chapter: the ways in which these saboteurs displace political and economic conflicts and fears associated with serious, widespread harm with less harmful and more narrowcast cultural conflicts that dissipate and exhaust our democratic energies.[29] We are developing these particular illustrations because these are salient today, not to suggest that sound-bite sabotage only occurs in the form of culture wars. In fact, our earlier analysis has already suggested a wide range of displacement strategies other than political and economic to cultural. Advertising culture wars is, however, a commonplace and widespread displacement strategy today (Frank 2004). As one reporter recently commented regarding the ongoing debates over intelligence failures leading up to the September 11 terrorist attacks, a $40 billion a year intelligence system failed, in part, as a result of an information system operating in ways that confuse and obstruct serious thought. He noted, quoting one intelligence analyst, that the rise of 24-hour news networks and omnipresent new media challenged even sophisticated intelligence agencies with widespread cultural expectations for instant analysis. Instant news spawned instant analysis and suffocated deep thought. "A number of intelligence officials have lamented that the practice of strategic intelligence has eroded" in "an emerging information age of instant news bites," Douglas MacEachin, the CIA's deputy director for intelligence from 1993 to 1995, wrote last year.[30]

Sound-bite sabotage is a complex political and cultural dynamic that cripples communication—from the operations of our most elite intelligence officers to our students' more modest efforts to better understand the conflicts we face. Saboteurs take advantage of opportunities created by normal conflicts to divert and concentrate our attentions in the ways we have outlined. Perhaps the best way to demonstrate our point, however, is through a more detailed case study. In the next section we use the case of tort reform advocacy to bring together our efforts to illustrate the ways that branded information is politically interested. Thus we argue that branded information is interested in two ways. It is designed to sow doubts, avoid communication, and undermine agency at the citizen-consumer level and at the macro structural level, where it sows doubt about both the possibility and desirability of democratic governance itself.

IV. Tort Reform Advocacy: Sound-Bite Saboteurs in Action

According to Lance Bennett, managing images in the news has become "an essential part of successful governing and politics. . . . The textbook on how to manage the news was written during the Reagan administration. . . . As former White House communication director David Gergen put it: 'To govern successfully, the government has to set the agenda: it cannot let the press set the agenda for it' " (1996,

146–48). The information management plan developed by the Reagan administration (and used skillfully by the Clinton administration and others) resulted in one member of Reagan's White House communication team (Richard Wirthlin) winning the *Advertising Man of the Year Award* in 1989. The public-sector communication strategy that won this prestigious private-sector advertising award included, among other, now commonplace strategies, regular meetings to decide what the government wanted the press to cover each day, how to encapsulate that message into one "line of the day" for each member of the administration to repeat, saturating communication channels with this official message masquerading as news, and then managing journalist deviation from this interested message by a combination of spin and political pressure.

Reporters fall victim to this for several reasons, ranging from the pressure to fill the news hole to the professional norm of objectivity that creates a journalistic preference for authoritative voices to legitimize the news, creating what we call an official or elite bias in the news.[31] Ironically, the more objective journalists try to be, the more official bias they invite into the news. This elite bias in the news results from public and private leaders who are willing and able to exploit these and other well-known structural characteristics of privately owned mass media organizations, including journalistic preferences for individualized, fragmented, dramatized, and normalized news.[32] What Bennett's analysis reveals is that while the mass media remains a powerful political and cultural force (and its private leadership remains one target of our analysis here), the biases and distortions we observe in our information system are not *primarily* driven by what reporters in competing newsrooms do each day. Public and private leaders devote enormous resources to trying to control the news. Understanding sound-bite sabotage, then, requires us to examine both the volitional activities of these interested public and private leaders and the structural factors—most importantly manifest in new and old media—that enable the amplification of some messages and the muting of others.

Haltom and McCann build on Bennett's work in their detailed analysis of the systematic, loosely coordinated construction of "tort tales" or fables about a litigation explosion that, despite scholarly debunking, are still widely circulated as news today. Their analysis focuses on how these stories about individuals injured through corporate negligence came to be framed as morality tales about individual greed and a permissive criminal justice system. We began this chapter with one infamous case of "distorting the law," the McDonald's coffee case, drawing heavily from Haltom and McCann's analysis. In this section we will discuss in some detail their larger argument about tort reform advocacy in general and what it demonstrates about information system distortion in particular. We will see in the tort reform case, as Tom Baker finds with regards to medical malpractice advocacy, that when powerful actors collaborate to market stories designed to represent their private interests as a public interest, even when their stories are contrary to the best available data, the messages they create still penetrate deeply into our political culture, where they reconstitute common sense, suffocate serious thought, and weaken democratic decision making.

> Built on a foundation of urban legend mixed with the occasional true story, supported by selective references to academic studies, and repeated so often even the mythmakers forget the exaggeration, half truth, and outright misinformation employed in the service of their greater good, the medical malpractice myth has filled doctors, patients, legislators, and voters with the kind of *fear that short-circuits critical thinking.* (Baker 2005, 1, emphasis added)

Haltom and McCann begin by outlining the case of Judith Haimes, a victim of medical malpractice who was awarded $986,000 for damages in 1986 by a jury of her peers—and, as we noted earlier, studies show that these jurors come to tort cases suspicious of plaintiffs but are often still persuaded that the serious harm caused was a result of negligence.[33] Haimes suffered "a severe allergic reaction to an injection of dye prior to a CAT scan at Temple University Hospital in 1976," after warning the radiologist and the doctor about previous severe reactions and having her concerns dismissed as "ridiculous." But she never received a dime of that award. A judge set aside her judgment (and a new trial was dismissed by a second judge). But the sound-bite version of her story lives on as branded information. "Although interest in the lawsuit receded quietly," according to Haltom and McCann, "the original story developed a robust life of its own in American mass culture and politics.... News reports announcing the dismissal of the award were soon overtaken by published accounts that selectively translated the event into an entertaining morality tale about excessive litigiousness.... The fable quickly became a symbol for the thriving national tort reform movement" (2004, 1–3).

   This demonstrably false story continued to be cited by CEOs, comics, the *Washington Post*, Presidents Reagan and Bush, in professional publications, by tort reform advocates Walter Olson and Charles Sykes, by Harvard Law professor Kip Viscusi, in a *Time* magazine article, in numerous editorials, letters to the editor, popular press books and book reviews, and by Peter Huber, who "repeated the anecdote in his widely recognized book *Galileo's Revenge* (1991) and a companion *Forbes* article (1991) as a classic case of 'junk science' that routinely permeates our courts. Somehow Huber transformed an unorthodox malpractice claim that was thrown out of court for lack of evidence into an example of routine failure by the civil courts and a subversion of law by fraudulent science" (Haltom and McCann 2004, 4).[34]

Haltom and McCann argue that stories like this one are designed by interested parties to circulate as "tort tales" expected to divert and reconcentrate public attention by reframing efforts to hold corporations accountable for serious harm done to individuals as, instead, a plague of frivolous lawsuits driven by greedy lawyers, immoral plaintiffs, and permissive jurors. These tort tales then become part of a larger background consensus critical of lawyers and personal injury litigation, fueled by lawyer jokes and interested anecdotes, forming a new conventional wisdom made salient as another weapon in the cultural war against more democratic use of the courts to challenge powerful elites.[35] Like the Willie Horton ads, these stories demonstrate a routine political dynamic in which public and private elites use sophisticated PR techniques and superior resources to control the news and advance loosely linked "lines of the day" that are amplified by reporters who are, according to Haltom and McCann, dependent on official or other interested sources for news content to *construct* "dramatic anomalies as a way of normalizing the atypical so that it becomes, over time, a matter of 'common sense' " (6).

Haltom and McCann contrast these designer accounts (forged by networks of lobbyists, think tanks, and columnists advocating a particular privatized approach to tort reform that could not otherwise be persuasively sold on the basis of our best available data) with what they call a realist account, which highlights the enormous gaps between what we know and the messages sold in these tort tales. Most importantly, they find that the inaccuracies are not random, since they nearly always tilt in favor of a single elite-supported—and empirically unsupported—tort reform position. The distortion constitutive of sound-bite sabotage is not random but coordinated; the information is interested and designed to carry advertisements that advance a private interest as the public interest. This is what we mean by branded information. In the realist account, scholars have repeatedly shown that plaintiffs rarely win large judgments against corporations for defective products, that the number of cases has not increased (that is, no tort litigation explosion can be persuasively demonstrated), and that the key players (lawyers, judges, jurors) consistently act in ways that filter out the frivolous cases.

Haltom and McCann examine how it is that the more accurate story is repeatedly and overwhelmingly trumped by the calculated messages propagated by interested advocates. To do this they first analyze the instrumental activities and techniques used by tort reformers, revealing a complex and multilayered, social movement-like approach to reform, and a public relations approach to political communication that overwhelms scholarly analysis (40). Tort tales, when contrasted with scholarly analysis, are carefully crafted to be more *available* than balanced; more *accessible* and *adaptable* than reliable and scholarly; and more *affirmatively actionable* than detached and analytical (68–72).

Being more available then balanced, branded information can more successfully exploit resources and access advantages to saturate communication channels and *make* interested messages readily available. Being more accessible and adaptable, interested messages can more successfully exploit the freedom that comes with being outside of the scholarly peer review process to find more innovative ways to, as Haltom and McCann put it, "make the popular and intellectual merge" (40). Taken together, these advantages allow sound-bite saboteurs to more effectively link their stories to familiar and comfortable morality tales designed to mobilize supportive publics, marginalize others, and disempower both.

While realists "aspire to alter citizens' empirical knowledge about law" they leave "largely uncontested prevailing moral frameworks for assessing law in modern society" (75). Advocates, on the other hand, construct complimentary packages of powerful images advanced by selected anecdotes that concentrate attention on the moral of the story that advocates are interested in peddling, in this case, that privatization is always better public policy. Scholars repeatedly demonstrate that the data do not support the universality of this claim, to little effect. The interested advocates, as Frank puts it, may "get the facts wrong, but they get the subjective experience right" (137), an experience of powerlessness in search of someone to blame, communities in search of affirmatively actionable moral tales that make sense in our everyday lives to help us make sense of the conflicts we face.

> Available, accessible, adaptable, and affirmatively actionable appeals are undeniably powerful in mass culture. . . . The

more available, accessible, adaptable and affirmative that proposals and arguments supporting proposals are, the more that reform populizers persuade themselves anew. This dialectic is common. Advocates sign on to tort reform efforts because they come to believe that reforms will address problems. They marshal arguments and information that reinforce their beliefs and their exertions. The tort reform ideas they sell are ones they themselves have already bought. . . . Beyond defining tort problems and espousing tort solutions, tort reform rhetoric contributes to a holistic critique of civil justice and sociopolitical culture in the United States. Stories, sermons, slogans, and statistics mutually reinforce one another. *The result is a coherence so factually elusive and morally resonant that is difficult to rebut. . . .* [And that coheres as a] moralistic politics of resentment that big business can embrace. (Haltom and McCann 2004, 70–72, emphasis added)

The tactics of tort reform activists are an illustration of one change in our information system that is rooted, in part, in changes to our interest group system. While public interest groups have been growing in the past forty years, traditional interest groups have come to dominate both the insider and outsider approaches to pressure politics. In the past, those with insider access exercised great influence by directly engaging with decision makers (over private lunches or golf outings), but as Mark Smith shows quite clearly above, business lobbyists have come to realize the importance of dominating the outsider game as well, seeking to make public opinion an instrument of business power. Tort reformers, like traditional interest groups in general, enjoy tremendous insider access and have effectively used this access to pressure policy makers for public policy favorable to their private interests. Increasingly, they also combine these insider tactics with powerful efforts to influence policy through managing public opinion (grassroots organizing, public information campaigns, supporting talk radio, Christian broadcasting, and a network of elite commentators dominated by conservative voices today).

The interested information management strategies mobilized in this particular illustration are built on three legs: (1) generous, often hidden financing from extremely conservative corporations, family foundations, and wealthy individuals; (2) a plethora of diverse knowledge production and marketing organizations, made possible by this funding and designed to produce parallel clusters of "arresting ideas," packaged to link the popular and the scholarly. Further, the leaders of these organizations keep the diffuse but ideologically linked players on message and maximize the mutually reinforcing potential of their multiple platforms; and (3) public leadership mobilized to provide these private talking heads with authoritative legitimation for their arresting, and interested, messages. "Organization, financing, and leadership are essential to the accomplishment of the pop tort reform mission, but ideas constitute that mission. Absent ideas that arrest attention, any knowledge imparted is more likely to sustain a trivia contest than a regime change.... [The key has been] their strategic coordination in promulgating big, attractive ideas" (Haltom and McCann 2004, 40).

In the tort reform case, the key advocacy organizations are the Manhattan Institute[36] and the American Tort Reform Association. The Manhattan Institute sponsors scholars and creates opportunities to narrowcast (using sophisticated public relations techniques to target increasingly discrete segments of the public with messages tailored to the narrowest set of concerns for those segments) in "controlled forums," often then broadcasting (in a still selective manner) proceedings to key opinion and decision makers to *organize a cerebral base for tort reforms.*" The American Tort Reform Association simultaneously coordinates the strategizing and lobbying efforts of over 300 corporate and trade groups and forty-five state organizations "to formulate and reformulate 'common sense' regarding torts in particular and civil justice in general." This coordination function involves primarily *"mediating between big ideas and everyday impressions"* (Haltom and McCann 2004, 42–44, emphasis added), embedding the cerebral into the cultural in the form of a soon-to-be-familiar sound bite.

Sound bites such as "tort tax," "litigation lottery," and "litigation explosion" "distill commonsense objections" and amplify selected aspects of these by deploying "hyperbole in service of defining problems and suggesting solutions" (54–56). They distill and amplify, in part, by fragmenting and decontextualizing stories selected for their dramatic human interest appeal, removing them from more concrete legal and political narratives about appropriate remedies for real harm done and recontextualizing these within familiar-sounding tort tales calculated to mislead and redirect public attention toward an alternative image of the primary harm done. Instead of individuals harmed by the negligence of the powerful, sound bites such as these reframe the story to highlight empirically doubtful claims about harm done by permissive jurors, coddling lazy individuals targeting corporations with deep pockets. In this case we observe interested parties with generous corporate funding creating an alternative information system to support public policy favorable to their private interests by reconstructing common sense about negligence, personal injury, law, and legal institutions in order to displace one framing of this conflict with another.

In addition to the *instrumental* dimension highlighted in the interest group activities above, the work routines common in the mass media provide a critical *institutional* dimension, focusing on how communication in the context of a commercialized mass media impacts instrumental strategies to reinforce the non-random distorting effects on our information system observed here. Haltom and McCann "demonstrate how routinized conventions of news reporting have contributed to scripted representations of civil disputing and tort litigation that closely parallel and support the narrative constructions advanced by pop reformers" (2004, 149). According to Haltom and McCann, Bennett's four information biases (journalist preferences for personalized, dramatized, fragmented, and normalized news stories), themselves developed from Bennett's analysis of the intersections of journalist work routines and leadership efforts to control the news, provide a foundation for understanding the institutional contexts for tort tales and, in our view, for sound-bite sabotage.

While actual personal injury torts were not rising, the saturation of communication channels with tort tales—stories ready-made and easily reshaped for commercial telling and selling—led to increased coverage, so that "attentive citizens" found "in the daily news considerable support for the commonly alleged but empirically dubious conclusion that actual rates of litigation have grown rapidly or 'exploded' " (174). Haltom and McCann found, however, that *the skew of news stories on tort reform was not random*. In this case, they found that news stories selected and neglected similar aspects of the legal narrative in describing the conflict, so that "faithful readers of news might come to surmise that products liability cases overwhelm civil courts . . . when in fact cases concerning auto insurance claims, contracts, divorce contests, and other issues are far more prevalent" (75).

> Even more significant, we think, news narratives are inclined to echo tort tales in their tendency to discount the role of legal principles and processes in formal resolutions of most covered disputes. Our data demonstrate that newspapers encourage readers to judge the civil justice process on the basis of assertions and events either prior to or subsequent to trials, thus largely ignoring the legal arguments and

> evidentiary proceedings in formal courtroom settings that
> shaped eventual judgments. As in tort tales, law is virtually
> eviscerated by news accounts of legal disputes, having been
> displaced by a focus on the adversarial contests waged by
> narrowly self-interested parties and by outcomes seemingly
> as arbitrary as any lottery. (175)

Tort reform advocates have succeeded in the instrumental struggle
to put tort reform on the policy agenda—through directly lobbying
and through public relations campaigns to concentrate attention on
particularly dramatic (and not illustrative) tort tales. Since their efforts
include priming reporters to consider these tales highly newsworthy
(163), media outlets increasingly chose to highlight the themes tort
reform advocates had already been saturating communication channels with—resulting in calculated messages, branded information,
circulating widely as news. News stories demonstrated a systematic
overcoverage of plaintiff victories (three times as often), in part because
reporters and key publics were primed to see "plaintiff victories as far
more newsworthy" (165). Haltom and McCann also found undercoverage of defense victories, overemphasis on the rare case that results
in a huge award, and undercoverage of the far more commonplace
reduction or reversal of awards and concluded that the instrumental
success of reformers' efforts to exploit the institutional biases in the
mass media effectively set the public policy agenda by making these
rare but newsworthy large awards the most familiar touchstones for
public deliberation.

   These news stories not only misinformed citizens about the
facts of specific tort cases and trends regarding tort litigation, but
they filtered out debates over legal principles, procedures, and rules
of evidence. These stories "virtually eviscerate" our understanding of
and respect for the law itself, *constructing* the law "as arbitrary as any
lottery" and creating a fertile cultural soil for the commonly heard,
usually misinformed, and now seen as branded complaints about
litigiousness and legal "technicalities." While the data demonstrate
that the instrumental efforts to prime journalists and citizens were
successful, it also reveals a powerful institutional force at play that
partly explains how inaccurate but branded tort tales trumped the
best available data. Haltom and McCann write:

> The challenge of contextualizing and characterizing civil
> justice accurately will weed out sources unwilling to simplify
> their remarks, so many scholarly specialists and dispas-

sionate analysts have probably removed themselves from reporter's Rolodexes inadvertently. Others will be muted again, either wholly or in part, by legally mandated secrecy. In addition, anomalies and absurdities jazz up articles in ways that regularities cannot, which imparts to those who brandish arresting anecdotes a worthiness to be quoted or cited that cannot be matched by those who would draw attention to law or legal procedures that shape disputes or to decisions and developments that are hundreds of times more common. (170)

As the illustration of tort reform advocacy demonstrates, reporters are more likely to pay attention to messages made familiar and designed for consumption than to spend the time and energy navigating through the complexities of legal and political debates to pull out the relevant parts of the story. The result is that news stories "play down the rational processes of civil disputing and play up the rhetorical excesses of arguing cases in the press, just as tort tales accentuate caprice or injustice in litigation lotteries" (172–73). Seen as a larger dynamic, beyond just advocacy efforts in this one area, we argue that this case provides a concrete illustration of how sound-bite saboteurs concentrate public attention on their preferred, private, and interested messages.

V. Opportunities to Construct Dependent and Cynical Citizens

To the degree that sound-bite sabotage dominates as a powerful instrumental and institutional strategy for interested parties willing and able to hawk branded information that fits easily into news stories, we have an information system that is constructing forms of common sense about the law and politics and democracy that not only misinforms citizens about specific issues but also encourages more cynical and dependent forms of citizenship more generally. The tendency to frame politics as a game or horse race is, for instance, often pointed to as a source of citizen cynicism about politics, but there is also evidence that this type of media coverage—in a context where sound-bite sabotage is commonplace—accurately reflects how our currently distorted information system works.

One lesson learned from the tort reform advocates is that while the power to frame the news might first appear to bolster concern about a growing and an unchecked power of the fourth branch (media), it is at least as much a marker of the unchecked power and agency of private-sector interest groups, think tanks, and allied public leaders. "News frames are of particular interest because they constitute an exercise (intentional, or, quite often, unintentional) of journalistic power; frames can draw attention toward and confer legitimacy upon particular aspects of reality while marginalizing other aspects" (Lawrence 2000, 93). While Lawrence is highlighting media power here, given that public and private leaders know well how the media works, they can and do take advantage of "unintentional" media power to attempt to get their own frames, spin, stories in the news, as we saw in the instrumental actions of tort reformers exploiting these institutional characteristics of news reporting organizations.[37]

As we saw in tort tales and sound-bite sabotage in general, Lawrence argues that game framing advances an implicit view of the role of government that "encourages the public to view all politics as self-interested calculation and cynical manipulation" (110).[38] What she adds to our understanding is the insight that while we might recoil at cynical manipulation, a sober perspective on how politics works supports the view that "politics *is* often about battle and strategy and winning and losing, after all, and the motives of politicians *are* at times cynical" (111, emphases in original). In this sense, more cynical forms of citizenship are an incomplete analytical category. We need to know the degree to which cynicism here is linked to acquiescence or apathy or power-poor and agency-impaired dependency, on the one hand, or to a better understanding of our information system, of how law and politics work, a healthy if sobering skepticism and increased confidence in our own capacity to understand the political-culture we live within.

Baumgartner and Morris analyze *The Daily Show* and present data that suggest this alternative dynamic, healthy skepticism, is playing out along with more acquiescent forms of citizen cynicism, which reminds us of the importance of analyzing the cultural contexts within which cynicism emerges, which we do at length in chapter 5. Lawrence notes that daily news stories must be seen as parts of larger meta-narratives, not unlike the ongoing struggle over tort reform, where we see an episodic willingness to work to fake the larger context by misrepresenting advertisements as news, self-interest as public interest, and public relations experts as disinterested scholars (96).[39] Interested agents construct commonsense sagas that brand information by linking fragmented daily stories to loosely clustered dramas of social control. These clusters are designed to facilitate or make automatic and internalized the reframing of individual policy debates according to the meta-themes woven throughout these clusters of conflicts: permissive parents or a permissive criminal justice system as the root cause of our deteriorating quality of life, for instance.[40] These themes privilege the formation of a public agenda focusing on cultural and lifestyle conflicts more likely to stir passion across the airwaves—especially among the frustrated, cynical, angry, and misinformed—and are more readily linked to an affirmatively actionable solution: punishment, privatization, and preemption.

"Policy-making is most newsworthy, therefore, when it is marked by clear conflict that promises a resolution, what Cook describes as 'conflict with movement.' Conflict without movement, in contrast, offers little that beat reporters recognize as news, since the *sine qua non* of news is not conflict in and of itself, but an endless series of conflicts and momentary resolutions" (Lawrence 2000, 96). This insight reinforces the importance of dramatization and controlling images in the news as a technique of sound-bite sabotage in a context where the mass media—particularly the new media—shortens the time needed to convert a new and arresting idea into common sense. "In short, the potential for diversionary agenda setting, empty 'symbolic politics,' and empirically ungrounded political lore to dominate the conventional wisdom of public discourse has become a familiar feature of contemporary public life" (Haltom and McCann 2004, 271). As politics changes with mass media, making image control and image-based communication a more important tool for agenda setting and salience struggles, the already powerful have "come to invest heavily in media campaigns aiming to mold public agendas" (271).

In the tort reform case, routine news stories defeated the legal narratives that won at trial in the struggle to construct common sense. Haltom and McCann "identify how mass-produced knowledge about the lawsuit crisis has worked to shape significantly the salience and terms—that is, the mobilized bias—of such public contests over legal policy among elites and before ordinary citizens" (2004, 271). Sound-bite sabotage, then, threatens to make "any rational discussion of the dispute and the policy issues raised virtually impossible, while providing a powerful boost to the dubious general claims of a partisan political reform movement" (184). Though it would be utopian to suggest that we have ever reached the ideal of independent citizens actively participating in self-governance, surely we have been closer to that ideal than we are today as consumers of reports on public opinion, a form of political knowledge produced by private-sector professionals and generally taken to represent a snapshot of our collective public judgment about the conflicts we face.

This linkage of market and electoral techniques is not new, but it does add a dimension to understanding the impact of sound-bite sabotage. To say polling data is public opinion, according to Salmon and Glasser, for instance, confuses *what* is being studied with *how* it is being studied. This confusion is based on seeing individual polling data, which is assumed to be like voting, as more valuable than analyzing elite interest group activities (insider and outsider) and preferences. George Gallup, concerned that interested minorities were overly influencing public policy, created the modern polling industry by applying commercial marketing techniques to neutralize the capacity of interest groups to represent their private interests as the public interest (Salmon and Glasser 1995, 440).[41] Techniques that were useful for predicting individual consumer preferences, however, mobilize forms of exclusion that undermine active and independent forms of citizenships.

Justin Lewis argues that notions of public opinion linked to polling data have "been used to delegitimate assembly by large groups of citizens," reframed in the shadow of scientific polls as irrational, unrepresentative, and "in opposition to public opinion." Further, polling data displaces citizen articulation of their preferences with professionally constructed messages designed to speak for relevant publics and systematically represent narrow, elite preferences as public opinion (2001, 26–28).

But leaders (including private leadership in the mass media) quickly amplify polling data as *available*, easily *accessible*, *adaptable* (because it is only quasi-scientific), objective data that appear to respect the value of individual opinion and increases *their* ability to speak with an authoritative voice about their own *affirmatively actionable* agenda (Salmon and Glasser 1995, 444). According to Salmon and Glasser, however, it also legitimizes a particular view of politics and democracy. It amplifies a negative view of freedom, self-governance as free trade and democracy as consumer choice. Citizenship comes to be premised on an individual right to speak *in* public, which only requires the absence of state suppression. The ability to speak *to* publics and *with* other citizens, however, comes to be distributed on the basis of resource superiority (445). The resulting information system distortions we have identified with sound-bite sabotage and branded information become, accordingly, both less visible and more potent.

In this market-driven view, communication is just a mode for delivering interested opinion preferences, grouped together as public opinion and displayed as disinterested options for citizens to choose from. "Political discourse in this context functions as advertising" (446) disguised as scientific data in the news. The goal for citizens is not participation but identification with preselected elite designer positions. This approach to understanding the complex, competing, and contingent menu of positions held by various publics illustrates how the substantive meaning of democratic deliberation can be reduced to a process driven by brand loyalty, even as its presentation as dramatic spectacle grows in our imagination.

This dynamic collaboration between public and private leadership creates an information system that makes it harder for us to understand the conflicts we face and the routine political dynamics that drive our efforts to address these conflicts as opportunities to lead. "An understanding of the public as responsible agents teaches the moral ambiguity and open-ended, provisional quality involved in the pragmatic tasks and communicative process of the public life, where the search is not for personal closeness, 'truth,' final vindication, or normative communal consensus, but rather for appropriateness, fit, and provisional if sound resolution of concerns" (Boyte 1995, 431).

Conventional wisdom says this interest-group-driven spectacle enables informed citizens to more effectively protect and promote their own interests and the public interest. But, Edelman argues, this is based on two untenable assumptions: background consensus on the facts and policy making driven by rational calculations. A more sober perspective would see the news as a "succession of threats and reassurances." Conflicts become political problems, not on the basis of a background consensus on the facts but precisely because "controversy over their meanings is not resolved. The debates over such issues constitute politics and catalyze political action. There is no politics respecting matters that evoke a consensus about pertinent facts, their meaning, and the rational course of action" (Edelman 1988, 3). Conflicts are opportunities to govern, opportunities to lead and opportunities to sabotage; the heart of political struggle thus becomes strategizing to win the meta-conflicts over which conflicts we ought to focus on as a society.

Combining the ability (superior resources) with a willingness to systematically fake both text and context and the powerful techniques outlined in our first three chapters, we argue that branded information peddled by sound-bite saboteurs is undermining both the possibility and desirability of democratic deliberation, scholarly inquiry, and meaningful citizenship today. As Edelman noted, "problems come into discourse and therefore into existence as reinforcements of ideologies . . . [and] the solution typically comes first, chronologically and psychologically" (12, 22).

An explanation for a troubling condition is typically more important to partisans than the possibility of eliminating the condition; the latter is a rhetorical evocation of a remote future time unlikely to arrive, while the explanation is vital to contemporary political maneuver. . . . The persistence of unresolved problems with conflicting meanings is vital. (18–19)

The leaders with the agency to determine which conflicts we will address also signify who is virtuous, useful, worthy, and rational . . . and who is not. They constrain or enable competing notions of citizenship and common sense. And they advertise perspectives on politics that favor their private interests, because they understand conflicts are opportunities, and branded information is a powerful tool for exploiting—and sustaining, rather than resolving—these opportunities in a mass mediated society.[42] We turn now, in the next chapter, to an examination of the role of new media and the influence of a postmodern ethos in enabling sound-bite sabotage.

Saboteurs, Sound Bites, and Simulacra

Democratic Agency and Academic Discourse in a Digital Age

Learners, for Dewey, are never passive, neither disinterested spectators of ideas nor idle absorbers of sensations. They are always active, implicitly working to reconcile . . . tradition and practice, emotion and reason, doing and thinking.

—Stephen Fishman and Lucille McCarthy,
John Dewey and the Challenge of Classroom Practice

Educators must challenge a voyeuristic reception of films by offering students the theoretical resources necessary to engage critically how dominant practices of representation work to secure individual desires, organize specific forms of identification, and regulate particular modes of understanding, knowledge, and agency.

—Henry Giroux, "Breaking into the Movies:
Pedagogy and the Politics of Film"

I. Introduction

There is a medical condition suffered by the morbidly obese known as micronutrient deficiency.[1] People with this condition consume drastically more calories each day than they need to survive yet still suffer from malnutrition. Though dangerously overweight, they are, in a very real sense, starving. Their bodies, though overwhelmed by calories, lack the *kinds* of calories—the nutrients—needed to maintain good health. Thus in a painful irony, the morbidly obese can suffer both the ravages of obesity (atherosclerosis, type 2 diabetes, high blood pressure, degenerative arthritis) and the deprivations of malnutrition (deficiencies in iron, iodine, zinc, vitamins A, B, and C).

Micronutrient deficiency is in many ways, we argue, an apt metaphor for understanding the digital media's impact on democratic agency, engaged citizenship, and academic discourse in the United States. In today's environment of multimodal communication and electronic simulacra, we have more information (calories) available to us and in more forms than ever before, but we lack the kind of quality information (nutrients) needed to maintain healthy participation in our democratic and academic cultures. Like the morbidly obese, we suffer from both excess and deprivation due, in part, to our consumption habits, specifically when we uncritically consume the calculated messages in branded information. And our suffering can be both amplified and potentially mitigated, as this chapter will argue, by the power of new media.[2]

Our consumption of new media, however, is complicated by an additional factor: the difficulty of discernment. While the morbidly obese could, with relative ease, distinguish empty calories from vital nutrients (most food packaging now displays nutritional breakdowns), deciphering quality in the fire-hose flow of information, images, and sounds constituting new media, separating the wheat from the chaff, the empty calories from the needed nutrients, is a daunting task. There is just too much information in the digital universe, a universe that does not come with readily available and objective "nutrition" labels, a universe that fakes the text with interested nutrition labels, brought to you by the architects of our fast food culture, and fakes the context with "free" educational materials (dominating our science classrooms) like the four basic food groups.

Consider, for example, the sheer amount of bytes and pixels that flows through, supports, and forms the information economy. No one has the mental resources to process all of that material. Indeed, the phrase "information economy" has a built-in, but often ignored, irony. As Richard Lanham explains, economics is the study of "the allocation of scarce resources. . . . But information is not in short supply in the new information economy. We're drowning in it. What we lack is the human attention to make sense of it all. . . . *Attention is the commodity* in short supply" (2006, xi, emphasis added). The challenge of critically engaging (consuming) new media, therefore, is not just to restrict consumption or even that too much of the "food" being consumed is empty calories. It is also that we could not consume all of the information available even if we tried, making the discernment and attainment of quality nutrients that much more difficult—and, more importantly, the exploitation of that difficulty for undemocratic ends that much easier. Critically engaging new media requires that we see the ongoing and interested struggle over the distribution of a commodity: citizen attention. This is a struggle where overload is not simply a problem but an insidious opportunity for public and private leaders, a precondition for exploitation aimed at filling citizen agency with empty calories. What we previously analyzed as a combination of distraction and reconcentration here suggests a dynamic that threatens—unless we fully unpack both the promise and the risks associated with new media—the construction of more entertained but less informed, more cynical but less engaged, overloaded but confused forms of citizenship.

We need a map, a guide, a series of nutrition labels on how to frame, negotiate, and critique new media, not a predetermined political agenda, not a blueprint, but a process for sifting through the volume. Without such a method the new media and those who would turn it to undemocratic ends can, through overload, starve the information base from which reasonable decisions are made. Interested distributions of attention can contribute to our being unwilling, uninterested, or incapable of analyzing and synthesizing the very new media deluge that is overwhelming us, encouraging us to turn away, as a rational decision, from critical engagement.

Indeed, it is the combination of media-induced starvation and the exploitative strategies of the sound-bite saboteurs that creates the greatest danger for our democratic and academic cultures. The confluence of interested messages and information overload, of branded information and new media technologies, results in what we have called sound-bite sabotage. Sound-bite sabotage, characterized by gross reductivism, decontextualized messages, free-floating signifiers, and nonrandom, indeed, calculated, caricatures of content, stunts the citizenship skills, the literacy, needed for careful deliberation, recursive analysis, and the formation/achievement of common ground. Worse, it enables and encourages other socio-cognitive processes that are antithetical to democratic deliberation. When citizen thinking and argumentation are driven by the ethos of sound-bite saboteurs—deliberate use of logical fallacies, privatization of political communication, disregard for data, decision making marketed as consumerism, expertise misrepresented as elitism, power inequities explained as meritocracy, spectacle masquerading as news coverage—they are likely to divide and polarize, and to erode, through lack of example and exercise, a citizen's ability and desire to engage opposing views, weigh evidence, seek expertise, and either persuade or be persuaded. Without these socio-cognitive processes, these sociopolitical agreements, democracy cannot function—and neither can academia.

In truth, we believe that the detrimental effects of sound-bite sabotage are especially profound for our students, inculcating what could be called an aggressive passivity,[3] a dogmatic indifference, a sense of entitled apathy where too many students feel little need to interrogate their own opinions, less need to turn those opinions into arguments, and the least need to engage the arguments of others. Instead, mimicking the pundits who pass for journalists on the cable news channels, these students use the branded and balkanized "infotainment" of the sound-bite media to justify idiosyncratic and myopic perspectives. This erosion of the active, democratic, and open-ended mind-set required for learning harms not only the discourse that occurs in our classrooms but also, more profoundly, the civic life our universities were, at their best, designed to maintain and advance. Without the critical intervention of academia—itself a target of sound-bite saboteurs—the deleterious effects of a sound-bite-infected media on student thinking, argumentation, and civic participation will only increase.

And yet, to fully understand sound-bite sabotage and to fully plan an effective intervention, we need to be careful not to conflate the deleterious impact of sound-bite sabotage with the power, problem, and *potential* of new media. While new media can be exploited by sound-bite saboteurs and can cause their own challenges for democratic and academic cultures, they also open up new sites for expression, new avenues for research, and new formats for education: blogs, podcasts, talk radio, streaming video, YouTube, and other interactive communication systems. To be sure, new media and the tactics of the sound-bite saboteurs are intertwined, but they are not the same phenomenon, and to make them so harms not only our understanding of each component but, more importantly, their current and potential interactions. In what ways can we/should we distinguish between the sound-bite saboteurs' use of new media and the new media themselves? Can one understand the effect, affect, and nature of sound-bite sabotage without understanding the effect, affect, and nature of new media? Does the nature of new media constitute, at least to a degree, the way and why of sound-bite sabotage?

Ultimately, our critique of sound-bite sabotage is not a critique of new media. But in some sense it has to be. While the phenomena of the new media are not reducible to sound-bite sabotage, sound-bite sabotage would not be the phenomenon it is without the power of new media. Of course, the diversionary tactics of the sound-bite saboteurs predate new media: faulty emotional appeal, ad hominem, ad populum, non sequitur, red herring, and others have been around for as long as humans have been able to communicate. But it is the combination of these fallacies, these rhetorical strategies from advertising, sophistry, and entertainment, with political discourse and news coverage *through* the new media—what we have called the branding of information—that has created the current toxicity. The speed at which sound-bite saboteurs can mobilize falsehoods, the ease with which digital technology can counterfeit both context and content, the balkanization of political opinion through Web sites dedicated to the narrowest political views[4]—all of this sabotage is enabled as much by the power of the medium forming the sound-bite message as by the message itself. If the majority of Americans still got their news from three television networks and a local newspaper, then we doubt we would be writing this book. It is the amplification and mutation of classical diversionary tactics through the power of digital media that make today's sound-bite sabotage so effective and devastating.

Moreover, the new media *themselves* are changing societal notions of such things as identity, literacy, agency, community, context, evidence, news, and citizenship. New media's ability to—by themselves—cause change does not mean that there are not actors exploiting these changes, employing this power to insidious ends. It simply means that, just like the written word before them, new media technologies create new socio-cognitive abilities, abilities that open up opportunities for some and close them for others. New media are not mere vehicles for the sound-bite saboteurs' rhetorical strategy. New media, in some sense, constitute the nature and effectiveness of that strategy. After all, they are *sound-bite* saboteurs, not just saboteurs. Consequently, it would behoove us to understand the power, problem, and potential of new media separate from the sound-bite saboteurs' exploitation, if only to better understand what it is the sound-bite saboteurs do to and with new media.

The remaining purpose of this chapter, therefore, will be to examine the conflicts (the problems and opportunities) new media create for our democratic and academic cultures. As Lance Svehla argues,

> The new media inculcates a powerful yet potentially adversarial literacy in our classrooms. This literacy challenges academic discourse while simultaneously opening

the academy to the possibilities of multiple literacies, democratic practices, and socially aware pedagogies—even if those possibilities occasionally seem more fractured than multiple, self-indulgent than democratic, hedonistic than socially aware. (2006, 84–85)

Rather than narrowly framing the new media's influence on literacy and democracy as destructive and deadening, we must consider how new media could invigorate and even enlarge our academic and democratic cultures. We must, in a Deweyan sense, nest the binary of media and print, image and word—find or create a Peircean third that values the new media experience, that embraces the power and inevitability of technological revolution, but that, at the same time, contests, refigures, and enriches the digital zeitgeist through commerce with print culture.

It is a project or "curricular agenda" that "demands that we engage with the young on the grounds of their experience, and at the same time show them with greater confidence than is usually the case now why in such an agenda reflection is essential for them" (Kress 2003, 175). If, as we argue throughout this book, the public square is decaying, then combating this trend requires more than intellectual critique. It requires intellectual leadership, both within the halls of academia and without. It requires a public pedagogy, a refiguring of our roles as scholars and of our relationships to students, knowledge production, and information systems. We must be willing to get ourselves ideologically and professionally dirty, to engage the pop culture mediums that are forming and reforming democratic life. If we can seize the opportunity *and* the challenge of digital democracy, then we might be better able to wrest the power and potential of new media away from the sound-bite saboteurs.

And as rhetoricians, why shouldn't we engage in such a project? If capturing attention is the key to the digital age, to democratizing it, then rhetoricians are uniquely qualified to perform that task. As Lanham argues, "The devices that regulate attention are stylistic devices. Attracting attention is what style is all about" (2006, xi). Style as a substance rather than window dressing, medium as part of the message, rhetoric "as a force in society and a factor in the creation of knowledge" (Bizzell and Herzberg 1990, v) is what rhetoricians do, what we believe, and who we are. Indeed, the short supply of attention in the new media age links students, citizens, and leaders to the power of rhetoric and, we might add, the major themes of this book: framing, socio-cognitive schema, shared language, knowledge production, and discursive analysis. How do corporate and political elites manipulate our strained attention spans in order to bamboozle us? How can we marshal the attention needed to resist these framings? How can we penetrate the flood of information, disinformation, and indifference that demarcates sound-bite sabotage? Unlike the old Soviet model, which sought to control the public by minimizing information to official state channels, making information itself the salient power of the Cold War, the free market model overwhelms its citizens with information, making the operative controlling mechanisms, the rhetorical filters and schema, the salient power of the digital age.

We must not, therefore, let fear of new media, the radical changes they bring, and their exploitation by sound-bite saboteurs drive us into retreat. We cannot abandon the public square to those who do not truly believe in it. If we are to effectively work against sound-bite sabotage, then we must be prepared to confront it in more places than the classroom and with more tools than traditional academic discourse. In order for our intervention to be successful, however, we must first deal with three fundamental problems that new media exacerbate and sound-bite saboteurs exploit: the fear of literacy, the modernist nostalgia for print, and the question of agency. If we cannot deal with these issues, then any hope for a successful intervention is futile.

II. The Fear of Literacy

> One might say the following with some confidence. Language-as-speech will remain the major mode of communication; language-as-writing will increasingly be displaced by image in many domains of public communication, though writing will remain the preferred mode of the political and cultural elites.
>
> —Gunther Kress, *Literacy in the New Media Age*

Many in academia are afraid, afraid that the end of modernity signals the end of literacy as they know it. Barbara Maria Stafford explains:

> The end of modernity is marked precisely by this uneasy sense that literacy has come to an end. For many, meaningful sounds and coherent texts have been drowned out in the fire-hose flow of data. Pedagogy's venerable scribal skills seem defiled by hidden systems of connected, but variously

formatted, electronic apparatus that manipulate, modulate, synchronize, and digitize information by numbers through endless entertainment channels. (1996, 58)

In many ways, we empathize with this sense of unease. Literacy often does seem under attack by the new media. The communication systems of postmodernity sometimes do seem to be overwhelming institutions, socio-cognitive abilities, and democratic practices sacred to the academy and academicians.[5] Is it surprising that this sense of being overwhelmed results in a corresponding sense of trepidation? As Kress asks, "What do we lose if many of the forms of writing that we know disappear?" (2003, 7). And yet there is something about this fear that also strikes us as disingenuous, futile, hyperbolic, and somewhat ahistorical.

First, we believe the fear of the new media's impact on literacy often masks a deeper fear—one of being replaced. What is the job of an academician, what is his or her purpose, in a world where scribal skills are defiled—both by new media technologies and by public relations experts and think tanks providing an alternative knowledge production system? What place does he or she have in a culture where the written word is not revered? Gunther Kress and Theo van Leeuwen write:

> The opposition to the emergence of the visual as a full means of representation is not based on an opposition to the visual as such, but on an opposition in situations where it forms an alternative to writing and can therefore be seen as a potential threat to the present dominance of verbal literacy among elite groups. (2006, 17)

Lest we forget, literacy is also an economy, an industry, and we, as academicians, are major players in and beneficiaries of that economy. Literacy production provides us not only with material goods but, perhaps more viscerally, with personal and professional identity. If the digital media continue to reshape literacy, then we may find the very core of what we value in the culture and why we are valued by the culture marginalized—economically, socially, and existentially.

To put it crudely, the digital trumping of text threatens our university monopoly. As Lanham argues, "In the digital writing space, words no longer have it all their own way. They have to compete with moving images and sounds" (2006, xii). Many of us are not willing to compete and find the very notion of engaging in public argument (i.e., arguing in nonacademic settings under nonacademic rules using nonacademic tools) distasteful, even distressing. So, rather than framing the new media's challenge to traditional literacy and academic culture as a Veynian or Deweyan opportunity to link the popular with the scholarly, we withdraw, labeling new media barbaric and backwards and leaving them to the tender ministration of the sound-bite saboteurs.

Second, the fear of the new media's impact on literacy is, in the end, futile, and, consequently, damaging to an academician's cultural credibility and agency. The technological revolution has already happened. The coup d'etat has already occurred. Indeed, "it is no longer possible to think about literacy in isolation from a vast array of social, technological, and economic factors" (Kress 2003, 1). The only real questions left are how much more change will occur, whether or not the academy can adapt, and how much it should adapt. Continued change caused by digital technology, however, is inevitable. If we ignore the reality of these technology revolutions, then we run the risk of seeming both isolated and irrelevant. As Cynthia Selfe argues, "If we continue to define literacy in ways that ignore or exclude new media texts, we not only abdicate a professional responsibility to describe accurately and robustly how humans communicate, and how they compose and read in contemporary contexts, but we also run the risk of our curriculum holding declining relevance for students" (2004, 55). The declining relevance of our curriculum *for* students could trigger a corresponding decline in our ability to impact the culture *through* students. Rather than fearing technology-induced changes in literacy, we must engage them, if only to ensure our continued value, relevance, and agency.

Third, the fear of the new media's impact of literacy is often hyperbolic, even irrational. It is a caricature to portray new media as barbaric, parasitic, debilitating, and corrosive.[6] Such caricature misses the true problem and opportunity of the twenty-first century's digital drama: the simultaneous expansion and restriction of democratic culture and complex socio-cognition. While granting some of the harm (change?) caused by new media and especially by their exploitation, the new media have also opened up incredible new spaces for debate, expression, analysis, grassroots organization, and advocacy: blogs, myspace.com, and podcasts, to name but a few. And while each of these new mediums has limitations and causes problems for academic discourse and democratic culture, each also represents more people empowered to speak about more things and in more ways than ever before. For example, while we are sure that WebMD has led to incomplete, even dangerous, applications of medical information by laypeople and has fed hypochondria, we are also sure that it has led to life-saving checkups and to patients challenging, in empowering ways, the supremacy of the medical establishment. While the quality and veracity of the "news" reported on blogs must always be questioned, it cannot be questioned that blogs cover stories that the corporate media do not or will not cover.

While the speed and simulatory nature of these electronic mediums often make maintaining hallmarks of academic discourse (the fact/opinion distinction, the ethos of expertise, the need for data, evidence, and verification, sensitivity to context) difficult, this difficulty should not result in academicians leaving the mediums to the unchallenged manipulations of the sound-bite saboteurs. Instead, we should help students negotiate these new spaces, help them understand how meaning is made in and with the new media—what Kress and van Leeuwen call " 'the grammar of visual design' " (2006, 1). Yes, we must also show students the limitations of those makings and how visual grammar mirrors, diverges from, and resists the grammar of the written word, but we would benefit by listening to what our students already know about the new media, to what they can teach us about media's conflict with print.

Finally, the current fear of literacy's end is merely our civilization's most recent nostalgia for a time when we supposedly were not concerned about eroding literacy skills, technological change, and cultural identity. Indeed, the "death" of some central feature of our humanity caused by the advent of some new technology is a fear as old as Western civilization itself. Some 2,500 years ago, Plato feared the advent of writing, the new technology of his day, and the very technology we worry the digital media are harming.[7] He writes (ironically enough):

> For this invention will produce forgetfulness in the minds of those who learn to use it, because they will not practice their memory. Their trust in writing, produced by external characters which are no part of themselves, will discourage the use of their own memory within them. . . . [Further,] they will read many things without instruction and will therefore seem to know many things, when they are for the most part ignorant and hard to get along with, since they are not wise, but only appear wise. (2001, 165)

Key to understanding this passage is Plato's fear that writing was somehow inauthentic ("produced by external characters which are no part of themselves"), and that it lacked quality control ("they will read many things without instruction and will therefore *seem* to know many things"). These criticisms sound eerily like many of the criticisms leveled against today's digital media and the students who revel in them; criticism, to some degree, we have made ourselves and will make in chapter 5. New media discourage real analytical thinking. The Internet makes students dependent on technology rather than competent researchers. Pop culture makes students obstinate, indifferent, and unwilling to engage materials we value in ways we value. Rather than enabling discernment and authentic knowledge production, new media encourage students to cut and paste.

How comfortable are we with such criticisms of new media when they are set in juxtaposition with Plato's criticisms of writing? How comfortable should we be? Hard as it might be to fathom, Plato saw writing as being every bit as harmful to his students as many current academicians see blogging, text messaging, and viral advertising to theirs. Writing, Plato believed, was going to stunt his students' spiritual fulfillment by turning them away from their souls' memory of the Forms. It was going to delude them into putting their trust in the ephemeral instead of the substantial, the transitory rather than the eternal, the external rather than the internal.

Today, of course, most academicians do not worry about their students' spiritual fulfillment, but surely our concerns over students' socio-cognitive development, level of literacy, and interest in print culture sound a similar chord. Some academicians are almost fervent in their belief that the new media are injuring students' ability to think, argue, and connect to the academic community.[8] While we are sure this fervor comes from a deeply held belief that the technologies reshaping literacy today are inherently inferior to writing, passion does not always equate with clarity and nuance. Passion may make one certain, but it does not make one correct.

After all, the technology of *writing* was, according to Plato, inherently inferior to the dialectic—and no one doubts Plato's fervor.[9] He writes:

> Writing, Phaedrus, has this strange quality, and is very like painting; for the creatures of painting stand like living beings, but if one asks them a question, they preserve a solemn silence. And so it is with written words; you might think they spoke as if they had intelligence, but if you question them, wishing to know about their sayings, they always say only one and the same thing. And every word, when once it was written, is bandied about, alike

among those who understand and those who have no interest in it, and it knows not to whom to speak or not to speak; when ill-treated or unjustly reviled it always needs its father to help it; for it has no power to protect or help itself. (2001, 166)

How different are these criticisms of writing from the criticisms leveled at new media? Plato's belief that the meaning of a word will be "bandied about" sounds suspiciously like a professor warning his or her students about the dangers of the Internet for conducting valid research. The new media are often accused of being a collection of voyeuristic images with no real depth of meaning. But this accusation is strikingly similar to what Plato accuses writing of when he compares it to painting. Painting is, according to Plato, inauthentic, shallow, and treacherous. It seems alive, but in truth it has merely the semblance of life. It is a simulacrum. Writing, as another type of visual image, not only shares this nature but is actually worse. A painting is, at least, a copy of a material thing (which is itself already a copy of a Form). A painting, therefore, is only two removes from Reality. A written word, however, is three removes away—a copy of a copy of a copy. It is a visual abstraction of what was already an oral abstraction of what was already a material representation of something Real. Consequently, writing is a mildly amusing, sometimes useful, but ultimately dead thing to Plato. It cannot respond to our questions the way a living person can.

By conducting this analysis of Plato's *Phaedrus*, we are not trying to argue that his view of writing is correct, or, conversely, that all concerns about what new media are doing to literacy and to our humanity are baseless. New media do cause problems for print culture, just as writing did change the way human memory and humanity itself function. But that is not really the point we are trying to make here. Our point is that arguments against new media, especially ones that portray them as the antithesis or nemesis of print, sometimes seem based on a degree of selective historical or cultural amnesia. Plato feared writing for many reasons similar to why academicians fear new media today, and yet, writing did not destroy us, and we doubt new media will either (with all due respect to Neil Postman).

Indeed, our culture's fear of new technology, and its influence on literacy (and, thus, self and society), is hardly a new phenomenon in Western culture, hardly limited to the ancient Greeks. Every time Western culture sees an advance in technology that results in a change in literacy, the same specters of injury and loss arise. From the Guggenheim press, to the vernacular translations of the Bible, to the Renaissance panic over writing, to Wordsworth recoiling from the Industrial Revolution, to Heidegger's blistering condemnation of technology,[10] to the invention of the Internet we are warned that something essential to our identity is under threat. Such warnings, however, often overreach themselves. They collapse important distinctions between using a technology and abusing it. They ignore that we have faced conflicts of technology, literacy, and identity many times in our history, and that the resulting resolutions have usually made our lives better. In short, there is no time when literacy, technology, and sense of self were not in flux and/or challenged. For literacy, technology, and self are not static entities. They are dynamic and interactive. To present them as static is to ignore our history.

And yet the work of theorists such as Walter Ong, Eric Havelock, E. D. Hirsch, and John Goody can hardly be labeled as being unconcerned with or dismissive of history. Perhaps portions of the larger culture can be accused of historical amnesia, but these prominent academicians know our past and its challenges, even if they do not always agree with other academicians' interpretations. It is not, therefore, that they suffer from historical amnesia as much as they suffer from a form of historical utopianism, what we might call a modernist nostalgia for print.

III. The Modernist Nostalgia for Print

> Without writing the mind cannot even generate concepts such as "history" or "analysis," just as without print . . . the mind cannot generate portmanteau concepts such as "culture" or "civilization," not to mention "macroeconomics" or "polyethylene."
>
> —Walter Ong, "Literacy and Orality in Our Times"

Modernist criticisms of new media have focused largely on the damage they do to print culture, specifically to the supposed higher levels of cognition that reading and writing, and only reading and writing, enable.[11] Theorists as varied as Lucy Fisher, Jane Healy, E. D. Hirsch, John Leonard, Matthew McAllister, Walter Ong, Neil Postman, and Mitchell Stephens have all "documented" print culture's vulnerability to new media, writing books with such provocative titles as *Amusing Ourselves to Death: Public Discourse in the Age of Show Business* (Postman), *The Rise of the Image, the Fall of the Word* (Stephens), and *Endangered Minds: Why Our Children Don't Think* (Healy), to name but a few. Of all these works, however, we believe Ong's, inspired by Eric Havelock's research into the literacy of the ancient Greeks, to be the most thoughtful, influential, and controversial.[12]

Havelock argues that the Greeks' creation of a completely symbolic alphabet reduced their need for an "acoustically trained memory," and "as the memory function subsided, psychic energies hitherto channeled for this purpose were released for other purposes" (1986, 101). Print created a shift in the Greeks' mental functioning, resulting not only in more mental space and energy for abstract thinking but also in new forms of cultural production. They could, for example, write down their history, pass greater amounts of knowledge from one generation to the next, communicate across large distances with greater accuracy, keep detailed legal and financial records, and develop new kinds of art and commerce. Lester Faigley summarizes Havelock's argument thusly:

> The Greek invention of the alphabet allowed memory to be externalized, releasing the ancient Greeks from the burden of memorization and offering them new opportunities for analytic thought. By enabling the Greeks to compare texts and locate inconsistencies, literacy overturned the authority of the oral tradition and brought about new forms of cognition. (1992, 201)[13]

Ong will seize upon Havelock's research to argue that knowledge, power, and advancement in the West, since the time of the ancient Greeks, have been linked to a specific technology of production—writing. Writing, Ong believes, is not simply a form of communication; it is a way of framing (even constructing) the world with print.[14] Writing as a technology enables advanced forms of thinking, culture, and material production.

Specifically, writing allows the mind to generate what Ong calls "portmanteau concepts" (1978, 2). A portmanteau is a type of old, large, leather suitcase, one that opens out into two halves with many smaller compartments hidden inside. A portmanteau concept, by analogy, is a large or fused concept with many smaller concepts embedded within it and upon which it is dependent for meaning, intelligibility, and function. For example, concepts such as "culture" or "civilization" or "macroeconomics" or "polyethylene" have countless smaller concepts built into them—too many for the mind to hold all at one time. Print allows the mind to store these smaller concepts externally, to more accurately tuck away parts of experience in text for later retrieval, reuse, and recombination. Print allows us to more carefully and more fully build on our ideas, to make them more historical and analytical, to make them exponentially more complex and susceptible to rigorous interrogation and revision than orality does. Thus the very thing Plato feared writing was going to erode—memory—is the very thing Ong believes writing has *transformed* to create a more advanced mind and world. If we compare the human mind to a computer, then print is a limitless number of external hard drives.

According to Ong and many other media scholars influenced by modernism, however, the socio-cognitive and cultural gifts produced by print are threatened by the ascension of new media. While reading and writing are still dominant forces in our culture, new media are chipping away at that dominance, inviting either a regression into older forms of cognition and culture or the creation of mutated forms caught between the worlds of literacy and orality. For example, Ong, despite the prevalence of reading and writing in our culture, does not see the influence of orality as dying out. Instead, he sees it as expanding (albeit in mutated form) through dislocation, especially in urban areas.[15] Svehla explains:

> The saturation of American culture by radio and television created what Ong called a secondary orality. Secondary orality was a hybrid literacy caught between the worlds of primary orality and written literacy. . . . It was, as Ong argued, "to varying degrees literate" [1978, 6], but that literacy was confused, not fully formed, and dependent upon the technology of writing rather than its master. For example, while watching television afforded the opportunity to read TV listings, channels, and words on the screen, it did not require an active engagement with the creation or interpretation of those texts. (2006, 87)

Thus new technology has, once again, triggered a socio-cognitive shift, but this time a shift that, according to Ong, impairs higher-level thinking and cultural production.

Now by critiquing Ong's argument (and, by extension, other modernist epistemologies) on media and literacy, we could be accused of our own form of nostalgia. After all, "There are more current theorists researching the media's social impact, theorists who take into account advances in media technology and changes in cultural epistemology" (Svehla 2006, 86).[16] Moreover, critics such as Beth Daniell and Lester Faigley have already challenged the ethnocentrism and "great divide fallacy" of Ong's claims.[17] Is thinking ability in oral-based cultures really that different from thinking ability in print-based cultures? Is it writing that causes higher-levels of cognition or being socialized to write? While we feel these are valid criticisms and important questions, we also feel that critiques of Ong's work have not yet displaced the modernist aspects of his considerable influence—or the influence of modernist epistemologies in general. While new media technologies have created incredible changes in the way we see, understand, and manipulate our world, too much of the way in which we conceptualize these changes has not changed. Until modernist understandings of new media, print, cognition, literacy, and, most importantly, their interactions are displaced, we will not engage the conflict of media and literacy in profitable ways—and, as a consequence, we will not be able to effectively resist sound-bite sabotage. For while we concur that both learning to write and experiencing new media alters socio-cognition, and that "pedagogy must be reformed to connect to students' media constituted consciousness" (Svehla 2006, 88), we do not concur that the influence of new media must harm learning to write, argue, or think; we do not agree that it necessitates a regression—whether that regression is called secondary orality, the end of literacy, or some other pejorative concept.

First, explanations of how technology reshapes socio-cognition and knowledge production should be somewhat contingent and tentative. Often, modernist theories of technology's influence on cognition are overstated. Any technology would be, at best, only one factor, albeit a very important factor, in the evolution of how we think or produce knowledge. Moreover, the influence of a new technology will not be and historically has not been uniform. New technologies will contribute to advancements in some ways, for some people, at some times, but, at the same time, they may also contribute to forces or trends that constrain or distort socio-cognition and knowledge production. Consider, for example, the uneven distribution of Internet access in poor urban and rural areas.

Second, Ong's conception and representation of neurological functioning, specifically how the left and right hemispheres of the brain interrelate, is too static and discrete—especially when it comes to understanding the creation, interpretation, and processing of images. "Although it was once believed that the modules for processing images were located in the nonverbal right hemisphere, scientists have recently been discovering that *both hemispheres* contribute to this function, particularly the left, which also processes logic, reasoning, and language" (Innocenti 2002, 63, emphasis added). The effect of media images on socio-cognitive functioning, therefore, cannot be fully appreciated with a modernist model that locates the symbolic, the imagistic, and the nonverbal in the brain's right hemisphere and logic, reason, and print in the left. As Svehla argues, "Images, language, and reasoning are not particularized functions of discrete or static brain parts. They are holistic functions enabled by the rapid and dynamic interactions of the brain's dual hemispheres" (2006, 89).

Rather than being consigned to the domain of the primitive, the oral, or the preliterate, the creation, interpretation, and application of media images, as a subset of all the images we process, should be seen *as* and *as actively involved in* some of the brain's highest levels of socio-cognitive functioning.

Debra Innocenti, drawing from the work of neurologist Antonio Damasio, explains[18]:

> Images are not simple neural phenomena whose influence is limited to sensory input. They are actually generated by numerous, synchronous systems also responsible for perception, memory, and reasoning. . . . Patients with achromatopsia (damage in early visual cortices) not only lose the ability to *see* color, but also the ability to *imagine* or *conceive* color even if the damage occurs late in their lives. (2002, 63, emphasis in original)

Media images do not have to erode higher-level thinking; they may even enable aspects of its very existence. The new media do not have to simply happen to students; students do not have to be passive victims. Students can and often do play an active, even artistic, role in the generation, understanding, and application of new media, especially with critical guidance.

This admittedly optimistic perspective, however, does not mean that students always do or will engage new media in active ways. As we will discuss more fully in chapter 5, sound-bite sabotage has made many students dogmatically apathetic, perhaps even ideologically narrow. When these students can be bothered to treat media images seriously enough to "read" them, they often read them in ways that willfully confirm what they already believe. When they come up against media images that are not easily lent to that task, they often retreat—suggesting that we, the professors, are "reading too much" into the images, that they're just images and mean nothing. Such students, as we will argue in chapter 5, are uninterested in argument because they see it as always and only interested, and they want to avoid being "taken in"—a savvy, experience-based cynicism resulting, at least in part, from their constant exposure to sound-bite sabotage. We admit that such students are a challenge, but we also argue that this "reading too much" reaction is a teachable moment. It requires us to provide our students with multiple sources of information and competing approaches to interpretation that will empower them to find and create meaningful subject positions. It requires us then to provide these thusly empowered students with opportunities for media image production—a distinction that leads to our final critique of the modernist aspects of Ong's work.

The modernist model of literacy (what literacy is and what it should do) is too constricted, puts too much value in the analytic capacity of critique, in the ability to separate one's self from a text or a concept or an object in order to assess it. As we have seen in our first three chapters, however, literacy in the digital age must be as much about design as it is about critique, about construction as it is about deconstruction, about framing as it is about dissection. As Kress argues, "critique is anchored to the ground of someone's past agendas: design projects the purposes, interests and desires of the maker into the future. Design is prospective, constructive not deconstructive, utopian and not nostalgic" (2003, 50). The meaning of media images is not just something we discover lying prostrate within the image; it is something we must create for the image. If we want students to understand how media images are created, branded, manipulated, interested, decontextualized, ideological, and persuasive, then we have to let them in on the process of making media images and not just the product of what has been made. As Donald Murray argues concerning students learning to write, studying the product of literature is not enough, because "conscientious, doggedly responsible, repetitive autopsying doesn't give birth to live writing" (2003, 3).

This argument does not mean that analyzing product is not important. Engaging new media images is not an either/or situation. Design *or* interpretation is a false choice. Of course, design is not done in a vacuum. Rather it is co-constituted with and by context, thus it is always co-design, or re-design, and critique is always a part of invention. Indeed, the relationship between design and interpretation, as with the relationship between media image and meaning, is what Kress might call motivated (2003, 42)—or what Louise Rosenblatt might call transactional.[19] A motivated relationship stresses agency, and a transactional relationship stresses reciprocity. And unlike the interested relationships promoted by sound-bite saboteurs, relationships that stress agency and reciprocity depend on more transparency to communicate in ways that we might expect to effectively coordinate social action. Thus the intention of a media image is not self-contained, not enclosed in the image itself, not an essence students discern by careful analysis. Media images signify because, in part, students "create or design their meaning in the very act of experiencing them" (Svehla 2006, 93).

Despite modernist fears, literacy has not come to an end, even to an end as we know it. The human story goes on, even if the mediums through which we create, conceive, and tell it change. However, literacy is evolving at a rapid, even hyper, pace. Because of the speed of these changes, many adhere to unproductive conceptions of literacy, but we do not have to. Rather than fearing the shifts in socio-cognition and culture instigated by new media, we could see them as opportunities to set the popular in conversation with the scholarly—to the potentially mutual benefit of both. Yes, Wikipedia, hyperlinks, and MTV all cause problems for print culture, but as we have argued throughout this book, conflicts, depending on how they are framed, are also opportunities. They are invitations to lead by framing questions, to enable meaningful public participation, rather than to "dissipate public energies by focusing on more trivial issues." The struggles over how to frame conflicts and the power inequities that demarcate those struggles are at the heart of both sound-bite sabotage and the exploitation of new media. Sound-bite saboteurs have transmogrified the admittedly complicated opportunity of new media into a series of diversions, empty spectacles, moral panics, half-truths, and outright lies. But just because they have corrupted new media's potential and have exploited the difficulties new media create does not mean we have to accept either. We can resist both the tactics and the ethos of sound-bite saboteurs.

But what is resistance in the postmodern, multimodal, digital world of new media? Our critiquing modernist epistemology and ontology should not be seen as synonymous with wholehearted support for postmodern theory. Postmodern conceptions of self, literacy, and language also cause trouble for academic discourse, democratic culture, and curricular intervention, particularly the postmodern complication of agency. What is agency in the multimodal world? Is framing or design possible in the hyper simulations of new media? Does the historical consciousness required for resistance exist in the digital age? If not, how can we wrest new media away from the sound-bite saboteurs? More profoundly, why should we even try? Is there even such a thing as sound-bite sabotage in a universe of free-floating signifiers, decontextualized positions, and digitized simulations? Or is what we have called sound-bite sabotage merely a reflection of our inability to let go of concepts that no longer have any real meaning in a postmodern age?[20] It is to these questions—specifically the question of agency—that we must now turn.

IV. The Question of Agency

> The truth of an idea is not a stagnant property inherent in it. Truth *happens* to an idea. It *becomes* true, is *made* true by events. Its verity *is* in fact an event, a process: the process namely of its verifying itself, its veri-*fication*. Its validity is the process of its valid-*ation*.
>
> —William James, "Pragmatism's Conception of Truth"

> There is no true word that is not at the same time praxis. Thus, to speak a true word transforms the world.
>
> —Paulo Freire, *Pedagogy of the Oppressed*

It has become almost a cliché among scholars, intellectuals, and pundits of the popular culture to write that we are living in a postmodern age. From MTV to the United Nations to the hallowed halls of academia, there is a belief that things are fragmented, devoid of overarching meaning, and, ultimately, beyond our ability to control, that our agency is an illusion and perhaps even culpable in our impotency. In Blacksburg, Virginia, a disturbed young man enters a college classroom and executes twenty-seven college students and five teachers, while outside another student captures the sound of gun shots on his cell phone. Hours later, NBC broadcasts parts of the killer's video manifesto. In New Orleans, Louisiana, Hurricane Katrina turns an American city into a third world nation, as government incompetence turns fellow citizens into refugees. In St. Petersburg, Florida, politicians use streaming video to spin a catastrophically brain-damaged woman's final hours into a political stunt and a media spectacle. In New York City, Islamic terrorists fly hijacked Boeing 767s filled with passengers into the World Trade Center.

Everywhere we turn new media betray and portray the crumbling meta-narratives that once offered at least the hope of meaning, progress, and justice. We watch—literally—as the once-sacred programs and institutions of high modernism fall apart. The integrity of democracy is shaken as aerial photographs of centrifuge tubes are presented as evidence to the UN Security Council. The promise of

Western civilization and the utopia of the United Nations are mutually stripped of credibility as journalists uncover the mass graves filled by Saddam Hussein and the new cemeteries filled by the doctrine of preemption. The rule of law fades as pictures of torture and humiliation at Abu Ghraib speed through the Internet. The moral certainty of economic progress drowns in movie images of the polar ice caps melting. From weapons of mass destruction, 800-mile boarder fences, Rodney King's beating, the Los Angeles riots, the burning of Malcolm X's widow, and the Menendez brothers' trial to massacres in Darfur, drug-resistant viruses, massive deforestation, suspension of habeas corpus, and suicide bombers, the world, more than ever, seems "a darkling plain. . . . Where ignorant armies clash by night" (Arnold 1993, 649), the "confused alarms of struggle and flight" (649) made visible this time, however, not by a poet's pen but by the light of a CNN camera that does not allow retreat into a distanced self or high culture refuge. The technology that was supposed to increase our control of the world has instead revealed the fragmentation of our lives.

And yet what exactly all of this fragmentation means and, more importantly, what we are supposed to feel and do about it are not clear. The postmodern theory that has arisen to describe our condition has critical power but offers little comfort and even less direction. As Albert Borgmann argues, "The idiom we have favored since the beginning of the modern era fails to inspire conviction or yield insight; the language of those who are proclaiming a new epoch seems merely deconstructive or endlessly prefatory" (1992, 2). Indeed, there are almost as many views on the postmodern condition, as many conflicting opinions on the usefulness or futility of postmodern theory, as there are theorists.

Yet this cliché, this now casual, commercial, and controversial use of the term *postmodernity*, still marks a very real sense that something important has changed in our understanding of ourselves and the world—a change found not so much in our fear of fragmentation and incoherence but in our sense of powerlessness in the face of that fragmentation, in the relationship of our agency, individually and collectively, to that incoherence. From philosophers such as the Marquis de Sade, Søren Kierkegaard, Friedrich Nietzsche, and Jean-Paul Sartre to artists like Matthew Arnold, Franz Kafka, James Joyce, Sylvia Plath, and Albert Camus, we have confronted feelings of fragmentation and incoherence before. Indeed, the ultimately fragmented state of life is a fundamental conceit of high modernism.[21] The difference between their state and the postmodern is the modernist's belief in the ability of the artist, the agent, the individual to resist, as an ethical project, this fragmentation, to stand in opposition to it from the vantage of the removed self, to form within one's self a consciousness that derives its wholeness from its agency.

We have argued throughout this book that the way new media information is framed, who frames it, and who benefits from that framing must be seen and understood if the damage of sound-bite sabotage is to be resisted. In making such an argument, were we guilty of our own brand of modernist nostalgia? Did we assume a level of agency that the new media experience brings into question? Many postmodern critics and media theorists would, at the very least, problematize the necessity and/or possibility of framing electronic information in the ways we suggest.[22] As Jean Baudrillard might argue, the hyper-fluidity and abundance of new media images overwhelms our ability and, perhaps more importantly, our desire to frame, to discriminate, to historicize. He writes: "History has stopped, one is in a kind of post-history which is without meaning" (1993a, 95). This period of post-history is "without meaning not because we are situated within a context . . . that constitutes the meanings we assign any object but because context . . . no longer provide[s] meaningful constraints for interpretation" (Svehla 2006, 95). The simulated and hyper-object evades context, derides the need for historical intelligibility. There is no frame that can contain its fluidity, just as "there is no place outside the flow of images from which a historical analysis can or should be made" (95).[23] The new media do not require our critical participation, merely our willingness to enjoy, to drift from one spectacle, one creative juxtaposition, one free-floating signifier to another, creating what Paul Patton calls "a hyperreal scenario in which events lose their identity and signifiers fade into one another" (1995, 2). And many of us do not seem to care or to even have noticed.

In the new media age, the desire for the "real," the material, the authentic, the crafted has been replaced with contentment for simulation, a simulation that no longer remembers or requires the reality it replaces (Baudrillard 1983, 11). We do not learn to play guitar anymore; we *simulate* guitar play with the X-box 360's *Guitar Hero*. We do not read the research of trained journalists anymore; we bounce through the hypertext of pundits. We do not have sexual relationships anymore; we support a $13 billion a year porn industry.[24] We are not required to sacrifice in our nation's wars anymore; we are asked only to support the simulated death and destruction that flash across our television screens. While these examples (especially the last) are, admittedly, hyperbolic, the underlying point gives us pause. What is agency in a digital world? What is its possibility? What is its point in the avalanche of images, sounds, and branded information—a modernist nostalgia? Theory hope? The empowerment we feel in choosing Skippy peanut butter over Jiff? If radical media theorists such as Baudrillard are correct, then "we should just surrender to the supremacy of the image, find pleasure in the pieces of the deconstructed universe, and move on" (Svehla 2006, 96). We should just forget the quaint question and false hope of agency.[25] It is, we admit, a seductive argument in many ways, but we feel that the price for such forgetfulness is too high and not evenly shared.

While the postmodern critique of agency is both powerful and useful (especially for explaining our students' apathy and understanding the exploitative tactics of the sound-bite saboteurs), ultimately we reject it as debilitating and misguided. Postmodern theory has produced no persuasive theory of resistance, no replacement for agency, which might lead to political action and change.[26] It reveals previously unproblematized power relations, perhaps even offers a powerful means of critiquing those relations, but it creates no way to move beyond those insights. It cannot seem to "articulate" Patricia Bizzell's call for "a positive program legitimated by an authority that is nevertheless non-foundational" (1990, 671). In short, postmodernism seems like the great furnace in John Milton's hell. It casts flames "on all sides round . . . /yet from those flames/No light, but rather darkness visible/Serv'd only to discover sights of woe,/Regions of sorrow, doleful shades, where peace/And rest can never dwell, hope never comes" (1957, 213).

And to be honest, we would rather spend our energy refiguring agency in light of the postmodern critique than trying to prove agency's ontological existence or epistemological validity. As Henry Giroux argues, rather than lamenting postmodern theory's inability to explain agency, "it seems more productive to examine how its claims about the contingent character of identity, constructed in a multiplicity of social relations and discourses, redefines the notion of agency" (1994, 350–51). In other words, we could spend forever trying to defend modernist notions of agency in a postmodern world, or we could look at our actions and evaluate that some lead to changing, shaping, and framing the world in ways we want. Whether or not we have a preexisting agency that we apply to the new media experience is not as important to our argument as whether or not we have the ability to evaluate the effect of our actions.

For while agency may no longer emanate from a distanced self and may no longer be leveled against easily discernable and monolithic power structures, it can still exist, individually and collectively, in the multiple, even fractured, *things we do*: write a book, protest deforestation, raise a child. It is agency as the measurable effect of action, agency as an "action that is not separate from, but also not reducible to, language" (Friedman 1991, 472), a pragmatic agency.[27] Such a notion of agency does not rely on the hoped-for emanations of a unified self but examines actions to see how a multiple, fractured, and fluid self might have manifested effectively in particular situations to achieve particular ends. The question to us, therefore, is not how we have the agency to frame media experiences but which kinds of framing lead to a sense of agency.

Similarly, we do not believe that "the context of history" and the imperatives of framing are as "overdetermined" or as "easily escaped" as Baudrillard believes. As Svehla argues, "There is a significant difference between the argument that there is no absolute meaning and that meaning does not exist" (2006, 96), that the restraints of history are always in flux and that they do not restrain at all, that framing is a difficult and contested process and that framing is impossible. Svehla continues:

> Despite Baudrillard's claim that the intelligibility of the object escapes context, his own argument, his own text, is dependent on context, on a frame of historical influence for its own intelligibility. Baudrillard is *made* intelligible through his connection to and our understanding of the works of Marx, Freud, Saussure, Heidegger, Nietzsche, and others. Those writers initiated the discursive practices—the context or genre—that made Baudrillard's text possible, and those initiators' texts were, in turn, made possible by previous initiators of text. To accept Baudrillard's argument is to accept the dubious notion that history no longer provides meaning within an argument that depends upon a continual reference to and critique of history for its own intelligibility. If there truly were a collapse of history's ability to provide meaning, then we could never come to that historical understanding. To notice that history has disappeared is possible only from a historical perspective. (2006, 96, emphasis added)

Finally, we are bothered by the often apolitical nature of radical postmodernism. Its refusal to grant agency where material harms are being done by individuals and groups to other individuals and groups does real political work, work that we, and many others, feel must be resisted. Indeed, many theorists see postmodern theory as a questionable attempt to remove notions of agency, identity, and social justice just at the moment when marginalized groups have attained the power to inhabit them. For example, Barbara Christian sees postmodern theory as the "production of a theoretical elite at precisely the time when the literature of peoples of color, of black women, of Latin Americans, of Africans, began to move to 'the center' " (1989, 229). Ann duCille's critique of the "camouflaging" effect of the term *postcolonialism*[28] echoes the fear that many have about the term *postmodernism*. DuCille believes that "false universals such as 'the postcolonial critic' camouflage the variety of neocolonial circumstances in which masses of people live, work, and theorize" (1994, 33). In a similar way, it could be argued that terms such as "the postmodern condition," "postmodern theory," and "the postmodern critic" camouflage the hunger, color, and gender inequalities that make it impossible or at least unpalatable for the marginalized to fully participate in the discursive universe. As Cornel West argues in response to the implicit middle-class privilege of Baudrillard's theory, "There is a reality *that one cannot not know*. The ragged edges of the Real, of *Necessity*, not being able to eat, not having shelter, not having health care, all this is something one cannot not know" (1988, 277, emphasis in original).

There are even theorists such as Thomas Newkirk who question the very existence (or at least the extent) of the postmodern condition, seeing "in the frequent assertion by academicians that we live in a 'postmodern age' . . . something mildly coercive . . . as if the issue has been settled, the paradigm shifted" (1997, 101). While conceding that postmodernists raise "interesting questions that needed to be addressed" (ix), Newkirk sees the assertion of a postmodern age as a reinforcement of class-bound divisions. He points out that while terms such as *essentialism*, *transcendence*, and *universal truth* are discredited in academic debate, they are embraced by a majority of working-class Americans. He writes:

> Yet at the same time the "postmodern era" is being proclaimed, surveys show that an increasing majority of Americans claim to be religious, believing in a Supreme Being who transcends history and culture. I would guess an even larger majority would claim that some values—"self-evident" truths such as human equality—are enduringly and essentially true, not simply "constructs" of a particular culture at a particular historical moment. (Newkirk 1997, 101)

Newkirk believes, therefore, that "it is paradoxical, if not hypocritical . . . to argue for the centrality of 'class' in our understanding of students, and at the same time advocate a form of skepticism that is antipathetic to the sources of moral and spiritual power in many working-class communities" (1997, 101).[29]

The real question to us, therefore, is not whether people have the power or the agency to frame new media, but who has more power to frame? Whose framing counts? Whose framing makes particular perspectives or approaches to the conflicts we all face salient enough to dominate public agendas and mobilize supportive publics? That is the better question—the testable question. While agency is always in flux, always plays out in particular and fluid and overlapping and contingent contexts, it is clear that the branding of information, reduction of citizenship to consumption, and unequal distribution of power *observed* to be driving these processes distort our information systems in ways that benefit some and harm others. From our viewpoint, putting pressure on the human ability to frame new media means highlighting this *unequal* distribution of agency, not rejecting agency's existence. Yes, understanding agency in a postmodern age requires, to some degree, highlighting its indeterminacy—but surely not its erasure. We accept, even value, the contingency of agency, but we do not accept the camouflaging of its uneven distribution. The dominant culture and those who benefit from it are operating within power hierarchies that exist, in part, to reproduce those hierarchies and maintain the status quo. Denying the existence of agency helps them do so.

Still, whatever one's feelings on the phenomenon of postmodernism, on its usefulness as a project for political change, or on the extent of the postmodern condition, the previous center provided by the modern project—"the domination of nature, the primacy of method, and the sovereignty of the individual" (Borgmann 1992, 5)—no longer holds, no longer persuades, no longer provides a common life for many inside the academy and without. Those of us who have been influenced by the postmodern critique but who do not wish to surrender theoretically discredited yet pragmatically cherished concepts from modernism, humanism, romanticism, feminism, and Marxism must now do so not by ignoring or demonizing postmodernity but by engaging it. We must move beyond the often totalizing impulse of postmodern theory but not beyond its formative influence, because, as Fredric Jameson argues, "for good or ill we cannot *not* use it" (1991, xxii, emphasis in original).

Indeed, Friedman argues that we live in a "post-poststructural" moment, a moment in which postmodernity is both present and past, a moment in which questions of "ethics and politics, agency and action, intention and meaning" (1991, 465) are once again legitimate, but now must be performed in light of the postmodern critique rather than in ignorance or spite of it, but also performed, we would add, in a way that does not fall victim to the equally dangerous and dogmatic extreme of anti-foundationalism. In other words, to productively enact our interest in ethics *and* politics, agency *and* action, intention *and* meaning we should avoid dualistic, either/or, black/white extremes, be it the certainty of Truth or the truth of Uncertainty, be it by calcifying binary oppositions or by collapsing them. We would further add that this performance, this balancing act, is, ultimately, a pragmatic one, that Bizzell's search for "a positive program legitimated by an authority that is nevertheless non-foundational" can be found in the works of John Dewey, Charles Sanders Peirce, William James, Louise Rosenblatt, Cornel West, and other prominent pragmatic thinkers.

Consider, for example, the question of agency as it relates to new media. The pragmatic agent is still embedded within cross-cutting communities and intersecting subject positions. He or she is still part of a complex, interactive process that does not have stable resting points, like reified individuals or free subjects. But, conversely, this fluidity does not prevent us from also differentiating between what subjects do in a communicative process (shape, frame, act) and the ways inanimate processes or mediums or institutions also powerfully impact communication. Inanimate processes may enable this or obscure that agent; they might amplify this or mute that fear or concern, but this power does not make them the same as agents. Each factor has force and relevance and influence, and their interrelatedness must be part of our analysis, but we can also differentiate between agency and medium. The active verbs "to shape" and "to frame" need an active subject to drive their potential effect, to perform the critical, difficult, and time-consuming actions that might lead to measurable agency.

Thus the sound-bite saboteurs' amplification of overload, their manipulation of decontextualized arguments, their dishonest use of data, and their purposeful spreading of disinformation may be empowered, even enabled, by new media but should not be confused with them. It is the sound-bite saboteurs who defraud and dispirit the body politic, who suppress thought and patriotic dissent, who twist image into apathy. Sadly, we believe that sound-bite saboteurs understand the nature of new media and the power of postmodernity, for they have been able to exchange an economy of material need for an economy of image. They have created a rhetorical world where images of supposed morality are often more important to a person than the imperatives of his or her material want.[30] They have man-aged—acting with considerable agency—to, in a Baudrillardian sense, substitute "signs of the real for the real itself" (1983, 4).

This electronic slight of hand exacerbates the already difficult nature of new media, making our tasks as academicians that much harder. We need a method that will allow us to reveal the tactics of the sound-bite saboteurs without partaking of those tactics, which will allow us to reject sound-bite sabotage but not our engagement with it, which will allow us to see the problems generated by new media but also the potential. In sum, we need a method that will allow us to enact conflict as opportunity. We believe John Dewey's work to nest supposed dualisms provides that method and can serve as the basis for our critical intervention.

V. A Deweyan Alternative to Either/Or Thinking in a Digital Age

> Conflict should always keep in mind the goal of negotiation and even the goal of deciding upon a course of action. In this way, students learn not only that conflict is everywhere in their world—they have already learned this from their culture, from *Crossfire*, from talk-radio, and from the other prominent models of argumentation. They might learn also that the inevitability of conflict does not imply throwing up one's hands in despair and becoming merely a spectator to the arena of culture and politics.
>
> —Charles Paine, *The Resistant Writer*

Too often the new media's relationship to academia is cast in terms of binary oppositions: academic discourse versus new media, word versus image, print versus hypertext. Perhaps this dualistic approach should not be surprising, given the larger dualisms that define both our culture (self versus society, thought versus language, faith versus data, belief versus evidence, reason versus emotion, mind versus body) and much of our pedagogy (product versus process, object versus subject, curriculum centered versus student centered, argument versus narrative, research versus teaching). We would argue that such binary oppositions harm not only our understanding of each component in the dualism but, more importantly, our understanding of the components' interactions and our role in creating those interactions—the processes by which components come to mean, function, conflict, and change.

Each opposite contains its other; each opposite depends, in a reciprocal way, on the other to define and continually redefine its own existence. A focus on opposition without a corresponding focus on cooperation, therefore, only gives us half the picture, and a distorted half at that. It reinforces an autonomous and atomistic, rather than a constructed and cellular, view of entities in conflict. It erases the inter-related, interpolated, transactive, and mediated relationship that is not only the generative basis for the binary but also for each component in the binary. A focus on opposition alone betrays a creeping foun-dationalism that sees the components of a binary as somehow Real, independent of our construction of them—making binary conflicts not only Real, in a foundationalist sense, but inevitable, natural, and, perhaps, preordained. Entities, ideas, and people come into conflict not because of how they are related, the way and how of their framing, but because of some natural or innate or metaphysical essence: cats and dogs, women and men, Christians and Muslims. Dewey calls this reliance on supposed essence the "philosophic fallacy" (1929a, 27).[31] We call it the enshrinement of the epistemological, metaphysical, and ontological questions over the pragmatic.

Indeed, Dewey saw this reliance on essence to explain/justify conflict as so misguided yet so central to Western thought that he eventually rejected the term "interaction" in favor of the term "trans-action" as a way of emphasizing the constructed and co-conditioning nature of supposed dualisms. Louise Rosenblatt explains:

In *Knowing and the Known* (1949), John Dewey and Arthur F. Bentley suggested that the term "interaction" had become tied to the Cartesian dualistic paradigm that treats human beings and nature, subject and object, knower and known, as separate entities. In the light of the post-Einsteinian developments, they proposed the term "transaction" to designate a relationship in which each element, instead of being fixed and predefined, conditions and is conditioned by the other. (1993, 380)

The components of a societal dualism, even society itself, exist to Dewey not only "*by* transmission, *by* communication, but it may fairly be said to exist *in* transmission, *in* communication" (1917, 5, empha-sis in original). Thought and language, academic discourse and new media, reason and emotion exist in and *as* a process of transmission among members of a community. As constructions, they are mutable to human action and revision—and so are their conflicts.

Reliance on dualistic thinking, perhaps not surprisingly, is another attribute of the sound-bite saboteurs. Either/or, us versus them, red state versus blue state, good versus evil, straight versus gay, or with us or against us thinking is often how the saboteurs frame politics, economics, foreign policy, religion, and everything else that makes up our culture. Saboteurs encourage us to reject the search for common ground, common cause, and common sense (the shared and constructed nature of our reality) and focus instead on division as definition and definition as division. They portray conflicts not as products of our interpretive and communicative processes (and, as such, within our ability to revise and reframe) but as the inevitable clash of preexisting and independent forces, leading to disingenuous and debilitating pseudo-definitions of what should be evolving democratic concepts. For example, they often frame nuance as propaganda, complication as obfuscation, expertise as elitism, and patriotism as compliance. Fortunately, Dewey's work offers an alternative to either/or thinking—one close to Jacques Derrida's deconstructive method but ultimately not limited to what we believe is the dead end of deconstruction.

In *John Dewey and the Challenge of Classroom Practice*, Stephen Fishman and Lucille McCarthy claim that Dewey's "distrust of either-or choices, and . . . [his] attempt to integrate apparently contradictory positions, is both a continuing theme and an organizing structure of his work" (1998, 15). They continue:

> The motivating force of his [Dewey's] writing is always clear: his unrelenting effort to reconcile false dualisms. For example, whereas from many traditional perspectives the self is opposed to world, a Deweyan analysis, although acknowledging their tension, would stress ways in which self and world condition one another and are necessary for one another.
>
> This strategy of reconciling traditionally opposed forces by showing ways in which they cooperate and interact is central to Dewey's philosophic writing. (16)

It would not be self *or* society, curriculum centered *or* student centered, evidence *or* belief, academic discourse *or* new media for Dewey. Individuals, ideas, beliefs, and arguments are best understood as in constructed interaction rather than isolation. Or, more precisely, they are best understood as always already interactions. The basic social unit for Dewey is what Raymond Boisvert calls "cellular." Rather than society being "composed of indivisible, self-contained units . . . [atoms], a society is made up of smaller societies. The ultimate constituents, like cells, are themselves composite and porous to the surrounding environment" (Boisvert 1988, 54). Each component of a dualism, therefore, is always already permeated by the other component, bound in a recursive and mutually defining, though sometimes confusing and unequal, relationship of perspective and use. Fishman and McCarthy call Dewey's attempt to reconcile false dualisms "nesting."

Nesting dualisms recognizes that the terms that make up supposed dualisms do not correspond to an objective reality or a preexisting essence but to each other, each contains the other, through a reality mediated by human action and intervention. The objects, individuals, and ideas of the world do not have an independent reality we discover so much as an interrelated reality we construct. In this way, Dewey's method of nesting dualisms is somewhat similar to Baudrillard's critique of "the binary oppositions inherent in most theories of representation: authentic vs. synthetic, organic vs. mechanical, reality vs. representation" (Svehla 2006, 95). Yet Baudrillard's critique is different from Dewey's method in that Baudriallard does not nest the binary; he erases it—along with tensions, inequities, and conflicts that need to be interrogated and the agency required to do so.

Dewey does not want to either calcify or erase the tension in binary oppositions. He wants to engage it, to acknowledge that the tension is also the product of a transactive relationship. The components of a dualism depend on their reciprocity *and* tension for meaning, function, and revision. By erasing the binary instead of nesting it, Baudrillard also erases our ability, our desire, and *our right* to reconstruct it. We are left only with the "options" of surrender, drift, hedonism without guilt—with a certain pleasure in the irony of things. Baudrillard dismisses any other response as delusional theory hope. Consider, for example, the real versus synthetic binary that Baudrillard collapses. Baudrillard would have students see the emptiness of this binary and then enjoy simulation—albeit with an ironic awareness. Dewey would maintain that students are still subject to images in very *material* ways, ways focused around the twin motors of consumer advertising: anxiety and desire. Dewey would have students investigate how the supposed dualism of real versus synthetic is actually a codependent relationship mediated by their intervention.

In this book we have attempted to nest such binaries as faith and reason, belief and evidence, academic discourse and new media, and postmodernity and agency. For instance, in chapter 5, we will offer a critique of belief that is not really a critique of belief itself but of belief severed from a mutually defining and co-interrogating relationship with evidence. It is not that evidence-based arguments are inherently better or truer or more authentic; it is that belief without evidence is removed from the transactional process that is the ground of its creation, function, and validation. The reverse is also true. Evidence depends on belief just as much as belief depends on evidence. Indeed, we would go so far as to say that belief is a type of evidence and evidence a type of belief.

Without this interaction, this recursive interrogation and validation, our arguments must leave out some part of our experience, some part of our potential agency, some part of our community, and, therefore, some part of our humanity. If reason requires the sacrifice of emotion for its validity, then it becomes its own kind of unquestionable deity. If evidence must be devoid of belief, then where will the wonder come from that drives us to seek out evidence? If faith cannot be seen as a type of data and data as a type of faith, if they cannot mutually contextualize, complicate, challenge, and ameliorate each other, then what is their value for solving human problems? The problem with sound-bite saboteurs' application of belief is that there is no corresponding, critiquing, fulfilling tension with honest evidence—the result being an imbalance that weakens what are supposed to be democratic deliberations.

Finally, nesting dualisms is also an attempt to counter dogmatism and epistemological calcification, an attempt to see the process of how we argue, how we make knowledge, as more important than any single, particular outcome. Fishman and McCarthy explain:

> [Dewey] offers us, not a series of truths about reality . . . but a method, a set of categories or questions with which to probe any perplexing situation. Faced with a problem—personal or professional, practical or theoretical, in the school or marketplace—Dewey's approach leads us to ask: What are the dichotomous activities at work in our situation? How might they be better integrated and balanced? In other words, Dewey's approach helps us attend to the conflicting activities within our dilemma and to approach our problem with the goal of reconciling its underlying forces. (1998, 17)

If we do not try to reconcile our dualisms, try to keep our minds and arguments open ended, we lose the desire for common ground, the need to look at situations, ideas, and conflicts from a variety of angles. Most importantly, we lose the ethical imperative to test the validity of our ideas by examining their effects, because instead of constantly *seeking* answers we will spend all our time *defending* them. In short, we harm our ability to learn, to grow, and to change and, so, we become willing, if unknowing, participants in sound-bite sabotage.

Consequently, our willingness to test the validity of our ideas by examining their effects has both functional and moral benefits for our culture. As Dewey explains:

> A conviction that consequences in human welfare are a test of the worth of beliefs and thoughts has some obvious beneficial aspects. It makes a fusion of two superlatively important qualities, love of truth and love of neighbor. It discourages dogmatism and its child, intolerance. It arouses and heartens an experimental spirit which wants to know how systems and theories work before given complete adhesion. . . . Compelling attention to details, to particulars, it safeguards one from seclusion in universals. (1983 [1922], 308)

Reconciling dualisms means that we *never* stop questioning our beliefs, testing our theories, refining our methods, or collecting our data, for adhesion, answer, and certainty (the unholy trinity of the sound-bite saboteurs) are antithetical to growth and morality. "The process of growth," Dewey argues, "of improvement and progress, rather than the static outcome and result, becomes the significant thing. . . . Not perfection as a final goal, but the ever-enduring process of perfecting, maturing, refining is the aim in living" (1948, 177).

VI. An Objection to Nesting Dualisms

> We must preserve the possibility of universal connection. That's the fundamental challenge. Let's dig deep enough within our heritage to make that connection to others. . . . The quest for knowledge without presuppositions, the quest for certainty, the quest for dogmatism and orthodoxy and rigidity is over.
>
> —Cornel West, "Diverse New World"

> The Other is what allows me not to repeat myself for ever.
>
> —Jean Baudrillard, *The Transparency of Evil: Essays on Extreme Phenomena*

A possible objection to Dewey's concept of reconciling dualisms lies in the issue of inequity tied to hierarchy. As Derrida has shown us, cultural binaries are marked not just by opposition but also by power stratifications. One half of a binary is always privileged, always works to erase or suppress the dominated half. Such dualisms as word versus image, speech versus writing, mind versus body, white versus black, and man versus woman are "organized hierarchically: the first term is seen as higher or better than the second" (Johnson 1995, 43). How does the activity of nesting address this inequity? Why would nesting a dualism work to resist or reconstitute or revise the nonegalitarian way its components are connected? Even the word nesting has conflicting connotations, depending on how one ends it: nest(ing) implies an active agent working to reconcile a dualism; nest(ed) implies that the connection between a dualism's components already exists, and the job of the agent is to dig into the dualism to discover the how and why of that connection. In other words, one form implies a fluid nature to cultural binaries, a constructed and, therefore, changeable nature. The other form implies a certain level of calcification, problematizing our ability to alter the binary and encouraging passive (albeit sometimes "savvy") cynicism, which we discuss in depth in chapter 5.

Our response to these objections is threefold: First, Dewey's work to reconcile dualisms does imply both a project the agent must undertake and a preexisting condition the agent must discover. This discovery of an already existing nested relationship, however, does not mean that the dualism and its content preexist human construction. The nested part of the dualism is not an essence. It is simply that binary oppositions are also historical constructions. In other words, we do not just make and remake dualisms. We, to some degree, inherit them from our ancestors. But that inheritance does not mean that further construction and further nesting is not necessary or possible. Words, ideas, evidence, arguments, and so on are not static or fixed entities to Dewey. Even when the historical connections are being "discovered," they are still the product of human construction and reconstruction. They are always already being revised, rediscovered, and recreated through the very act of engagement.

Second, we must remember that Dewey's concept of nesting dualisms is a highly interactive process. If there is a hierarchy from one perspective in the binary, then that hierarchy is counterbalanced by a corresponding hierarchy from another perspective. This longer quote from Fishman and McCarthy explains:

> As Dewey presents them, the educational dualisms he works
> to reconcile are *nested*. In other words, as we explore student

and curriculum, we find beneath each dualism concentric circles of other dualisms. And, to make matters even more complicated for Dewey's expositors, when we study these more fundamental dualisms, we find ourselves amidst mirrors reflecting infinite regress. That is, to study these more basic dualisms is to find them reflected in the very process of studying them. For example, as Lucille McCarthy and I examine my classes for signs of continuity and interaction, construction and criticism, interest and effort, our examination itself—and, indeed, our writing of this book—displays tensions and transactions between continuity and interaction, construction and criticism, interest and effort.

Thus, as we approach Dewey, we should keep in mind that he is trying to describe a world of highly interactive processes, but he must do this in an English language based on strict subject-object distinctions, on the view that everything is what it is and not another thing. He must, that is, try to describe an Einsteinian world of relativity—a postmodern, Borgesian world—in a language tooled for fixed, unchanging truth and in philosophic genre characterized by linear, logical argumentation.... Put differently, Dewey's task is to speak of a reality which does not conform to the so-called law of excluded middle: that things are either A or not A. It is a reality in which past and future appear to be simultaneous in the present, where means are ends and ends are means, where education is intelligent practice, and intelligent practice is moral, and the moral is aesthetic, and—like the snake swallowing its tail—the aesthetic is educational. In short, it is a reality in which familiar distinctions are transformed. (1998, 16–17, emphasis in original)

The limitations of reconciling dualisms, therefore, may be more in the language used to explain our actions than in the actions themselves. Hierarchies are not static entities either. They contain other hierarchies and other supposed binary oppositions that can then also be nested—weakening the seeming inevitability or naturalness of the more obvious hierarchies, revealing that hierarchies are themselves constructed and answerable to human revision. Seeing the nested nature of binaries becomes the first step in resisting hierarchies, because seeing the co-constitutive and constructed nature of binaries makes the alteration of their hierarchies imaginable.

Finally, we believe that deconstruction does not have to be in opposition to reconciling dualisms. Indeed, we believe that the deconstructive method can be folded into the overall process of nesting. Dualisms, we admit, are rarely, if ever, connected or connectable through equal strictures of power. If we consider, for example, the dualisms of male/female, white/black, and self/other, then inequities in power and the material consequences of those inequities are readily apparent. We are in favor, therefore, of making Derrida's deconstructive method a reoccurring part of the nesting process, part of understanding the relationship contained in a dualism, and part of reforming that relationship. Students should work not only to reconcile a supposed dualism but also to revise or redesign the power inequities that demarcate that dualism. The hierarchies that mark dualistic relationships must be deconstructed. However, we believe the process must not end there.

We do not want our critical intervention to be endlessly deconstructive, to be afraid of putting forth arguments about what is true, right, good, and decent, because we fear we will be accused of putting forth arguments about what is True, Right, Good, and Decent. Deconstruction may be a necessary and continuous step of nesting dualisms, but ultimately we want our intervention to be constructive. The pragmatic method requires testing, trying, advocating, and revising ideas, not just deconstructing them. As long as we continue to look at the effects of our ideas, continue to prove their truth, value, and validity through their consequences, we do not fear the charge of foundationalism.

For the truth of an idea is best understood not by what it is but by what it *does*. Ideas such as justice, truth, freedom, democracy, agency, cynicism, media, discourse, and argument only become true, become real, in use. They can only be achieved, implemented, revised, reinvented, and resisted when they are dirty with the human fingerprints that created them. Faith and reason, belief and evidence, hope and cynicism, conflict and resolution, word and image are not just nouns but also verbs, interactions connected through human mediation. As verbs, they are alive with the transformative and validating power of human experience. They are answerable to the human voice, to human context and content. As nouns, they risk death, the distant repositories of memory and abstraction beyond human critique and revision. God is a verb, data is a verb, love is a verb, argument is a verb, faith is a verb, evidence is a verb, citizenship is a verb, and democracy is a verb—because humanity is a verb. And, as verbs, each is open to the constant scrutiny of human limitation, perspective, and verification.

In the end, Dewey's work to integrate the dualisms at play in our world does not offer us the answer to the new media/academic discourse dualism—anymore than it offers us the solution to sound-bite sabotage. Instead, Dewey's work offers us a method for engaging dilemmas, a set of tools and practices for conflict resolution. We believe that this process of seeking connection, of finding opportunity in conflict, is more important than the specific and necessarily momentary answers to which we come. This method, this never-ending process, is what we can take from Dewey to challenge, within the classroom and without, the sound-bite saboteurs, their exploitation of new media, and the crippling form of cynicism that their sabotage breeds. In the spirit of John Dewey, therefore, we would now like to turn to a deeper examination of the kind of informed and engaged cynicism we believe might lead to effective resistance.

The Possibilities of Engaged Cynicism

Ideals, Practice, and Citizenship in a Democracy

I. Introduction

Hope has two beautiful daughters. Their names are anger and courage; anger at the way things are, and courage to see that they do not remain the way they are.

—Augustine

On September 12, 2006, MSNBC's *Scarborough Country* led with a discussion about Comedy Central's *The Daily Show* and its host Jon Stewart. The banner scrolling at the bottom of the screen read *"Daily Show*: Damaging Democracy?" as host Joe Scarborough looked at the camera and asked, "Is Jon Stewart's *Daily Show* making cynics out of American kids?" The question addressed by MSNBC, Scarborough, and his guests was twofold: Does *The Daily Show* make cynics out of young American viewers, and does that youthful cynicism hurt our democracy?[1]

Scarborough's guests that day were Mort Zuckerman, editor in chief of *U.S. News & World Report*, and Rachel Sklar of www. huffingtonpost.com, a news and an editorial Web site. Zuckerman noted that *The Daily Show* has a "real sway and hold" on people

151

who are "interested in the news," and that most of Stewart's viewers fall in the 18–24-year-old demographic—a demographic, he was quick to point out, that has "never voted to any great degree."[2] Sklar, in her early twenties, countered that she found it "galvanizing" to have the information provided by the show: "Day after day you see what's going on, you have to get involved, you have to see the spin."[3] Both guests agreed that *The Daily Show* provides information to 18–24-year-olds interested in political news, though they disagreed on whether or not those viewers are moved by the show to any sort of political action.

Scarborough did not directly respond to his guests' comments, instead characterizing *The Daily Show* as a "mouthpiece for the moveon. org people," claiming that such people had "bred . . . a civic consciousness" out of "an entire generation."[4] His contention that liberal political organizations are responsible for a lack of "civic consciousness" is difficult to address, since he neither challenged his guests' assertion that the age demographic they were discussing had *never voted to any great degree*, before or after the advent of moveon.org and similar organizations, nor explained what, besides voting, he might mean by *civic consciousness*. The charge of "cynicism" was apparently all that was needed, in that it has become impossible to deny or otherwise answer, thus highlighting how the inescapable ambiguity of problem solving and deliberation is exploited by sound-bite saboteurs—exploited not by lying outright but by misinforming, misleading, and creating within the polis crippling, paralyzing doubt.[5]

The Daily Show, The Colbert Report, Politically Incorrect, and now *Real Time with Bill Maher* and other comedy shows are increasingly taken to task for the harm they are supposedly perpetrating on American democracy and American youth. In a 2006 *Washington Post* column titled "Is 'The Daily Show' bad for democracy?" author Richard Morin begins with this line: "Jon Stewart and his hit Comedy Central cable show may be poisoning democracy" (2006, A2). Morin appears to go beyond mere assertion, however, by citing the work of political scientists Jody Baumgartner and Jonathan Morris, which, he says, finds that 48 percent of college-age youth watched *The Daily Show*, "but only 23 percent of 'show viewers followed 'hard news' programs closely' " (A2). The results of this study, according to Morin, show that viewers rated political candidates "more negatively" and "expressed less trust in the electoral system and more cynical views of the news media" (A2) after viewing Stewart's program.[6]

The answer to Scarborough's questions would appear to be a resounding yes. *The Daily Show* and Jon Stewart are fostering cynicism among our youth, and this cynicism is bad for American democracy. And yet we believe this is neither a complete picture of the cynical turn in American public discourse, nor is it an accurate conclusion to draw regarding what that cynicism might tell us about knowledge production, information distortion, or more effective forms of active citizenship and pragmatic agency.

Scarborough's questions—and the answers that both he and Morin suggest—do not appear to gibe with the discussion in either Scarborough's televised broadcast or Morin's column. Both seem to be concerned that *The Daily Show* is undermining the *positive attitudes* that young people would otherwise have toward politics, politicians, and the media, though neither seems interested in whether a negative attitude might be a rational response to what is actually happening in politics and the media or, importantly, whether such negativity might be useful—perhaps necessary—in a democracy.

The public sphere is, as we have discussed in earlier chapters, filled with the noise of serial and overlapping sound bites, by branded messages that blur the distinction between public relations for private gain and the information so vital to a healthy democracy, and we are collectively alarmed by the cacophony. We should note, however, that this alarm is increasingly articulated as a response to what many describe as cynicism, a blanket term whose accuracy and political utility will need some unpacking before we can make any sense of it. We argue in this chapter that the *charge* of cynicism and the misapprehension of what cynicism is and might produce or lead to (as opposed to cynicism itself) has among its other effects two important results over the long term that may preclude effective citizen agency and democratic deliberation. First is the already discernable demise of the value of expertise in public discourse, and second—as the inevitable consequence of the first—each successive generation becomes less capable of self-governance, of holding its government and other institutions accountable, because the pedagogy of reasoned, well-supported argument within the public square is disappearing. We are fast losing the ability to recall what such deliberation even looks like.

In this chapter we attempt to nest particular and related sets of cultural dualisms, dualisms that highlight the tensions between popular and scholarly discourses, rulers and the ruled, public and private spheres, and, most importantly in this chapter, between engaged and disempowering forms of cynicism. We do this, in part, by expanding our use of Dewey's distinction between our often messy, concrete democratic practices and our democratic ideals and aspirations that drive and direct and coordinate those practices, even with the knowledge that the ideal is always never fully achieved in practice. We explore in this chapter select examples of public- and private-sector saboteurs singling out popular culture performances for criticism precisely when these performative moments likely enable citizens to see the spin, the strategy, and the brand behind the message. And this is a failure of leadership, we argue, in both the public and private sectors, encouraging a disengaged, immobilizing cynicism regarding the gaps between our everyday practices and our democratic ideals.

We begin this chapter by exploring the roots of Western cynicism in order to demonstrate the crucial importance for democracy of the unacceptable, inappropriate, and even offensive cultural performance—performances that require what Branham calls "outsider status." We are encouraged to fear cynicism precisely for its trademark incivility, but this chapter, citing multiple new media sources, argues that the performance of the inappropriate by cynics may be one of our most effective tools against sound-bite sabotage—in the classroom, and in the larger public square.

II. Cynicism

> There can be no healthy relation of modern-day enlightenment
> to its own history without sarcasm.
>
> —Peter Sloterdijk, *Critique of Cynical Reason*

A Historical Trajectory

Most scholars date the start of the Cynic movement in the fourth century B.C.E., and the leading figure in that movement Diogenes of Sinope. Diogenes was known for his simple lifestyle and shocking public behavior. He lived out-of-doors, argued with people passing by, and disrupted lectures by eating or farting openly. He was considered shameless, uncivil in the extreme. A biography of Diogenes, compiled during the third century C.E., offers multiple eyewitness accounts of him masturbating and defecating in public, actually urinating on people and, once, spitting on a man who warned him not to spit inside a palatial, private home. When asked to explain his outrageous behavior, Diogenes said he spit on the man because he was the basest spot available in those luxurious surroundings (Krueger, qtd. in Branham and Goulet-Cazé 1996, 222–26).

According to F. Sayre, the ancient Cynics "attacked and ridiculed religion, philosophy, science, art, literature, love, friendship, good manners, loyalty to parents and even athletics—everything which tended to embellish and enrich human life, to give it significance and to make it worth living" (qtd. in Branham and Goulet-Cazé 1996, 81). While Branham does not attempt to deny this, he calls Sayre's account of the Cynics "humorless" (104), and persuasively argues that Diogenes' rhetorical method, characterized by its pragmatism, improvisation, and humor, suggests its uniqueness among ancient philosophical traditions, as well as, we argue, with Peter Sloterdijk and others, its utility for contemporary democratic discourse (Sloterdijk 1987, 91–92). Drawing on the work of Mary Douglas and Mikhail Bakhtin, Branham contends that the unifying (and thus hegemonic) experience of social rituals is undercut by parody. Douglas, he points out, notes that standardized rituals assert "hierarchy and order." Ritual is understood as an expression of "what ought to happen" and is, therefore, "not morally neutral." Jokes, on the other hand, "denigrate and devalue hierarchy and order. . . . The message of a standard rite is that the ordained patterns of social life are inescapable. *The message of a joke is that they are escapable* . . . for a joke implies that anything is possible" (qtd. in Branham and Goulet-Cazé 1996, 94, 95, emphasis added). Rites and rituals, in other words, are "socially consolidating and conservative," whereas parody and satire—humor that is often termed cynical—are "antiritualistic and disruptive" (95).[7] Strong, resilient democracies need healthy and interactive doses of both.

Diogenes eventually became a commonly known literary figure in ancient Rome, admired for his self-imposed poverty as well as reviled for his obscene behaviors, his lack of restraint. He was a complex figure, to be sure, in terms of morality. In addition to what was considered his appallingly uncivil behavior, Diogenes was renowned for publicly criticizing social mores, revealing hypocrisy, and "refusing to respect undeserved reputations" (Chaloupka 1999, 4). He observed that the distinction between the public and the private leant itself to hypocrisy, and he was determined to enact private behaviors in public in order to reveal the spin, the strategy, and the hypocrisy of representing private interests as public. As we discussed in previous chapters, he did this by nesting the dualism—albeit in a transgressive manner—to reveal the powerful impact on the distribution of citizen attentions and effective agency. The distinction, Diogenes insisted, was artificial and served the interests of the powerful, the well heeled.

Diogenes lived in a large city, slept, it is said, in a barrel or tub in full public view, and begged for a living. Thus, Branham reasons, neither self-sufficiency nor nature appears to have been a driving principle of ancient cynicism. Rather, freedom—freedom of speech (*parrh sia*) in particular—is "imperative" to the Cynic philosophy (96, 97). Rejecting work, Branham explains, the hallmark of what society considers a productive life, is necessary to "avoid becoming subject to society's rules and authority" (96, 97). The roots of cynicism, then, are found in rhetorical acts that "assert freedom in some particular context," a "performance premised on freedom" (98) and requiring outsider status for the rhetor.

Today we hear the charge of "cynicism" from virtually every quarter and in every possible context. Politicians are cynical, as are the journalists who cover them; our young people are cynical—because their music and their icons are cynical, maybe their teachers and cultural role models are as well. Parents are cynical, institutions are cynical. No one is exempt, and everyone seems to fear the inevitable decline of America that leaders suggest is being driven by cynicism. According to columnist David Broder, cynicism "saps people's confidence in politics and public officials, and it erodes both the standing and the standards of journalism. If the assumption is that nothing is on the level, nothing is what it seems, then democratic citizenship becomes a game for fools, and there is no point in trying to stay informed" (1994, A19). But as we discussed in the first four chapters, political communication is inescapably about strategy, meta-conflicts, and displacement: it is confusing because it is defined by disputation, argument, and deliberation about *what* we ought to be arguing about, and it is made more confusing by sound-bite saboteurs who encourage us to fear conflict itself and read cynicism as only and always disengaging and alienating. According to the vision of American democracy embedded in the current fear of cynicism, institutions and individuals are understood as cynical in a powerful "circularity" that "covers our political and social arrangements like a blanket" (Chaloupka 1999, 10). We argue that the assault on cynicism is both part of a larger war on criticism in general, and a part of a larger loss of our ability to understand and defend, in deliberative practices, the principles and ideals constitutive of a democratic society.

The charge of cynicism carries so much weight, however, that we are still left wondering what, exactly, cynicism is or, indeed, if it can retain any meaning or political utility amid such pervasive and ambiguous, albeit negative, usage. Cynicism is implicitly or explicitly defined as crippling contempt, low expectations, incivility, satire or parody, anger, the antithesis of idealism, or simply realism, among others. It is portrayed as a kind of skepticism gone bad, or too far. While the skeptic can be admired for not being naïve, the cynic is reviled as a kind of crippled skeptic, a dangerous figure who threatens stability and agency through her or his extreme pessimism, negativity, even paranoia, resulting in democracy-killing apathy. The common thread here, however, seems to be, as Chaloupka states, a "condition of lost belief" (xiv).

One reading of the concerns over cynicism, articulated in the Seditions Act of 1917 and the Patriot Act today, for instance, is that cynics are a threat because they challenge a carte blanche acceptance of the claims made on behalf of existing sociopolitical arrangements. Such acceptance naturalizes both the moral and pragmatic *rightness* of those arrangements, thus (re)producing both stability and belief—not to mention the status quo—ad infinitum. Understanding the fear of cynicism in this way sheds some light on what is meant by the "civic consciousness" referred to by Joe Scarborough, the consciousness that has been "bred out of an entire generation." Scarborough is afraid we are losing our collective ability and willingness to simply believe our public and private leaders—despite any evidence that might lead us to do otherwise. While the state of our democracy may give cause for concern, we argue that the problem lies not in cynicism per se but, rather, in the insistence by our leaders, which is subsequently taken up by some publics, that belief in our traditions, institutional arrangements, and constitutional principles is *the same thing* as approval of the policies and practices of any particular leadership regime currently controlling these (public and private) institutions. In the current context, publics are increasingly, aggressively encouraged to privilege beliefs that support passive and dependent forms of citizen agency, because such beliefs are divorced from a dialectical relationship with evidence and reason—they are neither seen nor performed as nested, in Dewey's terms. Instead, belief is framed in opposition to deliberation and reasoning as democratic practices. Belief itself becomes a sound bite and a public litmus test that may not be interrogated, insulating elite decision makers from criticism through sound bites constructed to saturate what we understand and accept as common sense with interested messages like "Individuals who sue corporations are greedy, looking for a litigation lottery," or "They hate us because we're free." What is certainly lost are the crucially important aspects of democracy that reside in critical interrogation and argument.

The Humor and Incivility of Cynicism

In his address to the audience and television viewers at the White House Correspondents Dinner in May 2006, comedian Stephen Colbert said this in reference to President Bush:

We're not so different, he and I. We get it. We're not brainiacs on the nerd patrol. We're not members of the factinista. . . . I give people the truth, unfiltered by rational argument. . . . I'm a simple man with a simple mind. I hold a simple set of beliefs that I live by. . . . I've never been a fan of books. I don't trust them. They're all fact, no heart. I mean, they're elitist, telling us what is or isn't true, or what did or didn't happen. . . . The greatest thing about [President Bush] is he's steady. You know where he stands. He believes the same thing Wednesday that he believed on Monday, no matter what happened Tuesday. Events can change; this man's beliefs never will.

Much to the chagrin of actual conservatives, Colbert, who plays a conservative talk show host on Comedy Central's *The Colbert Report*, had appeared at the White House Correspondents Dinner in character. His 30-minute "roast" of the president focused on the now-frequent criticism of Bush for being "out of touch with reality."[8] Drawing on the similarities between the president and the character he plays, Colbert boasted, "I give people the truth, unfiltered by rational argument." President Bush, sitting a few feet away, fairly squirmed, trapped quite literally on television and by the hundreds of press corps members sitting in the live audience. It is certainly worth noting that the following year's White House Correspondents Dinner featured the affable and utterly inoffensive Rich Little. Colbert's outrageous performance bit both hard and deep, and its lasting effects will not be forgotten soon by those responsible for booking the evening's entertainment.

The comedian, as one agent of Murray Edelman's cultural antidote, helps us see the spin and strategy of interested messages, of branded information, by occupying a particular place from which he might, as Douglas and Branham argue, disrupt hierarchy and order, even create in the cultural imaginary the possibility of escaping the "ordained patterns of social life" in a way that mainstream news media simply cannot. The comedian can disrupt the orderliness of presidential power to the degree that we might imagine, for example, a president who is disdainful of neither books nor facts; able and willing to incorporate new events and information into his decision-making process; disinclined to tout the moral superiority of *simplicity* in the context of what is surely one of the most difficult and complex tasks: being President of the United States.

According to Branham's research, Diogenes of Sinope was a rhetor with persuasive powers that few, if any, could withstand. The majority of anecdotes that cite Diogenes' words verbatim reveal that "almost one in six depends for its effect on some kind of pun or wordplay" and depict him as a man "whose philosophy grew out of a continual process of ad hoc improvisation" and whose "most brilliant invention was . . . himself" (87). And, while it might be pleasant to imagine that it was his wit alone that enabled his persuasive abilities, we cannot ignore the other side of that coin: his shocking incivility, his shamelessness, his rudeness, his completely inappropriate public behavior. He revealed the spin and strategy of the interested messages constructed and disseminated by elites in his day by intentionally nesting public/private and popular/scholarly dualisms to enable informed and engaged forms of learning, critique, interface, and knowledge production.

The idea of self-improvisation in the service of critical performance that we have been discussing may be fruitfully understood as the flip side of, or at least linked to, bullshitting—faking the context—discussed in earlier chapters. If by faking the context it is possible to persuade people to believe irrationally or demonstrably false things, might it not be equally possible, through interrogating the context, to enable people to imagine a very different, and perhaps more positive, or effective, reality, as a means of bringing it to life? This would suggest that the cynicism such satiric or parodic performances are often charged with are not in themselves either positive or negative; rather, they offer generative possibilities that may be realized in any number of different ways. We see in Digoenes the kind of active and engaged performance of cynicism that nests the popular and the scholarly, the experiences of the ruled and the strategies of the rulers, and it nests or links these by making the implicit explicit—linking our high-minded, shared aspirations to our often low-brow achievements in practice, without being dismissive of the cultural artifacts used to mobilize this critique, thus creating no opportunities for sound-bite sabotage.

Can we not then view the current spate of bitter criticisms about not only the cynicism that always already permeates our discourse but the incivility as well, in a more subtle and nuanced light? If the power of cynical critiques ot that which we hold most sacred—and that which is thus most invisible and most powerful—lies at least in part in the engaged and informed performance of the inappropriate, then how should we answer those among us who cry, "For shame! Neither Colbert nor anyone else should ridicule the president!" or

"Maureen Dowd should not be allowed to use disrespectful nicknames for the president and his staff!"?

There appears to be a disjuncture between the notion of critique as a valuable and necessary democratic tool (i.e., checks and balances among the three branches, a free press, democratically held elections) and the insistence by so many that cynicism, one of Western culture's most powerful, albeit harsh, forms of critique, is necessarily an unproductive and undemocratic force. Further, those who simply assert that cynicism cannot be productive and democratizing displace a focus on leadership failures (implied by engaged democratic cynics) to mobilize socio-cognitive schema that redirect our attentions to a putative need for leaders to more rigorously enforce an abiding belief in our institutions and practices.[9] Indeed, this insistence makes a false choice, a binary in which we must choose either dangerously narrow idealism or poorly defined cynicism. For while a particular case for the destructive potential of branded or disengaged cynicism might indeed be made, cynicism is too often the name we give reasoned, informed critique of institutions and policies in power—critiques that may be calculated, scathing, and performative but that are necessarily cynical. It is the charge of cynicism, however, that lends weight to a dismissal of the critique, which is surely more dangerous to democracy than a bad attitude. The charge of cynicism, then, strategically linked to a lack of faith in the possibility and desirability of democratic ideals, may crush the very communicative dynamics so necessary to democratic practices. We would argue that one aspect of the so-called culture wars, including the split among red states and blue states, is just this: an artificial and unproductive split between a narrowly idealistic grip on belief that places it at odds with well-supported argument, thus creating a striated and calcified dualism. The reciprocal relationship between belief and evidence, public scrutiny and private liberty—a relationship necessary for each one's existence—has been severed in messages calculated to fake the context and to divert our attention from leadership failures to concentrate on more trivial conflicts that divide average citizens from one another, rather than from their failed leaders.

Acknowledging that reciprocal relationship, nurturing it and emphasizing it rather than collapsing or exploiting the binary, reveals how democratic beliefs depend upon evidence and how evidence itself may be a form of belief. Consider, for example, the persuasive strategies of Martin Luther King Jr., Mahatma Gandhi, and Abraham Lincoln. The power of their rhetoric depends as much on belief as it does on evidence, as much on public scrutiny as on individual freedom from government. It depends on belief *and* evidence, on the relationship between the two. If we believe that all human beings are created equal, if we believe in the rule of law, in our inalienable rights, when we make our implicit beliefs in these things explicit, then we cannot as comfortably support the practices constitutive of slavery, colonization, or discrimination because those beliefs are *arguments against them* when coupled with sound evidence, expertise, and skilled rhetoric. The beliefs of these men were not severed from evidence but justified by it.[10] These men used belief *and* evidence to make powerful, world-changing arguments. They connected the two, used one to interrogate the validity of the other. And democracy benefited. It is the assault on that interrogating validity that sound-bite saboteurs mobilize; it is the need for a recursive relationship between belief and evidence that they seek to obscure.

It is entirely possible that the more we insist on belief and civility at the expense of evidence and expertise—a particular method of sound-bite sabotage that constructs messages to highlight their mutual exclusivity—the more narrow and rarified becomes the space from which critique (and thus the possibility of effective reform) might flow, and the more important outrageous, cynical, cultural performance becomes. If we accept at face value the simplistic explanation that everyone is either with us or against us, then only those who stand outside accepted social customs in some sort of uncivil and shameless performance may level any sort of meaningful critique. And that, we argue, is where *The Daily Show* and others offer some sociopolitical utility. In fact, beyond utility, we argue that what Stewart does on *The Daily Show* is modeling good citizenship in that it furthers the democratic practice of analysis and dissent and insists on contextualizing political speech. Stewart makes sound arguments that are cynical and that simultaneously reflect an underlying belief in both democratic action and the freedoms afforded individuals and the press in democratic principles, and a belief in creating thoughtful, popular opportunities for these to interface, and mutually interrogate one another.

Cynicism and (Out)Rage

The oft-noted incivility of our current public discourse is accompanied by dismayed observations of how angry we all seem to be, and of the cynicism that is part and parcel of that rage: "Confronted with cynical institutions, cynical media commentary, and intractable public predicaments, Americans are an angry lot," Chaloupka contends, conflating the public's rage over the cynicism that surrounds them with cynicism itself in a fairly convoluted rhetorical move that commits a most basic logical error: that of defining a term by the term itself (1999, xv). Chaloupka's description of the corruption and increasingly inequitable policies affecting citizen's lives in turn elicits their anger; one might argue that anger is a rational response to corruption and inequity and might even be, under the proper conditions, a precursor to action, a precondition for change. Scholars from a variety of disciplines in the humanities and social sciences have argued for the political utility of rage, shame, and even despair among and within social groups.[11] We would argue that the outraged incivility often associated with cynicism may be equally useful as a vital component of democratic action.

When Pat Robertson, a powerful leader of the Christian Right and intimate of the Bush administration, called for the U.S. government to assassinate the democratically elected president of Venezuela, the mainstream media certainly covered the story. On the August 22, 2006, broadcast of his Christian Broadcast Network show, *The 700 Club*, Robertson identified President Hugo Chavez as a threat to U.S. interests because of that country's rich oil reserves, and Chavez's socialist policies. Robertson, a former presidential candidate and ordained minister with a following of millions, publicly advised assassination: "We have the ability to take him out, and I think the time has come that we exercise that ability" (see Robertson, mediamatters.org). Two days later, Robertson "clarified" his statement on his official Web site, admitting that it was wrong to call for an assassination, and that he had done so out of frustration and concern for America. Besides, he "didn't say 'assassination' " he clarified further on *The 700 Club*'s August 24 broadcast. "I said our special forces should 'take him out.' And 'take him out' can be a number of things" (see Robertson, CNN). He went on to ask his viewers, however, if it would not be "wiser to wage war against one person" if that person is a dangerous dictator than to become "locked in a bitter struggle with a whole nation" (see Robertson, patrobertson.com).

On August 25, CNN reported the apology and clarification, along with a brief recap of the original story (see Robertson, CNN).[12] It did not take long for Fox News to trot out its political analysts, who insisted that Pat Robertson had been politically "irrelevant" for some time, that he was not really a "player" in conservative politics anymore—that, in fact, nobody really listened to him. And yet, despite giving lip service to Robertson's supposed irrelevance, Fox News continued to invite Robertson as a guest political commentator over the next few months and continues to do so as of this writing.[13]

Here is the point: to comprehend the depth and breadth of this story requires context. Yet other than brief references to the prior story of Robertson's call for Chavez's assassination, each of these news events featuring Robertson was articulated as a largely isolated moment, fragmented news that was never put fully into context; such is the structure, pacing, and priority of mainstream news media, with its obligation toward a bottom line and the claim of objectivity that often results in a nonrandom, interested bias in our news.[14] The only way for the nonresearcher, casual news media consumer to have perceived these isolated but certainly related news moments as a coherent story about information system distortion was to have been careful and intensive viewers/readers over a period of no less than five months of Fox News broadcasts, *Hannity & Colmes*, CNN broadcasts, *The 700 Club* on CBN, the news broadcasts of ABC, CBS, and NBC, PBS's *The News Hour*, and Pat Robertson's official Web site—an unreasonable and unrealistic expectation of news consumption, given the time it would take, for most working adults.

Or they could just watch *The Daily Show*. While it had addressed the Robertson-Chavez story earlier, it was *The Daily Show* that offered in the opening monologue of an episode airing in late February 2006 a recap of not only Pat Robertson's call for political assassination but the media's treatment of him in the aftermath, and his position as a religious and political leader courted by the press before, during, and after the actual event. In a montage of clips left to speak for themselves, viewers of *The Daily Show* watched Robertson himself use the word "assassination" and call for Chavez to be "taken out"; Robertson insisting that he had in fact *not* used the word "assassination"; Robertson apologizing for calling for Chavez's "assassination"; Robertson advocating war against one person as opposed to war against a whole nation; Fox News analysts insisting that Robertson had become politically and culturally irrelevant; Fox News hosts *that same week* fawning over Robertson as he offered his cultural and political views; and so on. All the while, Jon Stewart sat, saying nothing, eyebrows raised, lips pursed, his exaggerated, knowing look aimed at his television viewers.[15]

The effect of this montage of the mainstream news media's coverage of the Robertson-Chavez story was, of course, *to call attention* to the hypocrisy embedded within Robertson's outrage at the challenge he believed Chavez presented to U.S. policies and interests—and outrage that, left unexamined, would likely stand as the voice of Christians and, as such, enjoy an enormous amount of power among conservatives and the Bush administration. *The Daily Show* montage also revealed the hypocrisy, spin, and strategy playing out and through a news media system that covered the story by dutifully reporting what Robertson said—each time he said it—with virtually no context or analysis. The montage, by contextualizing each and every claim made by Robertson and, by implication, every claim supported by the media, served as a more informative venue for a thorough analysis of what had actually happened, and what it meant, than any noncynical news coverage by the big-city print news, the major networks, PBS, and cable. Comedy Central's *The Daily Show*—a show that Stewart famously pointed out to the hosts of *Crossfire* is preceded by puppets making crank telephone calls—mocked every individual and institution involved in such a way that viewers were compelled to experience the discomfort of reconciling multiple outrages, without any one being automatically privileged as common sense. As a result, viewers were better informed and armed against the sound-bite sabotage inherent in this case than if they religiously watched what media experts refer to as the "serious" news (Zuckerman, in Scarborough 2006).

Is *The Daily Show*'s treatment of the Robertson incident cynical, resulting in viewer cynicism, or did it contribute to informed democratic debate? Are there any circumstances in which we might consider them to be one and the same, or at least inextricably linked? Can we—and should we—place our faith, separated from evidence and reason, in institutions and cultural arrangements in the name of anti-cynicism, when the very structure of those institutions and arrangements insists that we can only recognize through critique and open debate the possibility of effectively addressing corruption and injustice? Chaloupka argues that "Cynicism clashes with familiar and powerful ways of characterizing social life. It resists and subverts the important social themes, such as faith, rationality, utopia, or reform. It undermines how we think about important concepts: freedom, authority, society, self-change, and stability" (1999, 12). How very different we might feel about this "resistance" and "subversion," however, if we replace the pejorative "undermines" with "complicates" or "deepens" or "nests."

III. Knowledge, Power, and the Failure of Ideology Critique

> Democracy [is] no simple thing but infinitely complex, not a rigid system or an implacable doctrine but an attitude of mind and a habit of conduct.
>
> —Henry Steele Commager, *Commager on Tocqueville*

The Fear of Knowledge and the Power of Confidence

We are all aware, and likely share, to some degree, a concern over the universally perceived lack of confidence the public now has in our institutions and practices, which appear to consistently fall far short of our democratic aspirations.[16] And while many are certainly outraged by failed leadership, our leadership seem oddly less concerned about the undemocratic practices dominating these institutions than about our loss of *belief* in them. We lament declining respect for authority far more vehemently than we seek to understand the atrophy of democratic decision making, or insist on a public discourse aimed at effective problem solving in order to regain a deserved confidence, grounded in an *achieved* legitimacy. But it is not belief that is the problem—in fact, we would argue that belief in the possibility of improving practices based on the best available data is a vital and necessary component of our notion that cynicism can be a productive, democratizing moment. The desire for reform and the willingness to act to make things better—whatever that might mean for particular groups and individuals—require some level of belief in the value and usefulness of our democratic and institutional ideals as linked to practice. The problem lies in belief separated from evidence, belief that is simply *interested*, serving privileged interests and thus rejecting any evidence to the contrary as threats to power: belief that is *branded*. Such belief can be isolating, crippling—every bit as worrisome as the crippling, isolating cynicism we hear so much about. But cynicism bears the brunt in the current public discourse of responsibility for many of our social ills; given the power of an informed, engaged cynicism, then, it should not surprise us that in current public discourse we may observe calculated efforts to conflate cynicism with amorality, permissiveness, relativism, and selfishness.

In our view, the problem lies not in cynicism but in a wholesale and calculated rejection of criticism based on the deliberate miseducation of the polis about the relationships between enlightened self-interest and the duties of citizenship, between public scrutiny and private liberty. It is this miseducation that allows sound-bite saboteurs to vilify serious engagement with data when they peddle popularized, naturalized "common sense" myths that serve particular interests. The end result is any knowledge that sits uneasily with the desired confidence in our institutions cannot but be invalidated by incoherent accusations about self-interest, thus representing private positions as if they were in the public interest. We are left, then, only open to being persuaded by branded messages designed to feel familiar—which, we argue, leads to a disparagement of expertise, data, analysis, and the inescapable discomfort, ambiguity, and disorderly contestations constitutive of an evidence-based, deliberative political culture.

We corner ourselves in this way into embracing an anti-intellectual approach to addressing the problems we face—persuasion becomes duping, recognizable by the accompanying feelings of challenge and discomfort, and argument is reduced to chicanery when it is practiced by experts, gutting the very concept of democratic deliberation and even the most basic critical epistemological approach to the challenges we share. And when we cannot hear the evidence, the analysis, and the conclusions of those with expertise—when evidence and argument are no longer used in decision making because, for example, a mere "theory" of gravity makes it automatically suspect as biased—we are left with only a deformed *ethos* of belief and a profound confusion about politics and conflict. And while it does not necessarily follow, the door is certainly left open for us to *also* be left with a lack of curiosity, a preference for the simplistic, and a disdain for the intellectual and community-level work required to continuously and reciprocally turn information into knowledge, knowledge into effective action, and action into useful information. We are left believing on Wednesday what we believed on Monday, no matter what happened on Tuesday.

Evidence of this increasing disjuncture between belief and expertise, the privileging of belief at the expense of the best available data, abounds in contemporary media, where news organizations regularly eschew complexity, context, and analysis for entertainment that avoids the charge of "interestedness" by muting the challenges to official pronouncements manifest in engaged cynical analysis. The media increasingly emphasize and confirm what we already believe to be true through sound bites and entertainment masquerading as news. Joe Hardin observes the following:

> Mainstream media is complicit . . . and are themselves now too disorienting and chaotic to provide any ground for sensible analysis and critique. Their methods are exploiting catastrophe, highlighting novelty, and sensationalizing scandal; their form is the juxtaposition of the trivial and the horrifying. Plugged in to the current that flows from television, the Internet, magazines, and newspapers, our heads quickly become inflated with an immense and disorienting charge of synthesized information all designed to encourage personal identification with the least amount of analysis. In

fact, the news now comes pre-analyzed and analysis itself becomes ground for skepticism. (Hardin 2006)

The seemingly never-ending flow of images and information operates alongside late-twentieth-century theories of ideology within the academy and has resulted in pedagogies that focus on producing savvy readers. Students are taught to produce smart cultural interpretations—to perform ideology critique—in order to avoid being "duped" by sound-bite saboteurs. We have already argued in chapter 4 that new media do not have to be used this way; we recognize that, too often, they are—and the results of this pedagogical juggernaut (which often resides underneath the umbrella term *cultural studies*) may be questionable, at best.

Cultural Fatigue and the Failed Promise of Ideology Critique

Peter Sloterdijk contends that ideology critique is exhausted (1987, 3). Indeed, we are ourselves exhausted by ideology critique.[17] We have learned its lessons too well. We already know that the system is corrupt, the man has his boot on somebody's neck, and co-optation is inevitable. Led Zeppelin sells Cadillacs. Dennis Hopper is a pitchman for a high-end investment firm targeting well-to-do boomers. Faith in our institutions has collapsed, and the disengaged cynic is unsurprised—worse, entertained—by lying liars and the lies they tell. Political and cultural substance are no longer required for celebrity. Left with the meager payoff of Sloterdijk's enlightened false consciousness, the cynical American does not believe anybody's argument, because argument itself is suspect, a sucker's game.

What happened? Why has the promise of ideology critique failed, both in our academic efforts to send our students into the world, fully aware of and armed against structural reproduction and the nature of power, and at the mass culture level as well, where progressive intellectuals expected to see this particular tree bearing fruit? Hardin argues:

> Popular wisdom has it that the reason progressive critique doesn't get much play in the mainstream media is that such critique is less appropriate for the sound-byte world of television talking heads, the format of angry white-guy radio, and the "gotcha" culture of Internet news. Progressive critique, the argument goes, is much too nuanced

and complex to be reduced to bite-sized pieces of quickly memorized and easily repeated platitudes. . . . Nuanced critique is not called for. And the pace with which we are barraged with scandal and tragedy has increased to the point where no sustained critique could keep up anyway. We are exhausted. (Hardin 2006)

Ideology critique as an end in itself (progressive pedagogy done badly) has rendered our consciousness both "well-off and miserable"—enlightened but unable to manifest that enlightenment in effective practice (Sloterdijk 1987, 5). As we noted in chapter 4, information overload can result in being well fed and yet malnourished; we suffer both the ravages of obesity and the deprivations of malnutrition.

Further, the Right has learned the language of ideology critique and has turned that language against progressive discourse.[18] Several months ago on an episode of the CW's *America's Next Top Model*, a young contestant from Texas proclaimed herself a "hard-ass, hard-line Republican," announcing that she did not like gay people because she did not "agree with their lifestyle." Further, she believed that affirmative action "is the biggest load of crap" she had "ever heard of." She concluded her self-representation by assuring everyone that she was "not racist."

The panel of five judges for the competition she had entered included two openly gay members. Only two of the five judges were white. They gently asked her if she understood not only what she had said but to whom (and in what industry) she had said it—did she understand, they asked incredulously, with whom she would be working if she was successful in the competition. The young woman replied that she did, in fact, understand all of the above, and the judges and other contestants should be "more tolerant" of her views.

This is an example of the Right deploying the powerful language of ideology critique and turning it against progressive discourse. Here the Right is claiming a foundational standpoint and attempting to link its standpoint to truth, rationality, and a common sense that is even shared by progressive purveyors of tolerance. In the sound bites of the young woman on *America's Next Top Model* we hear tolerance of a homosexual lifestyle reframed as intolerance of family values. Similarly, the environmental movement has been "unmasked" by the Right as an ideology opposed to private property in ways not unlike those used by progressives seeking to reframe property as a crime. Evolution becomes "only a theory," and fiscal responsibility is reframed as cold-hearted cruelty to the poor. Calls for economic justice become "class warfare," and "support our troops" becomes support for a hegemonic war-making machine. Clearly, sound-bite sabotage is not the hallmark of only one side of the partisan political aisle. Taking these very few examples together, and the onslaught of chaos, misrepresentation, ambiguity, and hypocrisy they engender, cynicism seems justified.

Predictably, such use of the language of ideology critique by the Right can also be seen as one consequence of the radical anti-foundationalism unleashed by parts of the Left. But we should not be surprised by this subversive use of progressive discourse, of ideology critique turned against itself. Foucault has taught us that within every discourse resides the means to disrupt that discourse—even those discourses whose political ambitions we support. Despite the promise of twentieth-century ideology critique—the hope embodied in the very fact of our ability to conceive of ideology and hegemony—we have now come to the realization that unengaged cynicism is the product of our limited critical intellectual practice rather than the "true" consciousness, equity, and social justice on which we were counting. Replacing faith and hope in right-utopian ideals with left-utopian ideals, similarly fragmented from action, encourages a disengaged and disempowering cynicism that is blamed for both the decline of our institutions and the faith in them to which we long to return. Cynicism, we seem to fear, necessarily manifests in apathy, and in a participatory democracy that has become overwhelmingly cynical, the only thing left to hope for is entertainment, and the self-congratulatory smugness of not being fooled by anybody, even if we accomplish this by disengaging and miseducating.[19]

But consider what Jesus would do—or, rather, consider the Christian marketing campaign "What Would Jesus Do?" from a few years ago. This brilliantly crafted sound bite, complete with youth-oriented merchandise sporting the WWJD logo, encouraged everyone to think about the daily decisions they made themselves, and witnessed others making, in the context of the Gospels, to make Christ's teachings a part of their everyday lives. But it only lasted a couple of years. What happened?

The answer may lie in this sound bite leading to a powerful, public analytical moment in which belief and evidence were not separated but, rather, remained bound in a nested, dialectical relationship. The Christian Right may have dropped the WWJD campaign because what Jesus would do in many policy instances was understood by nearly everyone to have likely been the polar opposite of assassination, no new taxes, or other actions preferred by powerful leaders on the Christian Right. It was impossible to fake, to bullshit, because the general public—including nonpracticing Christians and non-Christians—is so well schooled in what Jesus would do, what he did do, and what he said, that everybody got the contradiction immediately. This sound bite unexpectedly performed the engaged, cynical function of revealing the spin, distortion, and strategy of its intended, interested message. This was evident in how quickly we saw the shockingly cynical T-shirts and bumper stickers that asked, "Who Would Jesus Hate?" and "Who Would Jesus Bomb?"

It seems apparent that ideology critique has not led us where we wanted or expected to go. What we wanted, of course, were knowing citizens, enlightened by the unmasking of ideology (an activity that is in itself ideological), pursuing knowledge and truth (as opposed to Truth) to fortify their civic engagement and create a sustainable future for us all. But perhaps the decay and stagnation we are beginning to feel do not lie in the pervasive cynicism we now experience but, rather, in our inability to see *the democratic possibilities of cynicism itself.*

The limits of ideology critique alone may be, we contend, more a failure of progressive intellectuals to link the scholarly and the popular, the symbolic and the material; when we have worked toward that end, we have done so almost exclusively within the context of institutional classrooms, ignoring those popular sites where intellectual approaches to cultural needs are so desperately needed. Many intellectuals have failed to heed Gramsci's contention that we have a responsibility to participate in public deliberations, to bring the scholarly and the popular together, and, to struggle along with everyone else to productively address the conflicts we share. Specifically, intellectuals must see (and persuade others to see) the cynicism resulting from ideological critique as a pedagogical moment—not an end point but a new beginning that makes democracy both possible and desirable. When we successfully bring our students to see the interestedness of branded information, we cannot stop there unless we want to create only the unproductive and alienated forms of cynicism in our students. We must provide our students with more tools, from across disciplines, to enable them to see information sources and analyze the potentially distorting impacts of competing interpretative frameworks. We must also, as noted in chapter 4, provide our students with methods—such as nesting dualisms—to support their more productive engagement with the real-world challenges we face, once ideology critique contributes to providing a richer framework for understanding these.

Instead, progressive intellectuals have invited and allowed the anxiety and malaise of failed expectations and the pressure and scrutiny from an increasingly anti-intellectual public to erroneously define the work it does as an egg-headed embarrassment, and the cynicism resulting from the ideology critique we have been teaching for over thirty years as both immoral and a democratic dead end.

Cynicism need not be disempowering (though it certainly may be), particularly if we understand it as part of democratic practice—necessary, ongoing, never fulfilled or fulfilling. Ideology critique as a limited, non-nested form of progressive, worldly praxis creates unhealthy cynics without the skills to be productively engaged, constructing new media as opposed to the academy. We need not only to make the scholarly available, accessible, and adaptable, but we need, in the interest of an *engaged* cynicism that does not zealously believe in the transformative power of ideology critique alone, to make the scholarly affirmatively actionable. We propose revisiting John Dewey's distinction between the democratic ideal and democratic practices—signaling an important analytical and practical distinction in pursuit of understanding the reciprocal relationship between popular belief and scholarly knowledge—as a potential means to accommodate the pragmatic realism of the cynical-knowing-subject and to create a pedagogical space in which cynicism might itself serve deliberative public discourse.

III. Democratic Education and the Power of Public Pedagogy

> "Knowledge is Power." . . . Those who utter the sentence reveal the truth. However, with the utterance they want to achieve more than truth: They want to intervene in the game of power.
>
> —Peter Sloterdijk, *Critique of Cynical Reason*

Dewey, Chomsky, and Democratic Education

John Dewey argues that we must distinguish between democracy as an ideal and democracy as a particular form of government because the idea of democracy can never be fully realized in the state; it is an ideal, an aspiration. Even free elections, local and national representative government, and civil liberties—many of the practices we hold most sacred—have evolved in fits and starts, with advances and setbacks, over time and as a response to both needs that could no longer be ignored, and raw, political, and economic power, not always (perhaps not even often) in order to realize the democratic ideal, though often justified by that shared aspiration. The perfected, completed ideal of democracy must always be "distracted and interfered with by actual practice, and thus can never reach fulfillment, can never become fact" (Drew 2002, 924). Similarly, in her new book *Punishment and Political Order*, Keally McBride notes that "The polis is marked by a juxtaposition of idealistic or normative elements with the problems of administration"—political order, as one type of human collective, is distinct in its never-ending struggle between shared ideals and the practical considerations of administration. While McBride is referring specifically to punishment as a particular form of state administration, her contention that citizens should respond with skepticism to claims that worrisome practices of their government are directly related to the ideals they hold is useful here. When the state acts, she notes, "its ideals are on display and at stake" (2007, 4–6).

Working from Dewey's insistence on the analytical distinction between the ideal and practice, Noam Chomsky suggests that we run into problems when we collapse democratic ideals and practice together by implying current practice *is or must be already* ideal, which either insulates practice from critique or makes cynicism hopeless, futile, and ultimately disengaged. Collapsing democratic ideals and practice together, according to Chomsky, creates misleading myths about democracy—such as students mindlessly reciting the Pledge of Allegiance when in fact the United States has never provided "liberty and justice for all." These myths—where beliefs are made true by severing any link to actual practices—serve to maintain and reproduce the kinds of atrocities Chomsky documents in *Miseducation* and elsewhere, because, as Chomsky claims, they train students to turn a blind eye to what the United States *really* does and to accept instead the myth of a truly democratic United States, thus making it more difficult to achieve active participation and the necessary critique of democratic practices that (always already) need attentive and engaged citizens seeking to realize the ideal (Drew 2002, 924).

These two notions of how to understand how democracy works, what the role of education is and should be within a democracy, and what, if any, the possibilities are for change within a context of failed ideology critique offer some language with which to explore this question of cynicism. In Dewey's distinction between practice and the ideal we find the possibility for belief *existing simultaneously* alongside expertise (evidence, analysis, knowledge). In recognizing the necessity of both the ideal and self-reflective practice for Dewey's scheme, we may reconstitute the ideal (belief) from the unattainable, to a location from which we might continuously interrogate the validity of our practices. Similarly, practice (expertise) may be reconstituted as a location from which we might interrogate the meaning of our aspirations. Whereas Dewey, in this instance, is interested in an analytical distinction for pragmatic purposes, even while insisting simultaneously on a dialectical relationship between ideal and practice (interest and insistence creating what we have called a nested relationship), Chomsky's description of the myths created by collapsing the ideal and practice into dogmatic (patriotic) belief becomes a cautionary tale in which we can read the demise of anything resembling honest, effective deliberation in order to maintain corrupt and failing policies, institutions, and powerful elites who control and disseminate the increasingly branded information upon which we rely. And equally important are the dangers associated with severing the relationship between the ideal and practice.

"What Would Jesus Do?" failed, perhaps because it worked too well. The sound bite was successful in its initial purpose, as a religious slogan for Christian youth, because it evoked the kind of thin familiarity that sound bites generally rely upon, whereby consumers of the message are able to go only where the interested author of the sound bite wants them to go, and no farther. The WWJD sound bite was *not* successful as sabotage, however, because it was met with a *thick* familiarity among consumers—consumers who understood the complex historical and textual arguments inextricably linked to the question of what Jesus would do, based on their knowledge and understanding of what Jesus actually did, were capable of interpreting that question in extra-biblical contexts, such as current domestic and foreign policy questions, and capable of coming up with a variety of (for the saboteurs) undesirable answers to the question. The self-professed Christian politician learned that it may not be wise to ask constituents to think about what Jesus would do, because the public is already familiar with a context richer than, but mobilized by, the sound bite, and therefore knows too much to be easily fooled. The crucial importance of education—including affirmatively actionable ideology critique—thus becomes apparent as one means of resisting sound-bite saboteurs.

Democratic Practice and the Possibility of Reform

When Chaloupka writes that cynicism "resists and subverts the important social themes, such as faith, rationality, utopia, or reform," and that it "undermines how we think about . . . freedom, authority, society, self-change, and stability," (1999, 12) he calls attention to the fact that in collapsing the ideal with practice in these sacrosanct areas we risk, just as Chomsky warns, creating the myth that our practices are ideal, and that analysis of where practices may fall short places thinkers outside of the community of believers. The critic thus becomes popularly understood as a nonbeliever, a cynic, and cynicism threatens, through contagion and persuasion, those persons, institutions, and social arrangements we hold most dear. In such a climate, a pedagogy of ideology critique is considered harmful, at least in part, because it produces cynicism.

We disagree, but not wholly. If we recast the very notion of cynicism within Dewey's notion of democracy, and place cynicism in the analytical category of practice, we see that it is not only belief in our institutions without the interrogating power of cynicism that leads to Chomsky's myths. We see that cynicism without the interrogating power of belief is equally problematic. Where Dewey insists that in thinking about democracy as both an ideal and as a practice, simultaneously, the ideal serves as "a standard to which practice may aspire and by which citizens might criticize current democratic practices" (Drew 2002, 924). And this is very much about education—about teaching and learning—both within classrooms and in the broader public square. An engaged ideology critique thus becomes a component of democratic practice rather than the dead end of postmodern, agency-less citizenship, because as educators we can and should encourage students beyond just being savvy readers of consumer culture. In fact, we would argue that just teaching students to be savvy readers of consumer culture, without including as the essential next step some point of action or performance (think service learning or point-of-action pedagogical approaches) that engages the branded information they are learning to identify, we aid in the production of the kind of paralyzing cynicism so many of our critics accuse us of producing. In this Deweyan-inspired model, there is room for reform, because cynicism is anticipated and addressed within a framework that interrogates cynical observations and conclusions against the aspirations of ideals.

What might this mean in terms of the sound-bite sabotage we experience? Foucault says that resources for resistance exist alongside the nexus of power relations. They are always present—within social and institutional hierarchies—and they always leave their traces. This means also that they get caught up at some point within power relations, drawn into the system they are pushing against until they no longer function as resistances. Present forms of resistance are of course eventually and inevitably normalized, or recuperated, but recuperation in Foucauldian terms means also to invest in a discourse previously unrecognized. Present hegemony always changes, and since democracy as an ideal can never be fully realized, this is what we should be working toward—persistent movement and change. Argumentation and persuasion would accomplish this in an ideal world, but as our technological and discursive worlds evolve and we find ourselves increasingly inundated with sound bites rather than fully developed arguments, we argue that cynicism plays an increasingly important role in both imagining and occupying viewpoints at odds with dominant narrative. Further, we contend that while cynicism is a potentially stultifying product of ideology critique, it need not be.

Argumentation and Public Pedagogy

As with the young woman contestant on *America's Next Top Model*, who seemed affronted by the judges' intolerance of her intolerance, many of our students enter our classrooms with similar notions about freedoms and rights, evidence and belief, persuasion and dogma. We have each been teaching in public universities for over fifteen years, working with hundreds of eighteen to twenty-year-olds each year as they think through and discuss issues from our vast array of social and political challenges. They are required in our classrooms to listen and talk, read and write and reflect, summarize and analyze, and research and evaluate these issues and the various perspectives and rhetorical strategies that make up our cultural conversations about them. They are required to enter the realm of democratic deliberation. And while alarms are going off everywhere we look about the cynicism encroaching on their impressionable worldviews, we believe that a greater problem is both the forced separation and the strategic collapsing of the ideal and practice. The result is the kinds of myths Chomsky describes, whereby dissent and deliberation are eroded, and expertise is brutalized in a slow march toward anti-intellectualism.

Our students' are largely unimpressed by argument. Not particular arguments, or certain rhetorical devices—they are unimpressed by Argument itself, writ large. Statistics can be used to prove anything, they tell us; they are far more comfortable with familiar opinions—their own, and anyone else's who happens to agree with them. Our students believe certain things, and since no amount of evidence, including consensus among experts, is likely to persuade them otherwise, they are often at a loss to understand how making their own positions persuasive to others is either productive or necessary. And as we discussed in the previous chapter, the new media play a role in this, providing a mechanism for entrenchment—it is easy to only watch, read, and consume images that only support our positions, our interests. Moreover, the technology does not require, or even promote, distance, reflection, or discernment. It is just a massive wave of disposable information designed for instantaneous consumption—and do not worry, another wave will be arriving immediately. This does not mean the image is not a form of literacy, that reading images is not a complex and complicated act. It does not even mean that our students do not have critical standards; they do, but they are more fully articulated as issues of taste and appreciation. It simply means that those acts of literacy are not necessarily the ones we want, the ones democratic education depends upon. Sound-bite saboteurs know this, and they exploit it.

Our students have become adept (as we all have) at the language of progressive reform. Everyone, they insist with a shrug, is entitled to her or his opinion (an expression of tolerance, seemingly), and every articulated position is, at its heart, just opinion. Building on Lynn Truss's discussion of the demise of good manners, we can think of this view as a sort of trained autism, whereby a host of intertwining cultural, technological, political, and psychological forces combines to keep individuals "morbidly self-absorbed" (OED 2006) and, therefore, unable to adopt an even remotely other-oriented stance toward the world, the kind of stance required in order for things such as argument and evidence to have any serious meaning. This is another example of a hard distinction (as opposed to a soft distinction, for analytical purposes) between the ideal and practice; students observe current practices of persuasion divorced from the ideals of democratic deliberation, and the act seems indefensible—as well it should, in many instances. When we watch a legal drama on television, such as *The Practice*, we regularly witness defense attorneys struggling with the act of defending an accused murderer whom they know is guilty. Without the interrogating validity, the context, of our social aspiration to live within a judicial system where one is innocent until proven guilty, such legal work seems patently indefensible, outrageous, even offensive to our beliefs. But while the struggle is real, these fictional attorneys offer their best defense in order to consistently force the state to prove the guilt of the accused, so that our legal practice is kept in constant dialogue with our aspirations, our beliefs, because both practice and ideals, without the other, are pale shadows of what they might be in concert with one another, and we believe that this is true in our classrooms as well.

But in our classrooms, where students struggle to understand concepts such as "the best available data," "negotiation and compromise," and "consensus building" as a potential means to address difficult problems, we are beaten back from the teaching and learning we are trying to affect by political leaders who do not acknowledge that evidence is often complex and contradictory, and that it must be weighed carefully if sound decisions are to be made, a perspective then reproduced by community leaders and concerned citizens whose voices in our city newspaper insist over and over again that any position that contradicts their own is simply and irrevocably wrong, without bothering to offer a shred of rationale beyond "I believe."

If you think that students learn about logic, rhetoric, and argumentation exclusively (or even mostly) in the classroom, then you are wrong. They learn something every time public and private leaders say "I believe" and leave it at that, instead of "we know" accompanied by an acknowledgment of the supporting data compiled by experts, and an admission that there is now or may be in the future contradictory evidence that we are obliged to consider. And we cannot hold an evidentiary candle to what they learn every time the expertise of the scientific community is dismissed and shouted down by religious and political leaders who insist, for example, that biology teachers teach religion instead of science, their argument simplistically and disingenuously laying claim to Samuel Freedman's "false refuge of fairness."

Belief and evidence should be nested, in a dialectical relationship, in the same way and for the very reasons that Dewey insists on the dialectical relationship between the ideal and practice. Students learn something every time legislators offer their beliefs, alone or in combination with the anecdotes recycled in branded information, as the basis for policy agendas, laws, and wars—we all learn something. We learn that only the weak and the faithless consider other points of view, and that strength and leadership are found in the stagnant mire of "Even knowing what we now know, I wouldn't change a thing." We learn something every time someone with even a little power stands up and reinforces the value of belief alone—belief in creationism or ideology critique—over and above expertise, the best available data, and democratic deliberation based on our shared aspirations, which can and should continuously test both. We can certainly point to numerous examples where science has been used to put forth the evidence of supposed truths that later turned out to be grotesque lies: the supposed inferiority of both women and blacks, scientifically proven by "craniologists" and championed by innumerable Eugenics experts at elite universities. Such evidence was opposed by the beliefs of women, African Americans, and others; indeed, they used their belief to oppose such heinous notions long before they had the political power as groups to publicly interrogate the "science." Sometimes belief is the only thing the disempowered have to challenge the power of the dominant culture's evidence. What is alarming—what should be alarming—is when it is the dominant culture that insists on belief as the only rationale for important policy decisions, despite overwhelming evidence to the contrary.

In a recent appearance on *The News Hour*, David Brooks glorified Illinois Senator Barack Obama for his "deliberate mind" because he has what Brooks called "a thought process" in his approach to problem solving and decision making—despite his book titled *The Audacity of Hope*, an indication, perhaps, that indeed these are not mutually exclusive. That we have reached a point where identifying a political leader as a godsend because he has a thought process should tell us how far we must reach to climb out of this hole.

Some academics and thoughtful public leaders are, of course, raising the alarm, not about cynicism but about the diminishing quality of our public discourse, and calling for informed public debate.[20] In his October 2005 speech at the Media Center, former Vice President Al Gore said that "Americans in both parties should insist on the reestablishment of respect for the Rule of Reason. We must, for example, stop tolerating the rejection and distortion of science . . . for the purpose of intentionally clouding the public's ability to discern the truth" (Gore 2005, 7).

We can start by recognizing across public and private sectors that if we hope to encourage young people to effectively address in their lifetimes some of the crucial challenges we are and will be faced with, then we have to teach them, inside the classroom and in the much larger public square, what it looks like to gather and weigh evidence; recognize expertise as such, even as we note that bias often lurks in research funding sources and data-set frames; consider opposing views; and continually weigh these practices against their aspirations, ideals, and dreams, even while those ideals must be continuously interrogated by best practice and new information. None of this is easy; rather, it is the hard and ongoing work of democracy.

V. Belief, Expertise, and Cynical American Pragmatism

We are entitled to our moral, ethical and philosophical commitments. We are not entitled to our own facts.

—E. J. Dionne, "But, of Course, No Apologies"

What We Know and What We Believe

The above quote is somewhat problematic in that it suggests the possibility that facts are in a realm of human knowledge free from the
mess and ethical requirements of interpretation. This is of course not
the case; facts are the process and product of social interpretative relationships. Indeed, if Dionne means that our facts are not the product
of isolated human cognition, but instead the by-product of human
interaction and shared experience, then we have no problem with this
notion. While facts should not be used as a supposed alternative to
interpretation, as a means to elude or end the ethical imperative of
argument, we *can* often determine, through experience and deliberation,
what the best available data are. We can determine whether or not
experts have reached a general consensus and, if so, what this is. As
perplexing as it has seemed, however, poll after poll since the United
States invaded Iraq in March 2003 has shown us that misperceptions
about the events and situations leading up to the war abound among
the public—misperceptions that have, until quite recently, increased
support for the Bush administration's actions. The Program on International Policy Attitudes (PIPA) conducted a series of polls in 2003,
gathering data from June through September, in order to explore the
possible role of misperceptions in public support for our 2003 invasion
of Iraq, and to determine what, if any, role the media have played.
The study focused on the degree to which Americans believed one or
more of the following three demonstrably false claims[21]: (1) Weapons of
mass destruction (WMD) *have been found* in Iraq since the *first* Gulf War;
2) Clear evidence *has been found* that Saddam Hussein was working
with al Qaeda; and (3) World public opinion favored the U.S. invasion
of Iraq in 2003 (Kull, Ramsay, and Lewis 2003–2004, 570–71).

The authors found that while in most cases "only a minority
has had any particular misperception, a strong majority has had at
least one key misperception" (571). Just before the war, "68 percent
expressed the belief that Iraq played an important role in September
11th, with 13 percent even expressing the belief that 'conclusive evidence' of Iraq's involvement had been found" (571–72). The authors
also looked at public opinion after the invasion. Three months after
the U.S. invasion and occupation of Iraq, 33 percent said that "clear
evidence of WMD had been found in Iraq" (572). Importantly, the
question was not whether or not subjects *believed* Iraq had WMD, but
whether "clear evidence of WMD had been found." They "believed"
that in fact it had.

In March 2003, shortly after the war started, the authors asked
respondents "how all of the people in the world feel about the United

States going to war with Iraq" (573). Approximately one third of those polled believed correctly that "the majority of people opposed the decision," while one third believed erroneously that "views were evenly balanced on the issue," and another *full third of the population* "expressed the egregious misperception" that most people in the world supported a U.S. attack on and invasion of Iraq (573). A full *two thirds* of the population had it wrong, believing that world opinion was either ambivalent or in support of U.S. military action against Iraq. The question of why the status of the United States has sharply declined around the world becomes much less difficult to answer in light of this, and *they hate us because we're free* seems less persuasive as a rational response to that decline.

The authors of the study prefer to use the term *misperception*; in our view, however, the point is more clearly made, and the severity of the problem is more accurately communicated by stating unequivocally that fully 60 percent of the population (575) held at least one of these three *demonstrably false claims* to be true, and that these beliefs were, arguably, a significant cause of the popular support garnered by the Bush administration for its various policies toward Iraq. These demonstrably false claims, quite literally of life-and-death importance, led the authors to ask whether or not these "misperceptions" were "to some extent a function of an individual's source of news" (589). The results were instructive.

The study found Rupert Murdoch's Fox News to be "the news source whose viewers had the most misperceptions," while NPR/PBS listeners/viewers "held fewer misperceptions than consumers of other news sources" (582). Fox News, they concluded, "is the most consistently significant predictor of misperceptions" among all other news media (589).[22] And, most importantly, among those who believed these demonstrably false claims, support for the invasion was very high; among those who did not believe any of the three false claims, support for the invasion was very low.[23]

In addition to the Bush administration repeatedly saturating communication channels with messages branded to suggest that these claims were true, another explanation for the egregious misperceptions the authors found might be "the way that the media reported the news" (592). They found ample evidence that "many in the media appeared to feel that it was not their role to challenge the administration or that it was even appropriate to take an active pro-war posture" (592). When the media fail to challenge the government, it becomes simply a "means of transmission for the administration, rather than a critical filter" (592). The result of the media-as-administrative-lapdog is clear: this study found that Fox and CBS—the two networks that presented the least critical commentary before and during the war—had *the most viewers who believed these demonstrably false claims about the war and its context* (593, 594). And, in case any doubt still remains about the critical role of media as government watchdog, data show that "higher levels of attention to news did not reduce the likelihood of misperception, and in the case of those who primarily got their news from Fox News, *misperceptions increased with greater attention*" (594, emphasis added). In other words, if you get your information from Fox, not only are you more likely to get it wrong, but the more you watch, the less you will know and understand.

The phenomenal commercial success of Fox News is no doubt linked, at least in part, to its phenomenal success in reporting branded information across programming that benefited the Bush administration's policies and echoed Republican Party talking points. In terms of democratic processes, researchers point out, there is little to complain of if the president is able to move the public to support his decisions; but that is only true "to the degree it is the product of persuasion, based on the merits of an argument. What is worrisome is that it appears that the president has the capacity to lead members of the public to assume false beliefs in support of his position" (Kull et al. 2003–2004, 596). When the news media broadcast misleading, branded information masquerading as news, resulting in or encouraging or justifying a shocking majority of us to misunderstand our most vital policy issues, how can the republic function? If its media cannot do so, then how can the citizenry, inundated with sound bites and demonstrably false assertions supported by their government, step back from the order and hierarchy of social structures in order to identify the spin, the distortion, the strategy, and for whose benefit they are being bullshitted?

Enter Diogenes the Cynic: inappropriate, shameless, outrageous and offensive.

The Baumgartner and Morris study cited by Richard Morin of the *Washington Post* concluded, as we cited earlier, that young viewers of *The Daily Show* rated political candidates "more negatively" and "expressed less trust in the electoral system and more cynical views of the news media" after viewing Stewart's program. What Morin does not discuss in his brief column, however, are those findings from the same study that do not support Morin's fear-mongering suggestion that American youth are become increasingly cynical, and that this cynicism is hurting American democracy. We would argue that while some of the results of Baumgartner and Morris's research may be ambiguous, there is a stronger case to be made from the data they present that *The Daily Show increases the possibility* that viewers will believe themselves capable of understanding political issues, events, and conflicts, and that the confidence they have and/or gain from the show will surpass that of viewers of mainstream news media.

Political scientists use the words "external efficacy" and "internal efficacy" to distinguish the focus of citizen confidence regarding politics and politicians. External efficacy focuses on citizen confidence or belief in government officials and institutions—confidence in the degree to which the citizenry can count on the government to meet its needs and to otherwise be responsive to its wishes. Internal efficacy focuses on individual confidence in one's own ability to understand the complexities of politics, and to participate effectively (Baumgartner and Morris 2006, 352–53). Cynicism coincides with low external efficacy; the greater the degree of cynicism, the lesser the degree of confidence in government and institutions. *Engaged* cynicism coincides with low external and high internal efficacy and is therefore a critically important skill for democratic citizenship.

Baumgartner and Morris hypothesized only about external efficacy, and they found, as expected, a positive correlation: "*The Daily Show* generates cynicism toward the media and the electoral process" (353). What they did *not* expect to find was a correlation between *The Daily Show* and viewers' internal efficacy. What they found, however, was that "even though *The Daily Show* generates cynicism . . . it simultaneously makes young viewers more confident about their own ability to understand politics" (353); their data support the engaged cynic position we have been articulating.

Baumgartner and Morris's study of their 18–24 demographic also found that "frequent newspaper readers . . . have lower overall candidate evaluations than nonreaders," but that they "do not display cynicism toward the system and the media in the same manner as watchers of *The Daily Show*" (358). We would argue that this supports our contention that the "outsider" status of the uncivil, outrageous cynical performer remains as crucial today as it no doubt was in Diogenes' day—perhaps more so; newspapers are firmly entrenched within mainstream news media and, as such, subject to the structures and practices in which they operate. The authors conclude their paper by reluctantly conceding that "increased internal efficacy *might*, all other things being equal, contribute to greater participation," and "the increased cynicism associated with decreased external efficacy *may* contribute to an actively critical orientation toward politics. This *may* translate into better citizenship, because *a little* skepticism toward the political system *could* be considered healthy for democracy" (362, emphases added).

Just as creating a false separation between practice and the ideal may be destructive to democracy, both the PIPA and the Baumgartner and Morris studies suggest that when our democratic practices are presumed to be ideal—when practice and the ideal are collapsed as if they are one and the same, and the cynicism created by critique is vilified and effectively booed off the stage, our democracy suffers. It is easy—and serves particular interests—to claim that cynicism is destroying our institutions, but we would argue, like Barry Glasner, that we are afraid of the wrong things. If instead of fearing that cynicism is the dead-end result of all that critical thinking and analysis that ideology critique insists upon, then we might instead—especially as intellectuals and educators—insist upon our work as merely a part of ongoing, ever-evolving practice. Cynicism is part of effective democratic practice. We might in this way view the failure of ideology critique and its resultant cynicism as a pedagogical moment, both for the classroom and in the wider public square.

Cynicism only necessarily results in the kind of apathy suggested by Joe Scarborough and others if we believe that ideology critique—or any other practice—has reached its final form. The failure of ideology critique is an intellectual failure because *we believed we had found the answer*. From the first moment we took up the notion of false consciousness, we believed we could save the unaware through the unmasking of ideology. The religious zealotry with which some intellectuals have embraced certain of our most cherished Theories (capital T) may be seen in proportion to the fear now permeating our public discourse about the cynicism we have produced. Fortunately, neither ideology critique, nor cynicism, is the end of our struggle to improve what we do, how we do it, and how we talk about it.

Because we have neatly collapsed the ideal and practice (the ideal is our aspiration for a reformed sociopolitical structure, and our practice is ideology critique), our epistemological projects increasingly suggest that whether the object is "truth" or "best practices," that object exists out there in the void someplace. Our public discourse regularly features polarized assertions about belief rather than engaged dialogue that is notable for its willingness to negotiate and compromise for the sake of resolving shared problems. We look for ways to dismiss expertise and evidence that does not sit comfortably with our already established views, casting aspersions on expertise itself in a shortsighted anti-intellectualism that threatens to undo the very democracy we seek to strengthen.

But this is not the end of the story. "Truth" and "best practice" are only poison if we collapse the ideal and practice. They are not at all poison if we insist that truth and best practice can only ever be provisional and temporary as we constantly remake what "ideal" means through action, even as we understand that we must constantly strive for, but never reach, the ideal in our practice.

We thought, as intellectuals, that we were immune from believing in and reifying the never-realizable ideal—believing we could arrive there, and worse, that we had already arrived. The only reason we are mired in this depressed state of failed expectations is because *we believed we had found the answer*. We fell right into the trap of Theory, forgetting that theory making, like the democratic practices John Dewey talks about, can only ever be provisional and temporary. Like the ongoing, hard work of democracy, the ongoing, hard work of ideology critique, and the cynicism it produces *as public pedagogy*, requires intellectuals to link their scholarly work to the popular, to participate more fully in our most vital and open democratic deliberations in service of a knowing, engaged citizenry. The "knowing citizen" is deliberately constructed here in the present tense, as a figure that is both persuasive and persuadable, always. The knowing citizen is curious, informed, unafraid of contingency, skeptical—and yes, even cynical—and recognizes that these are necessary functions of participation in a democracy whose ideals inspire belief and demand ongoing, difficult work. The knowing citizen relies on evidence and effective argument and relies on expertise and the best-available data for decision making, with a full understanding that our ongoing, contested, vigilant, and often cynically critical struggle over both our aspirations and our observations and ideals and practices is the only way to better understand how these mutually constitute each other today.

6

Public Discourse and Democratic Deliberation

> We call a work of art trivial when it illuminates little beyond
> its own devices, and the same goes for political leaders who
> bespeak some narrow interest rather than those of the national
> or universal good. The fault is not in the use of theatrical acts,
> but in their purpose.
>
> —Arthur Miller, "On Politics and the Art of Acting"

I. Responding to Sound-Bite Sabotage

Frank Capra's classic 1939 dramedy *Mr. Smith Goes to Washington* has
become a cultural touchstone for both idealists and cynics. Jimmy
Stewart's character Jefferson Smith is often described as a wide-eyed
innocent. Head of the Boy Rangers, he is a political appointee whose
very decency and sense of fair play were supposed to make him an
easy target for Jim Taylor's corrupt political machine. But Smith's
goodwill, determination, and unflappable belief in the American
system of government ultimately triumph over Taylor's influence, or,
at least that is a popular reading of the film: one person can make a
difference. Unfortunately, it is the very idealism of this reading that
makes the film vulnerable to the charge of naïveté. Many of today's
ultrarealists see *Mr. Smith Goes to Washington* as, at best, quaint and,
at worst, misleading. One person cannot make a difference, and pre-
tending otherwise can work to mystify institutional corruption and
the potential means of resisting it.

Yet we feel reading the film as a *homage* to idealism focuses
on only half of its story, message, and, most importantly, method

for resisting anti-democratic influences. Idealism overcoming political corruption is not what Capra's film is about. Instead, it is about
idealism educated to agency by cynicism *and* cynicism awakened to
engagement by faith. It is the nesting of idealism and cynicism that is
the heart of the film's message: a message to which whistle-blowers,
grassroots activists, and those who oppose sound-bite sabotage would
do well to attend. *Mr. Smith Goes to Washington* is not *It's a Wonderful
Life* set on the Potomac.

Throughout the film Smith's idealism needs the cynicism of
Clarissa Saunders (Smith's aide) in order to be effective. Specifically,
he needs the expertise that cynicism has given her. Saunders knows
how the game is played. When Senator Joseph Paine, already corrupted
by Taylor's influence, falsely accuses Smith of trying to profit from
the creation of a national boy's camp, Smith initially folds under the
pressure. He cannot, by himself, stand up to the lies, the betrayal, and
the humiliation. The cynical Saunders, awakened by Smith's belief in
democracy, convinces and shows him how to fight back. Saunders also
helps Smith negotiate the webs of political power and the media and
guides him through the rules of a filibuster. She is the one who gets
his message and plight out through her journalist contacts. Yet she
would have done none of this if Smith's faith had not moved her to
engage, rather than simply survive and/or manipulate, the system. It
is the combination of Smith's passion and Saunder's cynical expertise
that makes for effective political resistance.

Thus Capra's film is not some fairly tale in which the good-
hearted triumph over those who are evil. Rather, it is a map for
bringing together those elements that allow us to negotiate conflict
within a democracy. Rather than turning away from the communication
systems, language games, and rhetorical techniques that a democracy
needs (yet that also complicate it), the film actually encourages us to
fight for and with them—and to resist those who would use such
systems to mislead and confuse. For example, Smith and Saunders
fight back with rhetoric, with filibuster, and with the rules of classic
and democratic argument. It is that which gives them a basis for
power. Media in the film (in this case newspapers and radio) are,
ultimately, portrayed as the hope of democracy. Yes, the film's journalists are cynical opportunists, but they are also teachers for Smith.
After Smith is tricked into being portrayed as a country bumpkin
in the papers, it is the journalists who open his eyes to the fact that
his appointment to the Senate is a sham; that moneyed interests, not
democracy, are in control of the Senate. When these same journalists

see real democratic argument in action (i.e., Smith's filibuster), they jump to report it.

When the Taylor machine tries to stop Smith—to break him—they do it by pumping out misleading, false, and slanderous newspaper stories and radio commentaries in Smith's home state. They shut down news outlets and muscle reporters, and they even use violence to stop the distribution of the Boy Ranger's newspaper. In short, they use their media conglomerate to falsely frame the context, to enact, sans the physical violence, what we have called sound-bite sabotage. Even in 1939, well before the advent of today's digital media, Capra knew that attempts to control the media were attempts to corrupt democracy, to frame issues in ways that favor cultural elites. What is even more interesting for us, however, is not simply Taylor's attempt to control the media image (to brand information) but how his tactic of violence reveals a shift in today's sound-bite sabotage. The Taylors of today know they cannot control the media any longer by shutting it down (too many outlets) or by using crude physical violence (too many lawsuits). Instead, the violence they use is hyper-misinformation, overload, white noise, and massive and systematic disinformation. The Taylors of today have gotten smarter. They have adapted to exploit today's electronic democracy. As journalists are increasingly replaced with pundits, experts with Foxperts, and news with branded information, the Taylors of today are increasingly in control of, and better able to corrupt, our democracy.

Capra's film is not and should not be viewed with a pair of rose-colored glasses. Rather than dismissing rhetoric and media as inherently evil or in opposition to democracy, the film valorizes both as indispensable to a democracy and the corruption of either as detrimental to the public good. And that message is central to our book. Just as Arthur Miller argues in regard to the theatrical arts, the danger in sound-bite sabotage is neither in the use of rhetoric nor in the use of old or new media; the danger lies in the degree to which these (and other techniques) are designed to confuse and mislead. If Miller's quote and Capra's film invite and support our claim that sound-bite sabotage is a powerful rhetorical strategy, a set of tools or mechanisms, then we must conclude that the thoughtful response is not to find fault with the skilled use of rhetoric or new media or cultural texts but to find fault with those usages designed to mislead and distort by branding information to dissipate public energies and systematically distort our information system, resulting in confused and confounded public discourse that undermines both the possibility and the desirability of actual democratic deliberation—disorderly, contingent, and vigorously contested as it must be.

If the "unforgivable sin in democratic politics is dissipating public energies by focusing them on trivial issues," then we suggest, following Miller, defining trivial as being less about content or substance and more about scope and consequences and framing and purpose. Sound-bite sabotage is sabotage because these designer messages represent narrow and private interests as public goods in order to mislead, misrepresent, and disable. In this sense, we want to state clearly that we are not suggesting that more or better use of sound-bite sabotage be considered even a remotely reasonable remedy to the information system distortion we highlight. This book is not a call for the Left to sharpen its sound-bite sabotage skills, nor a denial of the fact that some aspects of the Left are quite skilled already. Ours is not a call to fight fire with fire. Sound-bite sabotage, as both technique and political dynamic, is neither a simple nor simplistic Right/Left, Republican/Democrat, red state/blue state phenomenon. It is a multilayered, multifaceted, media-savvy attempt from competing ideological bases not to win an argument but to destroy the grounds on which argument can occur. Sound-bite sabotage is a cancer on the body politic, a systematic cultivation of gross reductionisms, decontextualized positions, free-floating signifiers, and caricatures of content. It should be cut out, not allowed to spread.

Furthermore, we believe that the tactics of the sound-bite saboteurs will, in the end, prove ineffective as a long-range political and rhetorical strategy. The saboteurs' reliance on pseudo argument, their contempt for legitimate disagreement, and their masking of narrow private interests as larger public goods will, ultimately, lead them to greater and greater isolation and more extreme forms of sabotage that seriously strain credibility. How will saboteurs form coalitions, the basic operating unit of democracies, when the lies they sell and the sliver of the public interest they serve are revealed? As we have seen, when a state's rights political leader in Congress (mis)diagnoses Terry Schiavo on the basis of a videotape to justify federal intervention in a state matter, or when the White House misleads us into war with innuendo and fear-mongering, it becomes, over time, increasingly difficult for a majority of Americans to see such leaders as either competent or truthful, and for such distortions to continue to be effective. The Republican Party, as a whole, has already paid a price for these particular distortions in the 2006 midterm elections, in the 2008 presidential election, and in a post-election struggle to redefine that party.

But even while we note that such distortion may not last, that those who perpetrate it may not continue to enjoy the public's confidence or even their jobs, we want to stress that this distortion—this sabotage—also makes it increasingly difficult for a majority of Americans to understand the complexities of the conflicts we face at home and abroad, and to develop a shared language for deliberation. We are all learning from the persistent, deliberate distortion of information we have highlighted in this book, and it is this public pedagogy of sound-bite sabotage that we find so alarming. The Bush administration, having misspent the goodwill of the American people on previous sound-bite sabotage, struggled mightily before leaving office to find support for an unnecessary war and to persuade Americans on a particular plan to move forward. When we should leave Iraq, whether or not we should leave Iraq, and/or how we should leave Iraq are all difficult and legitimate questions that require rigorous democratic debate. The consequences of these decisions will have major and long-lasting ramifications for the American people, America's position in the world, the Iraqi people, and the entire Middle East. Will we make these decisions based on the best available data, on the most persuasive arguments, on the premise of the greatest good—or has sound-bite sabotage so poisoned the well of public opinion, public trust, and engaged citizenship that honest debate is now impossible? Among all of the complex policy changes facing President Obama, this meta-conflict over our approach to political communication and deliberation over controversial issues may be both his most significant challenge and the area where, if his May 2009 commencement speech at Notre Dame is any indication, he may be particularly well prepared for success.[1]

In addition to the harms associated with sound-bite sabotage itself, detailed throughout the book, the saboteurs will, we believe, inevitably create a backlash that harms not only their private interests but, more importantly, the country's long-range interests—a damage more profound and more widespread than any setback caused by losing a debate, ballot issue, or election. As *National Review* columnist Jonah Goldberg wrote in regard to former Vice President Cheney's slash-and-burn style of governance:

> The act of building consensus often requires sacrificing your most preferred policies. But such consensus-building actually persuades the public, the bureaucracy and legislators of the necessity to act and reduces the chances they'll turn their back on the whole method. The Cheney method

> instead creates a blowback that hobbles one's efforts in the
> long run far more than compromise does. (2007, 7B)

And that, succinctly put, is another major problem with adopting
sound-bite sabotage. Sabotage does not encourage or enable more
engaged forms of cynicism or productive forms of citizen agency.
Instead, sabotage is designed to "dissipate public energies" to produce a
paralyzing confusion by emphasizing a calcified and dualistic thinking
that makes real compromise less likely. Saboteurs cannot afford to grant
legitimacy to those they caricature because their form of caricature is
a travesty, a diversionary tactic. Whereas cynics like Diogenes sought
to highlight the legitimacy claims of his targets in order to challenge
them and to enrich our understanding of the struggle over legitimacy
itself, sound-bite saboteurs seek to conceal inequities, distort data,
and divert attention. Therefore, just as we do not support saturating
communication channels with more branded information or encouraging more dualistic thinking or truncated ideology critique, we do not
support the use of sound-bite sabotage, even in the service of causes
we champion, as a productive or democratic response to the efforts of
sound bite saboteurs. Seductive as its results might seem in the short
term, in the long term it will bite the hand that feeds it. We strongly
recommend that we all, on both sides of the aisle, learn how to expose
and resist the approaches, indeed, any approach, to political communication that systematically distorts our information system.

But are we being hopelessly naïve here, or at least unrealistic?
Are we three Mr. Smiths without a Saunders counterweight? Some
realists might argue that power flows from where it flows; that power
in a democracy must often be wielded through manipulation; that
our idealism will leave us out of the game—co-opt the tactics of
sound-bite saboteurs, but use them to good ends. Do not throw out
a powerful strategy because you do not like the particular results it
creates. Change the results. Do not abandon a car that runs because
you do not like the destination. Change the destination. But such a
counterargument is not asking us to be Saunders; it is asking us to
be Taylor tempting Smith with the same Mephistophilean offer and
logic he used to corrupt Senator Paine.

Indeed, warnings against this type of counterargument are as old
as Western civilization and lead us to our final objection to adopting
sound-bite saboteur tactics: those who would endorse using sound-
bite sabotage for "noble" ends suffer from a shallow understanding
of the power of discourse, how disciplinary power works, how such
powers impact those who use them, and how such powers can and
should be resisted.

II. Language, Power, and the Danger of Co-optation

In Plato's *Gorgias*, Socrates warns Callicles against imitating evil rulers in order to gain power. He tells Callicles that he is "ill advised" if he believes that one can "have great power in this state without conforming to its government either for better or for worse" (1990, 103), and that this conformity is not merely cosmetic. Callicles "must be no mere imitator, but essentially like them" (103). In other words, to be recognized as part of a power structure's ethos, to gain access and wield its power, one must actually be or become part of that ethos. It is a transformation that, Socrates argues, can taint one's soul. The person who tries "to be like his unjust ruler, and have great influence with him" finds "himself possessed of the greatest evil, that of having his soul depraved and maimed as a result of his imitation of his master and the power he has got" (102). For Plato, mimicking the mechanisms of the unjust to gain power risks one's virtue.

One hardly has to be a spiritual foundationalist, however, to be wary of power's transformative nature. Michel Foucault, though operating from a wildly different epistemology than Plato, is equally as passionate in his warnings of co-optation. In *The Archeology of Knowledge & the Discourse on Language*, Foucault argues:

> Disciplines constitute a system of control in the production of discourse, fixing its limits through the action of an identity taking the form of a permanent reactivation of the rules. . . . None may enter into discourse on a specific subject unless he has satisfied certain conditions or if he is not, from the outset, qualified to do so. (1972, 224–25)

Like Plato, Foucault understands that to enter a discourse and to employ its mechanisms one has to be or become enough like its disciplinarians to be recognized by them. One must assume or be assumed by a sanctioned identity, embody a form of rules in order to enter a discipline's discourse, in order to speak and be heard within a structure of power.[2] And, also like Plato, Foucault argues that there is a danger in and a price for this transmogrification. We must confess the truth of the disciplines that we enter and that enter us. He writes:

> We are subjected to the production of truth through power and we cannot exercise power except through the production of truth. . . . We are forced to produce the truth of power that our society demands . . . we *must* speak the truth; we are constrained or condemned to confess or to discover the truth. (1980, 93, emphasis in original)

Thus if Foucault is correct, we cannot use sound-bite sabotage without, to some degree, becoming sound-bite saboteurs. We cannot simply use the tactics of the sound-bite saboteurs to achieve predetermined noble ends. The tactics, discourse practices, and language games of the saboteurs are themselves a form of knowledge, a way of framing the world, a production of truth demanding a transformative conformity and constitutive confession.

And while Foucault does not believe in a soul that can be tainted, he does believe in a political identity and cultural agenda that can be co-opted, a co-optation every bit as profound as Plato's tainted soul.[3] Indeed, Foucault's use of the word "confess" echoes Plato's use of the word soul—not in metaphysics or epistemology but in ethos. While Callicles' soul is "possessed," "depraved," and "maimed" for trying to imitate his unjust ruler, Foucault's subject is "subjected," "forced," "constrained," and "condemned" by the demands of discourse. This use of restrictive and violent language belies the idea that this trans-formation, this demand that we speak or discover the truth, is any more cosmetic than Plato's.

Discourse's demand for transformation and the corresponding danger of co-optation is why, for both theorists, so few revolutions actually change a culture's power structure. Too many people believe, as Callicles does (and as those who would urge the adoption of sound-bite tactics must), that they can use discourse, attain disciplin-ary knowledge, and enter power structures without that nexus using, attaining, and entering into them. Once the palace is seized, once *we* run the government, once the means of discourse are in ideologically correct hands, then the structure will change, and the mechanisms will be used for the public good. But resistance to state, economic, or cultural power structures is much more complex, and our actions are necessarily more complicit in maintaining those structures.[4]

This complicity, even duplicity, in maintaining what you are resisting results from power being exercised more than possessed. Foucault writes:

> Power is not exercised simply as an obligation or a pro-hibition on those who "do not have it"; it invests them, is transmitted by them and through them; it exerts pressure upon them, just as they themselves, in their struggle against it, resist the grip it has on them. This means that these rela-tions go right down into the depths of society. (1979, 27)

Resistance that does not change the structure of power contributes to reproducing that which it is fighting. As Victor Vitanza has argued

"The overthrow of a political position . . . is only a capitulation to eventual recapitulation. Revolutions-against-fascism only end up being new (political, critical, cultural, historiographical) fascisms" (1987b, 107). Consequently, Foucault argues, according to James Miller, that resistance begins at the level of the "micro-politic," at the level of what Vitanza has called "individual cells . . . of critical authority" (109). Miller explains:

> To change the world required changing our selves, our bodies, our souls, and all of our old ways of "knowing," in addition to changing the economy and society. To "seize" and exercise a dictatorial kind of power might thus simply reproduce the old patterns of subjectification under a new name. (1994, 234)

Changing the ideology of a power structure without changing the mechanisms that constitute it will not change all of that power structure's functions and will make lasting change less likely. For example, many socialist societies still treat homosexuals, women, drug addicts, illegal immigrants, and minorities harshly.[5] To truly resist sound-bite sabotage, we must change the restrictive yet productive discourse practices that currently constitute much of knowledge production and communication, teaching and learning, and democratic identity and debate.

The death of Socrates provides a good example of a Foucauldian understanding of power and a corresponding enactment of resistance at this micro-level. The Socrates of Plato's *The Apology* refuses to either escape, as Crito pleads, or to defend himself in the way of the clever rhetoricians—in a way that we today might call sound-bite sabotage. He does not assume, in other words, that he can use rhetoric in a manner he opposes, in a manner he finds unethical, without it also using him. He refuses, in effect, to resist in ways that sanction the power structure's mechanisms of knowing and that would make him complicit in maintaining and validating those mechanisms.

Instead, Socrates presents his way of knowing as an alternative and a superior way of existing in the world. He becomes a seducing object trying to persuade others by example. Friedrich Nietzsche argues this in *The Birth of Tragedy* (with, once again, striking religious imagery):

> From this point onward Socrates conceives it his duty to correct existence, and with an air of irreverence and superiority, as the precursor of an altogether different culture, art, and morality, he enters single-handed into a world, to

touch whose very hem would give us the greatest happiness. (1937, 253)

Socrates' seeming act of submission in drinking the hemlock is in truth an act of micro-level resistance. It is a rhetorical act that creates a new way of existing by transforming death into a different way of understanding the value of life. Indeed, Foucault argues that Socrates, in freely embracing death, establishes " 'the roots of what we could call the "critical" tradition in the West' " (qtd. in Miller 1994, 462, n. 15). Critical engagement requires not simply disagreement or critique but, more importantly, alternative ways of arguing. Socrates' critical example, albeit in less dramatic fashion, is how we want citizens (teachers, students, politicians, and the general public) to resist sound-bite sabotage. We need the courage to offer a different example of how to argue in a democracy, even if it means we might lose in our efforts to, as Gandhi put it, "be the change we wish to see in the world."

Such change, however, need not, must not, happen only in such high-culture texts as *The Apology*. As we saw with *The Daily Show*, popular culture texts are crucially important, not, per se, because of any particular content in a specific text, but because taken together they are more richly textured, more diverse than other information sources, more resistant to dissipating public energies, and more likely to sow doubt in ways that increase clarity as they make us laugh at ourselves and our leaders. In short, they are more supportive of active and engaged forms of cynicism and democratic citizenship. Popular culture texts can operate as antidotes to, or inoculation against, sound-bite sabotage, because they often perform the outrageous, the unacceptable, the offensive. And it is often exactly these performances that offer the information and perspective needed to counter the interested messages of interested elites.

Peer-reviewed data, science, and serious intellectual inquiry are all critical foundations of democratic prosperity, yet sound-bite saboteurs push public opinion away from the best available information when that information does not support their interests. The importance of vigorous inquiry in a free society, as we have seen through the work of J. S. Mill and others, requires that we reject claims of unique access to universally fixed and essentialist understandings of data and replace these with more sober, if less dramatic, understandings of data as the provisional agreements shared by communities of experts. This approach to data is the basis of liberty: Informed, vigorously contested public deliberation is a tool to resist sound-bite sabotage.

Effective democratic leadership, then, sets policy agendas in ways that recognize the collaboration between experts and others, as Schattschneider argues, not by increasing confusion and encouraging passive citizenship. Democratic leadership requires minimizing harm and distortion first. Second, both public and private leaders must seek to maximize public benefits. Leaders can and should act with the public interest in mind by taking seriously their responsibility to increase clarity and to support more engaged forms of cynicism and citizenship. This often involves (particularly for academic leaders) translating their specialized knowledge and disseminating it to a wider public, to better enable citizens to act on their own behalves—that is, we must do a better job of talking about what we do in the wider public arena.

Sound-bite saboteurs depend on the confusion that often predictably follows from their systematic efforts to sow doubt. Their superior resources command a level of attention in the new and old media that gives them a measurable advantage in controlling image and agenda, text and context, in and through the news. Elite noise machines see it in their private interest to cultivate citizens so confused that they cannot act on their own and so alienated that they are unwilling to trust any form of expertise, even so alienated from knowledge production that they often mobilize an elite-led, right-utopian relativism in rejecting the value of data, debate, and scholarly work itself. To the degree that sound-bite saboteurs succeed, they sow doubts that divide publics in ways that threaten to undermine active citizen agency, individually or in solidarity with others. The cynical yet engaged performance of public scrutiny can then become one core element of the checks and balances central to living in a democratic society—an element that is undermined by a systematically distorted information system.

III. Considering Countertrends and Cultural Antidotes

Understanding contemporary politics—what Edelman calls "the political spectacle"—requires attention to discursive struggles, because a careful analysis of language highlights the meta-conflicts over image and information control, venue, and agenda setting that are the core of how political power operates today. "News about politics encourages a focus on leaders, enemies, and problems as sources of hope and fear, obscuring the sense in which they are creations of discourse, perpetuators of ideologies, and facets of a single transaction" (Edelman 1988, 120). Language such as "irrational terrorists," "evil empire," or

"Osama bin Laden: dead or alive" dramatizes and personalizes conflicts in ways that mask the struggles over how to frame these conflicts, displace and reconcentrate public attention, erase both historical and political contexts, and mobilize more confused publics less able to achieve agreements that might resolve the conflicts we face.

According to Edelman, the core question in politics is *why we obey*, and the construction of political spectacles that "create anxieties and aspirations, insecurities and reassurances that fuel a search for legitimating symbols" is one of the central reasons we obey. We can only conclude, then, that understanding politics is *not* about knowing the best policy, or having all the facts, but rather learning to be aware of "the range of meanings political phenomena present . . . [and] the inevitability of distortion" (123–24). In contemporary political culture we obey because our leaders "determine our fears" in ways that dissipate our energies, fragment our perspectives, privilege the mobilization of interpretive frames favored by the already powerful, and encourage us to misunderstand both power and politics.[6]

> Rather than verifiability or falsifiability and the certainties and dogmatisms to which the search for definitive answers leads, a useful analysis must examine the consequences of uncertainties, unjustified certainties, the variations in response that diverse social milieus evoke, and the potentiality for multivalent responses to situations and texts. (Edelman 1988, 124)

Armed with this analytical framework, Edelman turns from a focus on the information distortions central to the construction of political spectacles to thinking about how we might move forward in progressive directions; he focuses, as we have attempted to do here, on the role that political culture plays in revitalizing the possibility and desirability of democratic deliberation. Like Edelman, we insist that a relentless focus on language is not myopic, nor should it be understood as the last-best strategy: "Though this analysis pays a great deal of attention to language, change in language is not a final answer either. The dissemination of new political terms, concepts, and phrases without concomitant changes in material conditions can only reinforce the old tensions and premises" (130). Our analysis here, and the analyses of others, are all part of an ongoing struggle—politics—that proceeds without guarantee and without final victories and, as we have seen in the work of John Dewey, it is precisely this lack of guarantee and absence of final victories that make democracy possible as the living, breathing, evolving system it is always becoming.

Still, the temptations (especially for academics) inherent in a concept of "false consciousness," or what Edelman calls the "triumph of mystification," are certainly abundant as we bear witness to the persistent and all-too effective threats to the communicative foundations for democratic prosperity and progress. *Surely, we think, an enlightened consciousness will finally achieve the changes we seek,* a consciousness like ours, naturally. We have seen, however, that this is not so, and, in fact, the theory-hope upon which this is predicated relies on the very collapse of idealism and practice, where we envision and put into play a practice that is deemed ideal, the very thing that Dewey warns of, and results in the kinds of myths that veil interest and agency and thereby weaken democracy, as Chomsky and others have shown.

But, as we have seen, art and humor, as particular aspects of popular culture, may act as key antidotes in this struggle against the triumph of mystification that threatens the communicative foundations for democratic prosperity and progress.

> Art helps counter banal political forms.... Art refuses to accept fact as truth and so liberates the mind from conventional presuppositions ... [displacing these with] complex associations and dense meanings as the hallmarks of the aesthetic. While political language focuses on the particular fear or hope, art evokes many concurrent levels of significance.... The popular humor that calls attention to the special subculture that binds disadvantaged people to one another can be powerful.... More generally, a potential for liberation from political texts and their rootedness in the present lies in the refusal to see any text or any form of discourse as paramount or essential; it lies in the sensitivity to the multiple and contradictory realities and the occasional transformations of reality associated with changed discourses, diverse social institutions, and different historical contexts. (Edelman 1988, 126–29)

Edelman illustrates the power of cultural antidotes by contrasting *Crime and Punishment* with a scholarly analysis of the causes of crime. The scholarly analysis justifies prevailing ways of framing crime and punishment, while in the other "Raskolnikov represents these things and others, but also their negations" (1988, 127). Today we might point to cultural texts such as *Dead Man Walking, Jesus Camp,* or *A Civil Action* as similarly challenging conventional discourses. We would certainly have to recognize the ongoing power of David Letterman and Jay Leno, and the even more disruptive humor found in *The Daily Show* and *The Colbert Report*, which studies show are the primary sources of news for significant numbers of young adults. We might also point to the counter-stories told by *The Innocence Project*, Michael Moore, or *An Inconvenient Truth* as powerful cultural antidotes in action today. In addition to these, there are also times that the dominant discourse delivers within it resources for resistance that emerge as powerful cultural artifacts demonstrating the close relationship between information management, as analyzed here, and civic education.

On the Media from National Public Radio, *Romenesko* at PoynterOnline, FactCheck.org from the Annenburg Public Policy Center, FAIR (Fairness and Accuracy in Reporting), TheOtherNews.com, Media Matters, RealClearPolitics, OpenSecrets, the Innocence Project, the Center for Media and Public Affairs, AlterNet, CJR Daily, Accuracy in the Media, Slate.com, and many other sites have already emerged as powerful forces for media literacy that counter trends toward sound-bite sabotage. The English language versions of news media such as *The People's Daily*, Arab News, or Al Jazeera, for instance, add to our ability to decode the news. And while it is clear to us that the trend toward branded information designed to sabotage effective public deliberation supports an information system that is less able to check and constrain elite actions, these countertrends are not insignificant and highlight the importance of lightly covered legislative battles—meta-conflicts—over how to regulate the Internet.

Further, this regulatory battle has a history in struggles within and around the Federal Communications Commission (FCC), particularly with regard to the Fairness Doctrine, that suggests that Internet regulation struggles are far more significant than their scant media coverage would indicate. Robert Kennedy Jr. argues powerfully in *Crimes against Nature*, for instance, that right-utopian success at deregulation, in this case persuading public-sector leaders to eliminate the FCC Fairness Doctrine, has contributed enormously to both information system distortion and, as a consequence, to unwise public policies made without public awareness or scrutiny. Similarly, Jeffrey Smith, in *Seeds of Deception*, finds overwhelming pressure from private-sector leaders seeking to prevent reporters from informing the American public about the potential dangers of genetically modified foods and the widespread failure of public and private leaders—on both sides of the aisle—to insist on even the minimal testing and laboratory standards experts routinely expect to protect the public health. This case included regulatory battles in the National Institutes of Health, the GAO, the FDA, and interest group pressure from media outlets, the Dairy Coalition, and others.[7]

It is also important, however, to recognize (as one aspect of understanding sound-bite sabotage) those times when our leaders succeed in modeling open-minded approaches to the conflicts we face, with respect for those holding opposing views, manifesting a shared aspiration to achieve agreements, and providing us with the timely, detailed, balanced information needed for citizens to make informed choices. These illustrations, which are neither characteristic forms of political communication nor insulated from the abuses we have documented in this book, demonstrate the ways leaders can, and do, seek to reduce fears about conflicts likely to cause serious harm by leading us through public deliberations as a form of civic education.

When anthrax was discovered in government mailrooms and leaders wanted to reduce citizen fear and prevent chaos, we were subjected to a month-long national seminar on the various ways anthrax can spread, subcutaneous or otherwise, and we did not stop using the postal service or stop going to work and school. In this case, we contend that our leaders concentrated our energies and fears by increasing our understanding of the challenge we faced.[8] When forest fires or cell phones in crowded theaters or smoking or litter were identified as problems that the public did not fully understand, public information campaigns (however imperfect or unpopular) were created to teach us, empowering us through enhancing our own understanding, to change our behavior or support new legislation mandating air bags or bicycle helmets or protecting the unborn from secondhand smoke or alcohol. When leaders chose to publicize risk factors contributing to heart disease or obesity, public health improved.

These examples demonstrate that it is possible to use the tools of modern advertising and public relations to construct familiar and authoritative slogans, saturate our communication channels, and persuade citizens to understand and support those changes that mark a particular path toward a particular set of agreed-upon goals. But this is not *simply* true, nor is it always true, because the contexts in which we use such tools are always changing, and the traces of previous, overlapping contexts always already remain, in us and *in the tools themselves*. The tools of advertising and PR are, like any other tool, constructed and defined by a complex and an interconnected web of meanings related to their conventions, histories, and the uses to which they are put. Tools, including rhetoric itself, are value-neutral in the abstract, but they carry relatively greater and lesser traces of historical and political meaning that may make some of them less desirable as tools than others. We might think of tools as neutral in their abstract form, but in practice—in use—they will necessarily be more or less ideological; it is only in studying the context of their uses (i.e., who wields them and to what ends) that we may determine both their effectiveness and whether or not it is even possible or wise to use them for quite different purposes (Eagleton 1991, 1–31).

This is an important question: Are tools, rhetorical and otherwise, neutral, or do we invent new tools, define them, with their use in specific contexts, inventing new tools each time we use them? If we think the former is the correct answer, then any technique used by sound-bite saboteurs is fair game, should be learned, and used well to the user's advantage. If we think the latter is the correct answer, then those tools that have been used to what we consider a bad outcome, and from an immoral or unethical intention, should be off-limits, since the tool itself is corrupt and corrupting, and we are more likely to wind up with a similarly bad outcome.

But what if there is some value, some sense, some truth in *both* of these propositions? We argue that this is the case. For example, a dictatorship may have what it calls and what looks like, on paper, a constitution: the rule of law, a judicial system, a congress, and so on—and yet none of those tools are really the same as their counterparts in a democracy, even though the use of a constitution is, in the abstract, the use of the same tool. This is because a constitution is not defined by genre, by what it contains in its paper form, but by how it is used. One might call something a constitution, but that does not make it one in practice; one constitution might provide due process, while another might mislead and disempower the very citizens who look to it to frame their lives in just and equitable ways.

If we follow this logic all the way through, however, we might be tempted to locate those historical situations in which so-called constitutions are used in corrupt ways and determine that constitutions are at least *potentially* corrupt tools, and we should best steer clear of them. Such a conclusion seems unwise and illogical on multiple levels, and we are thus more inclined to see constitutions as tools that may be used for good or ill, a more-or-less neutral tool. Each use creates a different tool of "constitution." The tool itself, its definition, its ontology, is a practice within a context. Until it is actually used, the tool is an abstraction, just as "leaf" is an abstraction we create of maple leaves and oak leaves. To grant the abstraction ontological status is to miss crucial grounds from which status can be defined, critiqued, and changed, grounds that constitute a vital component in both recognizing and working against sound-bite sabotage.

But what if we consider the tool of torture? We would argue that torture is not only morally unacceptable, but that it corrupts democracy and—importantly—that it *carries its corruption within it*. The problem with torture is not found in how it is used but in the worldview it carries—its point of view, the agenda that lies within it.

Torture, like any tool, is both created within a context, created by its use within each context, and it *simultaneously* carries a context within it—histories, meanings, and perspectives.

Where does that leave us as we try to understand and grapple with the tools currently used in sound-bite sabotage? In our view, it leaves us with a more complex, ongoing problem that resists final solutions and requires the never-ending work of analysis and evaluation, within ever-changing social and political contexts and articulations. The particular communicative tools we address in this book may be in some important ways neutral, reinventable in other contexts; but in other, equally important ways they may be corrupted by the uses to which they are put, and they also may always already *be* a use: they have histories, functions, and traces of meaning before we even think to begin to use them. But in order to *act* we must remember that part of what makes these time-honored rhetorical techniques a threat today is their amplification in new media, their link to elite funding that is interested and skilled at representing private interests in branded information as public interests. These are not new tools, but new and more systematically amplified, calculated uses of them, so in combination they amount to the phenomena we call sound-bite sabotage, which is to say that the same tools can be used for many purposes, *and* that each use creates a different tool.

Our point is that greater understanding of the contexts within which these particular tools are used in particular ways today helps us see the sabotage and, along with other intellectual and political work, may enable us to work more effectively against our increasing inability to address the challenges we face, challenges that require the best available data, and open deliberation among citizens with opposing views. And, simultaneously, we must struggle to see the particular contexts *within* the tools we use, to see how some tools more fully enable the harms we have been discussing to deliberation and engaged citizenship, to learning and intellectual inquiry, and even to discard some tools on the bases of their histories and their perspectives. And part of that work resides in the public, intellectual, and political work of ideology critique—in making the implicit explicit.

IV. Making the Implicit Explicit

Democratic deliberation is a conversation that, unlike the public relations campaigns mounted by sound-bite saboteurs, depends on making the implicit explicit and seeing the inescapable, multiple perspectives on any issue as an invitation to dialogue with those who hold opposing views—dialogue that is designed to support the achievement of voluntary agreements. Such dialogue puts values and interests on the table, changing the dynamic in ways that make the assertion-and-saturation strategy less persuasive and less powerful, *without having to use similar techniques,* as Mendelberg found with regard to the use of race-coded, law-and-order language in political campaigns.

In "Executing Hortons: Racial Crime in the 1988 Presidential Campaign," Mendelberg analyzed the now infamous Willie Horton ads to argue persuasively that "racial campaigns affect far more than voters' behavior at the ballot box" (1997, 134). The author asks about the degree to which public reactions to these campaign advertisements "cast the Horton appeal as a race card or, instead, as a straightforward vehicle for discussing universal, race-neutral concerns like criminal justice." In other words, did these ads prime whites' racial prejudice, as many have asserted? (136–38). In a controlled experiment, Mendelberg found that "exposure to Horton coverage increases the effect of prejudice, activates prejudice where it was nearly dormant, inclines prejudiced whites to reject the legitimacy of welfare programs, and endorse the idea that African Americans can do without them" (145–47). Further, "without Horton exposure, prejudiced individuals are 25 percentage points more likely than unprejudiced people to oppose racially egalitarian policies; with exposure to Horton, prejudiced individuals are 40 percentage points more likely to do so than unprejudiced people" (145). Testing the alternative hypothesis, that the Horton campaign activated people's concerns about crime, Mendelberg found that "Horton did not bring out the power of crime salience [and] did not move perceptions of the importance of crime as a problem" (151).

The Horton campaign was about race, mobilizing an implicitly race-coded, law- and-order message, but in her subsequent book-length analysis, Mendelberg offers us an even more intriguing insight:

> The racial message was communicated most effectively when no one noticed its racial meaning. . . . When society has repudiated racism, yet racial conflict persists, candidates can win by playing the race card only through implicit racial appeals. The implicit nature of these appeals allows them to prime racial stereotypes, fears, and resentments while appearing not to do so. When an implicit appeal is rendered explicit—when other elites bring the racial meaning of the appeal to voters' attention—it appears to violate the norm of racial equality. It then loses its ability to prime white voters' racial predispositions. . . . Political communication

that derogates African Americans does little harm if it is widely, immediately, and strongly denounced. In an age of equality, what damages racial equality is the failure to notice the racial meaning of political communication, not the racial meaning itself. (2001, 4)

Thus we see the value of critical, savvy, informed, and even cynical readings of culture; we see the value of ideology critique, but as one tool within democratic deliberation, one component of our ever-evolving practice that fails us only when we understand it as an end in itself.

We see through Mendelberg's work that sound-bite sabotage depends on the cultivated inattention central to implicit messaging for its success, and that cultivated inattention depends on publics that are either misinformed, confused, overwhelmed, frightened, or apathetic. When the values and interests at stake are left invisible, unexamined, one foreseeable consequence is confusion about what is at stake, even (or even especially) among more attentive publics. When coal company lobbyists provide free teaching materials to impoverished public schools that misinform our children about the environmental degradation associated with strip mining, or other forms of branded information invade our classrooms through Channel One, for instance, we ought to expect that citizen struggles to identify who ought to be held responsible for the ecological and other challenges we face will be more confused.

Just as democratic deliberation relies on making the implicit explicit, sound-bite saboteurs rely on keeping the invisible invisible. This precondition makes mere repeated assertions more powerful, which increases the incentive to bullshit by insulating the rewards for bullshitting from scrutiny, reinforcing the links to parallel clusters of confusion and dependency and fear through public relations, fakery, and rancid populism.

Meaningful attention to these conflicts requires elite political and cultural leadership that combines the intellectual and the popular to mobilize publics in support of democratic deliberation, scientific innovation, education, and the serious scholarly analysis of the most important conflicts we face.[9] We must insist on leadership that supports (rhetorically, by example, and with funding) real public education, both in institutional settings and the public square. In this way, critical public scrutiny (characterized by both ideology critique and its resultant cynicism) becomes part of our public pedagogy, not as an end but rather as a precursor to open-minded debates, and informed deliberations that allow us to understand (and participate in influencing) the countervailing forces seeking to influence public policy. In this sense, we need a reform-minded elite that recognizes its own interest in educated and acculturated publics, with a cultivated respect for the rule of law, for intellectual activity, and for the conflict management skills that make democratic politics both possible and desirable. We must insist on elites that focus their own and our attention on how power and politics depend on compromise and collaboration, and how competition and individualism depend on community and achieving shared values, rather than on distracting us with the trivial.

Finally, a respect for law and intelligence forged in practice and modeled by leadership can mitigate against the violence of factions. We need a sober recognition of the power leaders have to frame debates, and how exercising this power over time constructs the forms of common sense that often silence, implicitly, unpopular or disadvantaged voices. This power is not new, but in a context of mass multimedia, increasingly cynical publics, and the saturation of our information system with branded information produced by sound-bite saboteurs, the public pedagogy it wields is strikingly potent.

It is the pedagogical question with which we conclude. In our view we can no longer think about pedagogy as what happens in our institutional classrooms, or even how we approach our intellectual work as academics. And while this is certainly not a novel idea among progressive intellectuals, in our view there has been precious little movement in this area. We must be a part of a wider effort that presupposes the interconnectedness of the classroom, the public square, and the technologies and agencies of the new media in order to reconceive what we mean by both teaching and learning. This requires leadership, both public and private, to acknowledge and respond ethically to the fact that resources and access do not just afford elites a louder voice in discreet, present-day conflicts (although they certainly do that); the greater resources and access enjoyed by public and private leaders also necessarily means that these interested groups and individuals are actively and directly teaching us all how communication and persuasion are deployed and valued, and to what ends. Elites are, necessarily, educators. We must ask ourselves if what they are teaching, and what we are all learning from them, is furthering our democratic practices, moving them closer to our democratic ideals, or not—and how we choose to use our various media to get our messages out, in both the private and public sector, set a particular course for our democracy, whether we choose to acknowledge it or not—and refusing to acknowledge it is, in itself, a choice with material consequences.

We all learn how the world operates and what kind of agency and effect we might have in that world by observing and participating in the flow of information around us, and by observing and participating in the multiple, overlapping, complex struggles over resources and representation, and the reproduction of cultural ideals and practices making up our world. We have attempted to connect the ways in which private-sector advertising techniques have become indistinguishable from public-sector information techniques, resulting in branded information that distorts and misinforms, masking both interest and agency. We have attempted to show that the new media, while not the cause of branded information, are a fertile ground for it, constituting new techniques, new agencies, and the saturation by sound bites of our information system, at times to the detriment of publics willing and able to understand and act upon the challenges they face. And we have tried to explore the possibility that while one of our most treasured intellectual tools—ideology critique—seems to have failed us by exacerbating the cynicism in part created by the widely felt experience of being bombarded by interested messages whose agents and purpose often lurk far below the surface, that cynicism itself, and ideology critique, too, must be and can be reconfigured as components and provisional moments in democratic practice rather than as either dead ends or final solutions.

But we cannot leave it at that. If we reconceive teaching and learning to not just *include* the public square as an extra-institutional pedagogical site but, rather, as an integral, constitutive, overlapping, and arguably more powerful locus of both teaching and learning impacting *everything* we do in our classrooms, then academics must do two things, and do them more often and better: they must increasingly bring the popular into the classroom (see Appendix),[10] and they must learn to speak to public constituencies about what they do and why they do it.[11] Finally, it is in Gramsci's notion of an "organic intellectual" that we find a framework for the kind of productive tension we envision, a "pessimism of the intellect, optimism of the will." Gramsci insists that intellectuals work on two fronts simultaneously: at the forefront of theoretical work, and within the community. The intellectual has a responsibility to transmit her or his knowledge for the explicit, pragmatic purpose of problem solving. Nesting the intellectual and the material and the intellectual and the popular is where our best hope, as well as our work, lies.

Appendix

While I understood that language is socially generated, I saw that it is always internalized in transactions with the environment at particular times under particular circumstances. Each individual, whether speaker, listener, writer, or reader, brings to the transaction a personal linguistic-experiential reservoir, the residue of past transactions in life and language.

—Louise Rosenblatt, "The Transactional Theory: Against Dualisms"

The most valuable political act any teacher can perform is not to impose particular political views but to teach students to see the words that society tries to inject into them unseen.

—Wayne Booth, *The Vocation of a Teacher*

I. Into the Multimodal Classroom: Nesting New Media and Academic Discourse

Reconciling the dualism of new media and academic discourse presents academicians with something of a dilemma. Letting the new media operate openly in our classrooms, letting them influence explicitly the way students argue, write, and research in our disciplines, could erode the time-tested standards and enabling constraints by which academicians produce and disseminate knowledge. Yet shunning the new media, banning them from our classrooms, not only makes our curriculum seem irrelevant, disconnected, and outdated but also "shut[s] out of our classrooms a broad range of students' rhetorical skills and experiences, some of which can help them become better writers" (Williams 2002, 6) and, we might add, better able to resist sound-bite sabotage. The question is: How do we reconcile the dualism of new media and academic discourse so that it enriches an interdependent and a co-constituting relationship yet also respects that relationship's tensions—tensions that are equally necessary for productive permeation? More importantly, how do we get *students* to reconcile this dualism?

First, we need to shut up for awhile. We need to listen to our students and validate their experiences as makers of meaning. We must recognize that students may be more familiar with parts of the new media experience than we are. After all, they grew up in the digital age. What do they know about the new media, corporate think tanks, and the blogosphere? What can they teach us? What are they already doing with digital technologies in their daily lives?

Second, we need to rethink the pedagogical theory that informs many of the attempts to incorporate some degree of new media into the college curricula. Academicians from a variety of disciplines have already written, quite eloquently, of their attempts to connect students' media-constituted consciousness to academic discourse, to include new media technologies in their framing of academic culture. But too many of these attempts suffer from what Bruce McComiskey calls the *"read-this-essay-and-do-what-the-author-did* method of writing instruction: read Roland Barthes's essay 'Toys' and write a similar essay on a toy of your own choice; read John Fiske's essay on TV and critique a show" (2000, 1–2, emphasis in original). Such models displace the student's own experience in favor of a distant theoretical perspective. They represent a top-down pedagogy that encourages teachers to rely on certain cultural theories as the content of the class, to emphasize a particular outcome without a corresponding emphasis on the process of creation. As Lanham argues, "[S]tudents so instructed are not being taught; they are being housebroken" (1974, 19).

A second yet similar pedagogical approach replaces student experience with the political content of new media. New media are used to show how, for example, corporations are destroying the environment, the medical establishment is keeping us ill, and Madison Avenue is perpetuating sexist stereotypes. Academic argument, research, and writing are then used to document these abuses, to communicate their pre-, if camouflaged, existence. The problem with this approach is not so much its ideological perspective (at least for us); the problem is, once again, that the pedagogy is one of displacement: "the definition of categories such as the disenfranchised and the dominant, oppressed and oppressor, should be a *product* of the pedagogical process, not its unquestioned *premise*" (Jay and Graff 1995, 207, emphases in original). Instead of nesting academic discourse and new media, curriculum and student experience, to create new and open forms of knowledge production, each component becomes a separate vehicle for a prede-termined yet "discovered" knowledge—effectively erasing the need for constructive agency. As McComiskey argues, such an approach "foreground[s] cultural politics as material to be mastered, and students write to demonstrate what they have learned" (2000, 2).

While such an approach might be appropriate in certain academic contexts, we favor an approach that creates a "zone of crude contact" between students and the dualism of new media and academic dis-course. Much like Mikhail Bakhtin's "internally persuasive discourse," our students would be able to "finger . . . [the dualism] familiarly on all sides, turn it upside down, inside out, peer at it from above and below, break open its external shell, look into its center, doubt it, take it apart, dismember it, lay it bare and expose it, examine it freely and experiment with it" (1981, 23). To nest the dualism of new media and academic discourse, we need a pedagogy that privileges their interac-tion *as* the critical core of the class, a pedagogy that allows students to "develop the sense that culture itself is a constantly changing process, and that their own writing can influence some of the changes that cultures undergo" (McComiskey 2000, 24).

Finally, the differences between new media and academic dis-course would neither be erased nor made into a fetish in our classrooms. The socio-cognitive skills of word and image are not transposable just because they are nested. As Kress argues, " 'The world narrated' is a different world to 'the world depicted and displayed' " (2003, 2). Instead, the relationship between new media literacies and academic literacies must be continually constructed and reconstructed. The rela-tionship has no unalterable antecedent. The relationship is and has to be something the classroom community actively designs.

Indeed, we started chapter 4 with a quote from Fishman and McCarthy stating Dewey's belief that learners are never passive. The key to understanding this quote is its first word "learners." *Learners* are never passive. But this does not mean that all students are learn-ers, or that we always treat them as such. When students are learn-ing and when we are treating them as makers of meaning instead of knowledge receptacles, they are not passive. Given that our book has documented the rise of more passive forms of education and citizen-ship in our culture, we wonder if there is a trend toward less learning, toward unlearning citizenship. Students often seem willing to embrace a passive, apathetic, spectator role in the classroom and the culture. Worse, aspects of the popular culture and our pedagogies may have trained them to do so. How do we break through that apathy, that training, that indoctrination?

In *John Dewey and the Challenge of Classroom Practice*, Fishman and McCarthy argue that "although many of us may agree that a more inclusive society, one which encourages individual growth in accord with the betterment of the least advantaged, is desirable, deciding which classroom structures best help us achieve this goal is not easy" (1998, 63). Accordingly, Fishman and McCarthy turn to the work of Dewey for inspiration—not to find the correct or eternal structures that will bring about this better world but to develop an ongoing method, a continual process for the construction, application, and revision of ever-changing and ever-adapting structures. As Dewey argues, education is "a process of development, of growth." He writes:

> And it is the *process* and not merely the result that is important. A truly healthy person is not something fixed and completed. He is a person whose processes and activities go on in such a way that he will continue to be healthy. Similarly an educated person is the person who has the power to go on and get more education. (1964 [1934], 4, emphasis in original)

Our purpose here, therefore, is *not* to tell teachers *what* to do to resist sound-bite sabotage. We do not and cannot know the particulars of their situations. It is they who must create the exercises, methods of intervention, and lesson plans to resist the bias and distortion in our information systems from interested parties, public and private leaders, and to simultaneously acknowledge and work *beyond* the inevitable creation of cynical student-subjects. What we can do is share what *we* do to nest the dualism of new media and academic discourse and to resist sound-bite sabotage in our classrooms. The applicability of our interventions to other situations is for others to decide. We can only offer indirect solutions.

II. Using Music Videos in College Classrooms

One of the most productive exercises we use to help our students use writing to unpack their image literacy is the analysis of music videos.[1] The exercise is designed to help our students unpack and transform the image knowledge they *always already* bring to the writing classroom. Specifically, the exercise seeks to (1) acknowledge and respect our students' image literacy, (2) inject writing and, thus, recursivity into the media experience, (3) design an interpretative context for the image extrapolated from our students' lived lives, (4) help our students translate or "code switch" media literacy into academically acceptable writing, and (5) "decelerate temporarily the rate of speed and motion with which the messages enter our students' lives" (Penrod 1997, 18). To conduct the exercise, we videotape a series of music videos and bring them to class. Good artists to tape include Eminem, Korn, Slipknot, Gwen Stefani, Snoop Dogg, Kanye West, NWA, Kid Rock, Marilyn Manson, DMX, Mudvayne, Audioslave, Britney Spears, Fallout Boy, Justin Timberlake, Avril Lavigne, and Madonna, to name but a few. Each of these artists represents a different facet of our students' lived experience: the ironic yet socially conscious rap of Kanye West, the personal and political desperation of Mudvayne, the sexually charged gender bending of Madonna. In an attempt to use writing to slow down the image experience and tie our students' reactions to academic expectations, we take our students through a multilayered process of "reading" and "rereading" the image. We also inject as much writing into the visual experience as possible.

To begin, we simply watch the videos and discuss them. We will usually show a series of four to five videos before discussion begins. These initial discussions focus on students' emotional reactions and first impressions. Do they like the videos, the artists, the songs, and why? Students often comment on a video's style, intelligence, stupidity, and/or creativity (what they call "taking it to the next level"). Occasionally, however, students offer more socially complex comments: the artificiality of former "boy band" aficionado Justin Timberlake, the "stealing of black culture" by Kid Rock, the blatant homophobia in Eminem's videos, the gratuitous sex and misogyny in many Snoop Dogg videos, the way Marilyn Manson and Slipknot use costumes and violent imagery to make political statements, the way Korn uses dark imagery to highlight the social pathology of child abuse. This discussion leads to our first rereading of the images. We play the videos again and this time ask students to write down particular impressions and reasons for those impressions.

After (re)watching the videos and giving students time to write, we arrange students into small groups to share their impressions. In the class discussion that follows, we play the videos again and point out many of their formal elements: lighting, camera angle, costumes, and so on. To enhance analysis and recursivity, we rewind the videos and freeze-frame them on particular images, allowing students to support and debate ideas. After the discussion, we ask students to revise their written impressions, this time focusing on a specific image. During the next discussion, we run the videos as background noise, stopping them whenever requested. We may now discuss the colors used in videos, the dance style (urban, rap, house, or the frenetic "moshing" of heavy metal), the quick cuts the camera makes and what this requires of attention span, the videos' fashion sense and what this tells us about race, class, and gender, the videos' material-ism (from the grotesque display of wealth in some rap videos to the sparse, almost anti-materialism displayed in others), or how the videos present sexuality. Most importantly, we discuss how writing allows us to refocus, revise, and slow down the video experience, and why the academy values such interpretive strategies. We then replay the video one last time as the students revise their writing.

A good music video to use for this exercise is Madonna's "Music." As her name implies, Madonna is an icon of our media culture, and this video is packed with irony and simulation. The video starts with Madonna and her female friends (her posse) in the back of a luxury car. They are dressed in loud, flashy, outrageous outfits, sport over-sized gold chains, and drink Crystal champagne. Drunk, Madonna and her companions head to a strip club and throw money at female strippers, inverting and, thus, subverting cultural gender roles while simultaneously reinforcing them. The overtly sexual, almost grotesque dancing of the strippers mocks the dancing found in videos by such rap artists as Jay-Z and 50 cent. When Madonna and her friends return to their luxury car, Madonna's driver, a racially nondistinct male with an English accent (know to his fans as Ali G),[2] tries to impress them with his rap prowess. Sporting gold teeth and speaking in a cartoon version of Black English Vernacular, he is dressed to look like an urban rapper. He wears a stocking cap, gold chains, and clothes made by either Fubu or Mecca (both popular urban fashions). The video ends with Madonna's luxury car driving away and displaying a license plate that reads "Muff Daddy"—a sexually charged, gender-bending play on the name of rap artist Puff Daddy, now called P Diddy.

What is particularly interesting about Madonna's video is that it consciously enjoys using the very clichés of which it is making fun: flashy cars, hip-hop clothes, hyper-masculinity, and scantily clad women. It simultaneously wallows in imagery and themes from rap videos and makes fun of that genre's materialism, objectification of women, and appropriation of "black street culture" by white rappers. If Baudrillard is correct in his belief that the image can only refer to its own system of simulation, then Madonna's video seems to show that circular referencing is still capable of creating meaning. While Baudrillard believes that the dominance of media images in our soci-ety has eliminated a space outside the flow of simulation from which analysis can be made, the blurring of signification could be seen as a visual intertextuality that allows analysis from within the simulation. Madonna is both a creator and reader of her own video, a producer and consumer of her own video as text. Whether Madonna's ironic use of imagery ultimately subverts or reestablishes the materialism, sexism, and racism of some rap videos is open to debate. However, her video displays the kind of conscious and sophisticated manipulation of media that we hope our students will display in their writing. In attempting to simultaneously critique and claim a genre's images, she displays the multiple literacies we want our students to display.

As an essay assignment for this exercise, we ask students to keep a journal, for one week, of the music videos they watch. After discussing their journals with us, students are expected to write a four-to-five-page analysis of a specific music video. Drafts of the essay are workshopped in small groups and in conference. The final part of the assignment requires students to give oral presentations, an attempt to have oral, print, and visual literacies interact. Our hope in performing this exercise is that students will see the immense amount of knowledge they already have about the images that fill their lives. We also hope they will see how writing can enhance and transform that knowledge, for while we disagree with much of Marshall McLuhan's and Quentin Fiore's argument in *The Medium Is the Message*, we agree that the student "instinctively understands the present environment—the electric drama" (1967, 9). Her or his difficulty lies in communicating or translating that understanding via the written word.

III. Media Literacy Exercises

Part I

Over the next week or so, please click on each of the six Web addresses that follow to find an analysis on each site that focuses on the *same story* across all six sites. You may choose any story that you find on all sites, as long as it is a story you would expect to be of interest around the world, not simply in the United States. Print each article as you find it (since it may not be easy to find the next time you search), and conduct the analysis that follows once you have six articles on one issue or conflict.

http://www.abcnews.go.com/
http://www.msnbc.msn.com/
http://www.cbsnews.com/

http://www.foxnews.com/
http://www.cnn.com/
http://www.pbs.org/news/

1. List the facts that appear on *each* site.
2. List the facts that appear on only *one* site.
3. Looking at how the facts are selected, filtered, and combined, how would you evaluate the *tone* of each site's coverage of this issue (pro/con; fair/one-sided; thoughtful/hysterical)?
4. Looking at how the facts are selected, filtered, and combined, compare and contrast the competing ways that this story is *framed* by the six sites.
5. What can you conclude about our information system and citizen access to information from comparing these stories?

Part II

Over the next week or so, please click on each of the four Web addresses that follow to find an analysis on each site that focuses on the *same story* across all sites. If you can use the same story you used for Part I, then this is the best-case scenario. If not, choose one story that you find on all four of these sites, as long as it is a story you would expect to be of interest around the world, not simply in the United States. Print each article as you find it (since it may not be easy to find the next time you search), and conduct the analysis that follows once you have four articles on one issue or conflict.

http://www.factcheck.org/
http://www.fair.org/index.php
http://www.mediamatters.org/
http://www.aim.org/

1. List the facts that appear on *each* site.
2. List the facts that appear on only *one* site.
3. Looking at how the facts are selected, filtered, and combined, evaluate the *tone* of each site's coverage of this issue (pro/con; fair/one-sided; thoughtful/hysterical).
4. Looking at how the facts are selected, filtered, and combined, compare and contrast the competing ways that this story is *framed* by the four sites.
5. What can you conclude about our information system and citizen access to information from comparing these stories?

Part III

http://www.watchingamerica.com/index.shtml
http://www.people.com.cn/english/
http://www.cjrdaily.org/
http://www.afp.com/english/home/
http://www.arabnews.com/
http://www.bbc.co.uk/
http://www.pipa.org/

Select two sites from the list above that also cover the same conflict, and print their analysis as your foundation for responding to the following three questions:

1. Compare and contrast the competing ways that this story is *framed* by all the sites in Parts I and II (or Part II alone, treated as one category) and these two additional sites (treated as your second category). If you cannot find coverage of your initial story on any of these Part III Web sites, then you can go back to the Part I and II sites and search for a new story that is covered on all sites.

2. What can you conclude about our information system and citizen access to information from comparing these stories?

3. What questions are raised in your mind about our news, news sources, and media bias that you might want to learn more about or do additional research on?

Note to Instructors: While you will be able to highlight many lessons to enhance media literacy by using this exercise, the most important lesson to highlight is the value of having more than one source of information, because this empowers students to see the spin and framing and begin to learn to make their own judgments.

Notes

Chapter One

1. These stories were condensed from Factcheck.org (November 4, 2006). Factcheck is a nonpartisan service provided by the Annenberg Public Policy Center at the University of Pennsylvania and one of the most valuable new resources available to help us understand the scope and bias of interested messages—private and public—distorting our information systems.

2. A recent nutrition study in the peer-reviewed, online journal *PLOS Medicine* found that studies funded by industry were eight times more likely than independent studies to generate findings favorable to industry (see http://www.medicine.plosjournals.org/perlserv/. In a press release from Corporate Accountability International, titled "Big Oil Follows in Footsteps of Big Tobacco," we see this phenomenon is not limited to foods we eat. The press release and supporting evidence can be found from the Union of Concerned Scientists at the two Web addresses at the end of this note. Interest groups representing the food industry successfully lobbied the House in March 2006 to approve legislation that prohibits states from requiring warnings on food labels beyond what is required in federal law (see "Food Industry Fights State Label Rules" 2007).

"For decades, the tobacco industry has misled the public about the dangers of smoking. One of its methods has been to challenge the overwhelming body of legitimate scientific evidence that smoking adversely affects health, and to fund questionable science of its own. Thanks to the ongoing support of activists like you, we have exposed the underhanded tactics of corporations like Philip Morris/Altria and put pressure on Congress to reject Big Tobacco's claims. Now, the oil industry is following the tobacco industry's lead by casting doubt on the facts about global warming. The industry has spent millions of dollars funding a few climate change skeptics whose 'science' has helped spread uncertainty about global warming." http://www. stopcorporateabusenow.org/campaign/bigoil; http://www.ucsusa.org/.

3. Our point here is rather simple. We are not arguing that American history is most accurately seen as one unbroken road to prosperity for all but using Phillips to demonstrate that one commonly articulated perspective on how politics has actually worked in American history is entirely inconsistent with the best available data. Those advancing this perspective, what Phillips

calls right utopianism, seek to mislead the rest of us into believing that the free market has worked best (that is, has been most productive, independent of the separate question of how the surplus generated has been distributed) when there has been little to no government intervention or regulation. This is not now, and never has been, an empirically defensible proposition.

4. We would like to thank Lisa Miller for her very thoughtful feedback on early draft chapters that included a discussion about the commodification of political discourse.

5. See Fiorina (2006), who argues persuasively that while culture wars—a deeply polarized red and blue state electorate—are represented as just common sense, as our prevailing conventional wisdom, the concept is also inconsistent with the best available data. Further, these inaccurate yet widely shared notions are neither neutral nor accidental. The concept is based on a misinterpretation of election and public opinion data, "systematic and self-serving misrepresentation by issue activists, and selective coverage by an uncritical media" (8). According to Fiorina, American elites are more polarized, and more polarizing, but "their hatreds and battles are not shared by the great mass of American people . . . who are for the most part moderate in their views and tolerant in their manner" (8).

6. See Bennett (1996), *News: The Politics of Illusion*.

7. See Mendelberg (1997) "Executing Hortons: Racial Crime in the 1988 Presidential Campaign" and (2001) *The Race Card: Campaign Strategy, Implicit Messages, and The Norm of Equality* for data on amplifying racist attitudes with law-and-order rhetoric. Using race as an analytical category for crime or welfare analysis is also contrary to well-known evidence that race does not determine criminality or work ethic, as explained by Conley (2000), for instance, documenting that for whites and blacks *with the same wealth* we observe that graduation rates, work hours, income levels, level of participation in welfare, and crime rates are either the same, or that blacks perform better than whites. See Conley "The Racial Wealth Gap: Origins and Implications for Philanthropy in the African-American Community." See also Chiricos, Welch, and Gertz (2004) on the racial typification of crime.

8. This is not just lying, though it might include this. More importantly, it is systematic phoniness that manifests a willingness to fake the context as well, what Frankfurt (2005) calls bullshit, some (often approvingly) call spin, and others call PR.

9. Sometimes leaders leak the story to one source and then refer back to this source as independent confirmation of the credibility of the news story. See Moyers (2007) for a detailed analysis of this tactic.

10. A 2004 study, however, claims that while campaign ads are described by one Madison Avenue pioneer as "the most deceptive, misleading, unfair and untruthful of all advertising" (Freedman et al. 2004, 724), they actually teach and inform citizens. But their evidence of learning was that they found a small increase in already anemic levels of awareness of the candidates' name. This is hardly evidence of teaching, learning, or even just being better informed.

11. Recent discussion of a "decoy effect" identifies clear incentives to both fake the context and to confuse citizens. See Vedantam (2007).

12. There is likely no need to defend or explain the importance of data for the kind of serious inquiry that has driven science and the free market, resulting in standards of living and ways of understanding our world today that were unimaginable to our ancestors. But it is also a core constitutive element of living in a democratic society where we struggle to replace private violence and superstition with public law and deliberations. And even at our best colleges, we struggle to persuade our students that, while data never speaks for itself, we cannot come to reasonable and shared agreements without relying heavily on the difficult work of producing and examining the best available data. In Light's path-breaking ten-year study of what accounts for student success at Harvard, he found that students report that challenging homework assignments that require collaboration to complete increase both their learning and their engagement in the class. Light found that it was critical for success that students learn that *sustained* work is necessary to accomplish anything—that, in fact, this is what *develops* self-confidence and self-esteem, and that faculty mentors and advisors need to model this and in their assignments teach students the value and skill of perseverance in the face of the difficult personal and academic challenges we all face as a part of our daily lives. A "failure to dig in and engage with one piece of work in depth for hours at a time is hurting students enormously" (Light 2001, 37) and must be addressed as a critical time management issue, as a challenge to teach students what hard work means in an academic environment, and as a challenge to prepare students to become free citizens in a democratic society.

13. In chapter 4 we will address postmodern positions that put pressure on our defense of data and agency and acknowledge the power of the postmodern critique without wallowing in it.

14. See Barabas (2004) on the preconditions for democratic deliberation.

Chapter Two

1. See Bogle (2005), *The Battle for the Soul of Capitalism*, especially pp. 13, 20, 22, 25–27.

2. The linkage of market and electoral techniques is not new (see Fiorina 2006; McGinniss 1988; Rich 2005b), but it does add a dimension to understanding the impact of sound-bite saboteurs that highlights the complex relationship between leaders and (potentially) mobilized publics.

3. While Schor (2004) does not add the rapid commercialization of religious activities that has followed changes in FCC regulations to enable televangelism and its gospel of prosperity, we suggest that this might also be part of the phenomena (see Hedges 2007, though we find comparing the religious Right to fascism both historically and conceptually suspect, we nevertheless find Hedges's argument useful for connecting to the more nuanced arguments in Schor). On regulatory changes at the FCC—and the

politics behind them—see both Brock (2004) and Robert Kennedy (2005). Both outline in detail a dynamic remarkably similar to the interest-group-driven effort to substitute branded information for news and use it as the basis for interested public policy making.

4. See Svehla (2001), "Philosopher-Kings and Teacher-Researchers: The Charge of Anti-intellectualism in Composition's Theory Wars," pp. 388–90.

5. Of course, some of these things are also having a negative impact on our society, especially as they interact with and may be, in part, the product of consumer culture. Prayer in school or the desire for it, for instance, can be seen as a kind of groping resistance to commercialism, a desire for something deeper and more meaningful than consumption, a misplaced anger at the growing superficiality and vulgarity of our culture. People in favor of school prayer might not always be primarily interested in religious imposition but in something to counteract a culture that is harming their children, though this is an empirical question beyond the scope of our inquiry in this book. So while one might disagree with school prayer as a remedy (see it as misguided, misplaced, or dangerous), one can still empathize with the motivation of at least some of those who seek this remedy. However, our point is about how a public discourse that focuses our attentions away from the roles and responsibilities of leadership—including private-sector leaders driving our consumer culture—is both aggravating the challenges we face and confusing our efforts to understand these challenges, deliberate about them, and productively problem solve.

6. Philip Morris gave more than $9 million to political parties from 1995 to 2002. AOL gave $4 million, Disney gave $3.6 million, and Coke gave $2.3 million. "Two decades of corporate monies have eroded the regulatory, legislative, and judicial environment, making it far harder to protect children" (Schor 2004, 29).

7. In an interesting analysis of *The Daily Show*, Baumgartner and Morris (2006) find that our children are increasingly distrustful of public- and private-sector leadership, though those who watch *The Daily Show* (compared to those watching regular news) are more likely to both be better informed and more confident in their own capacity to understand our political culture. We see this as strong contemporary evidence that Edelman (1988) got it right when he noted that the antidote for politics as spectacle will come from the cultural sphere, as we discuss in depth in chapter 5.

8. See Boyte (1992), "The Critic Critiqued."

9. Before Lewis Powell became one of President Nixon's nominees for the U.S. Supreme Court, he wrote a very passionate memo for the Chamber of Commerce, arguing that the business community needed to use its superior resources and access to develop its own information system by funding new think tanks, supporting journalists and television networks, building publishing houses to support conservative scholars, and coordinating an assault on the liberal bias in the press, campus liberals, and anyone critical of the free market. You can read this memo at http://www.reclaimdemocracy.org/corporate_accountability/powell_memo_lewis.html.

10. As noted in chapter 1, right utopian is a term we draw from conservative analyst Kevin Phillips, who argues that while we are all familiar with utopianism on the Left, we ought to also beware of this same malady when it appears on the Right. He contrasts it with liberal "utopias of social justice, brotherhood, and peace," arguing that "the repetitious abuses by conservatives in the United States in turn involve worship of markets (the utopianism of the Right), elevation of self-interest rather than community, and belief in Darwinian precepts such as survival of the fittest" (2002, xxi). He also demonstrates historically, in *Wealth and Democracy*, that while the wealthy often speak as if they prefer no government involvement in the private sector as envisioned by the laissez-faire notions embedded in right utopianism, their behavior reveals a decidedly contrary perspective, as our history shows clearly that the rich have not shunned government involvement in the private sector but have sought it and benefited enormously from it. While we prefer right utopian (see also Barber 2003 for similar analysis), the more commonly used term today might be *neoliberal*, which is generally used to refer to those who at least say they believe in the positive value of unfettered market forces. Political labels can be confusing, since the so-called neocons today are actually neoliberals in the sense that they are also likely to favor a return to neoclassical liberalism, meaning an unfettered free market.

11. It is possible that neoscholarly might be more accurate than quasischolarly, particularly given Veyne (1988). Think tanks can be seen as rival new universities, where scholars no longer write only or even primarily for scholarly communities, but specifically for larger publics, meaning that the standards of professional achievement differ, as the audience differs.

12. And more recently, funding their own private armies as well, further demonstrating our point that their efforts are about more than selling a product. They seek to sell a worldview and to use their superior resources in a coordinated effort to accomplish this, with initiatives ranging from think tanks to special forces. See Scahill (2007) *Blackwater: The Rise of the World's Most Powerful Mercenary Army.*

13. American Enterprise Institute, Heritage Foundation, Cato Institute, Competitive Enterprise Institute, Manhattan Institute, Hudson Institute, to name a few, funded by the Coors, Olin, Bradley, Smith Richardson, Prince, and Scaiffe family fortunes.

14. Of course, there is also something more insidious going on when sound bites are constructed to defraud and dispirit, to re-present the cognitive landscape in a way that makes turning away in disgust perhaps another form of "rational ignorance," or what Hancock (2004) referred to more recently as *The Politics of Disgust.*

15. See Barabas (2004) for a thoughtful and representative discussion of the preconditions for deliberation.

16. The court in *Kitzmiller v. Dover* is highly critical of the ongoing and intentional nature of this type of fakery, especially notable in this case, since one goal of ID proponents is the Truth. You can read the court's decision at http://www.pamd.uscourts.gov/kitzmiller/kitzmiller_342.pdf.

17. Bogle (2005) argues that the "fabulous compensation paid to corporate chief executives," particularly in the counterproductive form of fixed-price stock options, created a cult of individual celebrity managers, and he calculates that corporate management can "claim responsibility for an extra return of only 1.2% per year." He concludes that the data show that CEOs "failed to create value" despite the explosion of compensation (17–18). CEO compensation was 42 times that of the average worker in 1980, 280 times in 2004 (xx). It peaked at 531 times in 2000 (17). While CEO compensation grew 8.5 percent a year from 1980 to 2004, not including the large perks included in compensation, average worker salary grew only 0.3 percent. The collapse of Enron deleted $65 billion from the economy; WorldCom lost $165 billion (20).

18. Managerial capitalism is capitalism run to profit managers instead of the owners (stockholders). Managerial capitalism, according to Bogle (2005), combines the worst elements of planned economies and free markets: it is inefficient managerialism that, like communist states, encourages the misreporting of productivity data at the firm level, and it also lacks any linkage to a public trough, iron rice bowl, or public interested stewardship. It encourages a perverse concentration of wealth that is "antithetical to the long-term stability of our society" (7). The usual gatekeepers—legislators, regulators, rating services, attorneys, public accountants, and, most importantly, corporate directors—failed to anticipate and prevent the "profound conflicts of interest" that are omnipresent in corporate leadership, encouraging and enabling corporate managers to ignore the interests of the owners—the stockholders (xxi).

19. According to Bogle (2005), the commonly heard claim that fixed-price stock options will link management interest to shareholder interest, while widespread as a rationale, is a "bromide" that turns out to be false, while "creating unworthy centimillionaires" and "eliminating rewards even for worthy performers" (15–16). Further, what came to be euphemistically called "managed earnings" is, in Bogle's view, institutionalized misinformation. Quarterly guidance projections do not provide data that investors can depend on to make informed decisions. Managed earnings are premised on "rarely reporting earnings that disappoint" and instead constructing an "illusion . . . to inflate the stock price" (xviii, xx). Bogle describes managed earnings as "sleight of hand financial engineering" that encouraged, for instance, unstable short-term speculation and the widespread manipulation of pension funds (25–27). These and other distortions of information resulted in 1,570 publicly owned firms restating their financial statements since the crash (22).

20. We are using anti-intellectualism here to refer to the elite amplified hostility to data, deliberation, and serious thinking and not to power-poor challenges of the elite's efforts to use expertise to insulate themselves from critical public scrutiny that can sometimes be mischaracterized as anti-intellectual.

21. See Bakhtin (1981), *The Dialogic Imagination*, for another reinterpretation and application of Kantian ideas.

22. Most of us live as what Kuhn (1970) called "normal scientists," working out the puzzles—addressing the conflicts—made salient by conventional wisdoms thought of as the prevailing norms regarding the ways we arrive at truths, determine the best available knowledge, and construct the critically

important background consensus sometimes reified as common sense, but actually referring to ongoing processes more likely comprehensible from a communicative action perspective.

23. Part of our argument, building on Gramsci (1971) (for instance, his discussion of the village priest as a public intellectual) and, more recently, on Haltom and McCann (2004), contends that there is today a need for scholars to return to ancient practices of speaking to multiple communities.

24. While Democratic Party leaders cannot persuasively dismiss the charge that they are elites (see Greider 1992), it remains difficult to refute that, when compared to the alternative, the traditional Democratic Party *positions* are far more attentive to the concrete needs of average Americans seeking living-wage jobs, retirement security, quality public schools, safe food, clean air, and drinkable water. At the same time, exploding campaign contributions—in an age when old and new media have increased the cost of campaigning dramatically—clearly demonstrate that the leadership of both parties remains beholden to competing and somewhat overlapping coalitions of largely corporate, traditional interest groups. Open Secrets provides voluminous data on campaign contributions, and for the 2004 election cycle we see that the top five strongly Democratic contributors were Emily's List, Labor Unions, the IBOEW, and the University of California, while the top five Republican contributors were the National Association of Auto Dealers, UPS, Merrill Lynch, the National Beer Wholesalers Association, and the National Association of Home Builders. Interestingly, however, we also see that five of the top twenty contributors—all corporate—gave to both parties: National Association of Realtors gave $3.8 million (48 percent to Democrats, 52 percent to Republicans), JP Morgan Chase gave $3.1 million (53 percent to Democrats, 48 percent to Republicans), Citigroup gave $2.9 million (51 percent to Democrats, 49 percent to Republicans), Bank of America gave $2.7 million (47 percent to Democrats, 53 percent to Republicans), and General Electric gave $2.3 million (47 percent to Democrats, 53 percent to Republicans). See http://www.opensecrets.org/bigpicture/topcontribs.asp?cycle=2004.

25. Dye and Zeigler (2006) argue persuasively that the key division in American politics is not between Democrats and Republicans but between party elites and the rest of us. The "irony of American democracy," as they call it, is that it takes wise elite leadership for democracy to work. Of course, this caricature cuts both ways, since sound-bite saboteurs are trying, and for a time succeeding, to victimize red staters (constructing this as a meaningful category) by getting them to internalize and embrace the implied caricature of their own selves as gun-wielding, Bible-thumping, hard-headed hicks who would rather wallow in the muck than read a book.

26. We are reminded of an episode from Michael Moore's short-lived network television show *TV Nation* where, floating on a recreational lake made possible by federal tax dollars in Gingrich's Georgian district, he sees his crowd diminish as he moves from vague chants of "get the government off our backs" (where cheers were passionate and the crowd grew) to chants of "drain this federally subsidized lake" (where cheers dissipated, and the crowd began to thin).

27. For many Americans, of course, the stem cell debate is not a life-style debate—any more than the pro-choice/pro-life debate is about lifestyle. But Frank (2004) does not imply this, as we read him; rather, these issues, in and through concepts such as culture wars, are *framed* as lifestyle issues, as "us against them," and it is this distraction, this interested construction of a divided populace, that concerns us here.

28. On concentrated disadvantage, see Sampson and Bartusch (1998). See also Davis 1998; Lyons and Drew 2006; and Clear et al. 2003.

29. See Schlosser's (2002) *Fast Food Nation* and Smith's (2003) *Seeds of Deception* for a much more detailed analysis of the linkages between our disappearing family farms and this larger, long-term, and bipartisan mise-ducation process.

30. Schlosser (2002) demonstrates how this bait-and-switch technique is manifest in individual hypocrisy as well. He documents in detail how private-sector leaders, such as Walt Disney and Ray Kroc, repeatedly (and with a single-mindedness that suggests they considered it an entitlement) sought and secured government preferences (tax breaks, subsidies, legislative insulation from liability, and union busting support, among other forms), even as they both built public personas with passionate rhetoric about the evils of government involvement in the private sector. Krugman's (2005a–e) analysis of our stalled efforts to address the health care crisis highlights the role that ideological blinders play in this process: despite having the most privatized and lowest-quality health care system among the G7 (and with more government dollars per capital spent on health care in the United States than in Canada), our right-utopian devotion to all things privatized stubbornly insists that these inconvenient facts are obstacles to doing the right thing, resulting in a Medicare drug plan that has actually found a way to make the situation worse for elderly and tax-paying ordinary Americans. In one of Krugman's most powerful arguments in this series, he points out further that the ideological blinders preventing affordable health care in the United States also, when compared to allies such as France, support a combination of policies that results in Americans working 200 to 300 more hours a year, taking fewer vacations or sick days to spend with family, and other similar consequences that allow Krugman to make a strong case that our policy choices are both irrational and anti-family.

31. For discussions of such moral panics, see Hall et al. (1978), *Policing the Crisis: Mugging, the State, and Law and Order*, and Pearson (1983) *Hooligan: A History of Respectable Fears*. For a discussion of governing through crime as a more routine form of this phenomenon, see Simon (2007) *Governing through Crime: How the War on Crime Transformed American Democracy and Created a Culture of Fear*.

32. As Wittgenstein (1937) argues, perennial questions are more useful for keeping philosophers employed than for focusing our intellectual efforts on living: "The way to solve the problem you see in life is to live in a way that will make what is problematic disappear" (27).

33. Iyengar and Kinder (1987) find that television news plays a strong agenda-setting role (when broadcasts highlight a problem, viewers are more likely to list the problem as a priority), influencing the standards that citizens use to evaluate leaders (what they call the priming effect), and, therefore, that the power of mass communication "appears to rest not on persuasion but on commanding the public's attention (agenda setting) and defining the criteria underlying the public's judgments (priming)" (117).

The ability of the mass media to influence both the questions we will debate and the standards we bring to evaluating leadership and policy debates "depends not only on the message, but also on the audience. . . . Agenda-setting was greatest among those viewers with limited political skills and interests. In contrast, television news primes the politically involved just as effectively as it does the politically withdrawn. Involvement offers resources against agenda-setting [determining which questions to debate], but no protection against priming" [determining which issues we will focus on in evaluating leadership] (95). More personalized news primes more effectively (82). Repetition is more effective for priming than a single, concentrated exposure (72), which may account for the difficulty we have persuading our students of the importance of intensive study.

Citizens do not pay attention to everything, thus the importance of themes and frames. Further, "people ordinarily prefer heuristics—intuitive shortcuts and simple rules of thumb. One such heuristic is reliance on information that is most accessible" (64). At the same time, the ability of mass media to set the agenda "waxes and wanes with changes in politics. Events that weaken partisanship, interest, and participation reduce the resources the public could otherwise draw upon to resist television news influence" (62), thus making it easier to divert, distract, and dissipate their energies and highlighting the importance of grassroots work as public education.

So in amplifying one conflict over others, leadership can impact the standards we use in evaluating their leadership, which means that securing issue salience is also an investment in a starting point for deliberations over a wider range of issues, increasing the political value of a presidential bully pulpit and suggesting ways that parallel clusters of ideas are linked. If we establish national defense or punishing street crime as the standard, then we are likely to favor candidates or policies we might oppose had we established living wage jobs or affordable health care as the standard. Iyengar and Kinder find that "those with fewer political resources [party identification and political involvement] are swayed most by the network agenda" (59). "The verdict is clear and unequivocal. . . . By attending to some problems and ignoring others, television news shapes the American public's political priorities" (33). See also Glassner (1999), *The Culture of Fear.*

34. And the radical revolutionary nature of their right-utopian business allies is similarly made clear by simply reading their statements, starting with the now-famous Chamber of Commerce memo written by Lewis Powell just before he was elevated to serve on the Supreme Court. Jimmy Carter's 2006

book, *Our Endangered Values*, and John Danforth's 2006 book, *Faith and Politics*, both argue similarly, from opposite sides of the aisle, that the current form of religious influence on politics is anti-intellectual and a threat to American democracy. See also Hedges 2007.

35. See also Farsetta and Price (2006) from the Center for Media and Democracy on "Fake News" at http://www.prwatch.org.

36. See also Herman 2005.

37. Please note that describing conflicts over posting the Ten Commandments as fundamentally more trivial than living wage jobs is not the same as describing the Ten Commandments themselves as trivial. We are not saying that the Ten Commandments are trivial, but that fighting over posting them in a courthouse is a divisive distraction from addressing more broad-based, arguably more serious problems that destroy good jobs, undermine family values, and weaken communities. Further, it is entirely possible that some, perhaps many, Americans believe that our leaders' time is best spent fighting over posting the Ten Commandments in our courthouses. But we see no evidence that this is a widely held view among average Americans, since the data consistently highlight how serious and pragmatic most Americans are about family and community.

Chapter Three

1. This narrative account of the Stella Liebeck story is based on the highly recommended and very detailed analysis found in Haltom and McCann's (2004) *Distorting the Law*, especially chapters 5 and 6.

2. Clearly an amount equaling the profit of two days' coffee sales is neither a burden nor a punishment for McDonalds Corporation; instead, the value emphasizes the logic and reasonableness of the jury decision to award punitive damages in this case. Since McDonalds is not going to feel the pinch of compensatory damages, punitive damages are a way to get their attention, not to punish them, since it is possibly, if not probably, cheaper to litigate and pay the occasional award than to actually correct the problem.

3. According to Haltom and McCann's analysis of editorials, letters to the editor, and other feature accounts, "information pertaining to the litigiousness of the plaintiff drew the most sentences of any category, despite that category's having elicited not a single mention in the spot [news] coverage ... and despite the defense having presented no evidence that an octogenarian who had never before sued anyone was trifling with McDonalds or trying to pull a fast one" (2004, 207–208).

4. While there are no guarantees, Schattschneider (1975) productively focuses our attention on strategies (inviting an analysis of dynamics and the mechanisms through which power operates rather than creating a standard that is based on favored substantive outcomes) that can be deployed by individual citizens, interest groups, political parties, journalists, or government agents of any partisan persuasion. Further, even as the public has

grown more dubious of governmental agency (sometimes with good reason, as in response to the Hurricane Katrina disaster), publicizing or socializing our approach to conflict remains one strategy that can strengthen the hand of the weaker disputant and can offer at least the potential of greater and more representative democratic participation. At the same time, recent work by Lisa Miller (2007) argues that enlarging the scope of a conflict can also "result in new frames that are actually narrower than the old ones." This suggests (consistent with our analysis here) that while the analytical distinction highlighting strategic calculations and struggles over privatizing and publicizing our approaches to conflicts remains productive, it is neither the case that privatized nor publicized approaches are always superior, more democratic, or even more likely to strengthen the hand of the weaker disputant. Miller goes on, regarding her analysis of crime control politics, to note that "as the crime issue is broadened to include state-wide or nation-wide constituencies, the social problem origins of criminal violence atrophy, and what remains is simply the individual pathology of lawbreakers" (313).

5. Today it would be fair to say that this vision focuses on more exclusive and more extreme forms of punishment and more unilateralist approaches to national defense. While today this is a result of the particular elite faction holding power at this time, this extremist episode does not alter the notion that one long-standing vision of limited government in the United States highlights the need to minimize government regulation of the free market and support government action against street crime and in our national defense. Notice, however, that this vision, in its current form, does not highlight a need to minimize government intervention in the private sector generally, since the currently dominant leadership faction is also keen on increasing government restrictions on gay marriage, federal control over education, and conservative forms of judicial activism (see Cohen 2007 on judicial activism).

6. Danner (2007) notes in reference to Karl Rove's use of sound-bite sabotage that "The object has become subject and we have a fanatical follower of Foucault in the Oval Office." He argues that this "radical attitude" where Rove is quoted by Suskind bragging about "creating their own reality" by saturating communication channels with their particular vision of limited government to mislead those who mistakenly believe they live in the real world "is brilliantly encapsulated in a single sentence drawn from the National Security Strategy of the United States of 2003: 'Our strength as a nation-state will continue to be challenged by those who employ a strategy of the weak using international *fora*, judicial processes and terrorism.' Let me repeat that little troika of 'weapons of the weak': international *fora* (meaning the United Nations and like institutions), judicial processes (meaning courts, domestic and international), and . . . terrorism. This strange gathering, put forward by the government of the United States, stems from the idea that power is, in fact, everything. In such a world, courts — indeed, law itself — can only limit the power of the most powerful state. Wielding preponderant power, what need has it for law? The latter must be, by definition, a weapon of the weak. The most powerful state, after all, *makes* reality" (emphasis in original).

7. See Arendt (1999), "Excerpt from On Violence."

8. In a very thoughtful analysis of this dynamic in the global warming debate, Shnayerson points out that saboteurs need only provide a quotable sound bite that insinuates that the question is highly controversial: "With those doubts neatly planted in the press, the public shrugs, politicians push the problem off to another day, and ExxonMobil parries new fossil-fuel regulations, earning more windfall profits in exchange for a pittance to the skeptics and their work" for think tanks that depend on ExxonMobil funding (2007, 144).

9. We use "the news" here because of its central importance, though it would be more accurate to say our information system, since our analysis is clearly not limited to the news. Further, we are sensitive to the fact that new and old media are also different, and that the differences in new media raise important questions about how agency regarding framing is being (re)distributed today and about the degree to which the value and power of socio-cognitive abilities such as framing (at least in its old media, largely textual, form) are substantively transformed by new media privileging of image making often decoupled from language. Since these clearly complicate our argument, we can only take them on one piece at a time, so our analysis of the particular impact of new media, while informing our analysis here, is developed more fully in chapter 4.

10. While this list is meant to be illustrative and thought provoking, the displacing of place to race may confuse some readers. For those interested in this particular example, see Meehan and Ponder (2002), who provide empirical support for their contention that, in the case they study, despite police rhetoric about focusing on place (which would be a progressive form of policing), police tactics continued to focus on race. See also Clear et al. (2003), Fagan and Davies (2000); Chiricos, Welch, and Gertz (2004); Sampson and Bartusch (1998); and Wacquant (2001).

11. Whether amplification of any particular conflict serves an end we like or do not like is not our point. It is that we must be aware of this amplification process in order to participate more effectively in politics. Further, we are not suggesting that we just become more skilled at sound-bite sabotage or encourage allies to better use the techniques we identify with sound-bite sabotage in service of ideological or partisan ends we favor. This would simply expand the distortion and anti-intellectualism we are critical of in the manuscript. We need to be aware of this strategic struggle over amplifying some conflicts and muting others in order to participate in ways that will sow doubt to increase clarity, expose hypocrisy, reveal how power and politics work, base problem solving on the best available data, and support more engaged forms of cynicism, citizenship, and democratic deliberation.

12. Building on our reference to Danner in note 6 of this chapter, he helps us distinguish engaged cynicism (subject aspiring to be subject, to agency) from the distorted cynicism or symbolic cynicism or sound-bite repackaged cynicism to mobilize a war on criticism, expertise, and serious thought (subject as object, and agency poor, a subject only in the story more powerful agents

have saturated communication channels with in their efforts to "create their own reality," as Rove describes it in the Suskind piece cited by Danner).

13. As the argument in Chapters 2 and 3 highlights, this anti-intellectualism is neither a strictly private- nor public-sector problem, nor is it an entirely partisan phenomenon, though Shogan argues that "due to the amplified importance of forging an intimate connection with the American public, modern presidents must adjust their political personalities and leadership. To combat allegations of elitism, recent Republican presidents have adopted anti-intellectualism as a conservative form of populism. Anti-intellectualism is defined as disparagement of the complexity associated with intellectual pursuits and a rejection of the elitism and self-aware attitude of distinction that is commonly associated with intellectual life" (295).

14. Shnayerson highlights that this dynamic is well known to elite leaders when he reminds us that two U.S. Senators (Rockefeller, D-WV, and Snow, R-ME) recently asked the ExxonMobil CEO to "cease and desist from its global-warming-denial campaign" (2007, 162).

15. Christie (1977); Schattschneider (1975); Sennett (1970); Simon (2007).

16. For a powerful analysis indicating that this is more myth than reality, see Alterman (2003); Bennett (1996); and Brock (2004).

17. Information taken from throughout Brock's (2004) *The Republican Noise Machine* and Alterman's (2003) *What Liberal Media?*.

18. Evidence? "Given the success of *Fox News*, the *Wall Street Journal*, the *Washington Times, New York Post, American Spectator, Weekly Standard, New York Sun, National Review, Commentary*, and so on, no sensible person can dispute the existence of a 'conservative media' " (Alterman 2003, 9). Further, while there is also a liberal media, it is smaller than assumed. Liberal publications all employ and publish some of the most conservative commentators. *The Nation*, one of the most liberal publications, includes regular columns from liberal haters such as Christopher Hitchens and Alexander Cockburn. The *New York Times* features extreme conservative William Safire and conservative David Brooks as core commentators. The *Washington Post* is the home for George Will, Robert Novak, and Charles Krauthammer, among many other major conservative leaders. Somewhat liberal Web sites, such as *Salon* or *Slate*, feature the extremist and nearly always negative rantings of Andrew Sullivan and David Horowitz and Charles Murray and Elliot Abrams. While few would include CNN on a list of liberal media sources, if you do include it we find that its central commentators include Robert Novak, William Bennett, Kate O'Beirne and Jonah Goldberg (*National Review*), David Brooks and Tucker Carlson (*Weekly Standard*), and Ann Coulter and Pat Robertson. ABC? John Stossel, George Will, and Cokie Roberts. *Time* or *Newsweek*? Will and Krauthammer. But leading conservative publications do not similarly share their platform with leading liberal analysts. In fact, the more thoughtful liberal analysts rarely get any national coverage, and those liberals who do are among the most conservative liberal voices available (this endnote paraphrases Alterman 2003, 8–12).

19. It should be noted here that while Krugman (2005a–e) is helping us expose sound-bite sabotage on the Right, his dismissal of the Social Security crisis can be seen as sound-bite sabotage on the Left as well.

20. In this second *New York Times* commentary, Krugman provides some numbers to support this claim. "In 2002, the latest year for which comparable data are available, the United States spent $5,267 on health care for each man, woman and child in the population. Of this, $2,364, or 45 percent, was government spending, mainly on Medicare and Medicaid. Canada spent $2,931 per person, of which $2,048 came from the government. France spent $2,736 per person, of which $2,080 was government spending. Amazing, isn't it? U.S. health care is so expensive that our government spends more on health care than the governments of other advanced countries, even though the private sector pays a far higher share of the bills than anywhere else. What do we get for all that money? Not much. Most Americans probably don't know that we have substantially lower life-expectancy and higher infant-mortality figures than other advanced countries" (2005d).

21. See Lewis Powell's memo for the Chamber of Commerce for the full text and analysis at http://www.reclaimdemocracy.org/corpporate_account-ability/powell_memo_lewis.html, written immediately before he was elevated to the U.S. Supreme Court. We do not wish to suggest that deliberation alone will resolve all the problems we face. Surely various types of resource inequities must be central to any sober analysis, but we start with deliberation because it is a foundational decision-making process essential to any productive addressing of the conflicts we face.

22. "A major source of stability in political systems is the distribution of intensities of preferences. At any single time, a political system may feature many areas of privileged access to decision making, allowing powerful economic interests to secure advantageous treatment from the policy making system" (Baumgartner and Jones 1993, 19).

23. See Dye and Zeigler (2006).

24. See also Zipp and Fenwick (2006) on what the data show about liberal bias in the academy.

25. See Fish (2001), "Thoughts on September 11–October 15, 2001—Condemnation without Absolutes."

26. Hofstadter (1963) notes that American anti-intellectualism is "older than our national identity" (6). He further notes that part of the political utility of anti-intellectualism is that "its very vagueness makes it more serviceable in controversy as an epithet." At the same time, this trend mobilizes a "resentment and suspicion of the life of the mind and of those who are considered to represent it; and a disposition to constantly minimize the value of that life." Among elites it is traditionally associated with conservative business and religious leaders who are suspicious of "experts" outside of their control and hostile to universities because they house experts (12). Hofstadter quotes the Reverand Billy Graham, saying, "You can stick a public school and a university in the middle of every block of every city in America and you will never keep America from rotting morally by mere intellectual education" (15).

The leaders interested in amplifying American "ambivalence about intellect and intellectuals" are themselves not uneducated, "but rather the marginal intellectuals, would-be intellectuals, unfrocked or embittered intellectuals" (21). David Horowitz comes to mind today, but Hofstadter reminds us that "anti-intellectualism is usually the incidental consequence of some other intention, often some justifiable intention," and he points to "progressive education" as one such intention that included a "strong anti-intellectual element" within it (22). Hofstadter argues that anti-intellectualism has become an entrenched and a widely shared aspect of American culture. "It first got its strong grip on our ways of thinking because it was fostered by an evangelical religion that also purveyed many humane and democratic sentiments. It made its way into our politics because it became associated with our passion for equality. It has become formidable in our education partly because our educational beliefs are evangelically egalitarian" (23).

27. See chapter 6, for our complication of the phrase "these same tools," especially as it relates to rhetorical tools.

28. In the misinformation, for instance, from the still widely used four basic food groups (no scientific basis) to the interest group watered-down food pyramid, to the fast-food culture analyzed in *Fast Food Nation* and genetically modified foods analyzed in *Seeds of Deception*, we see this power used to dissipate public energies through misinformation that displaces a sober focus on agents causing enormous harm. De Luca and Buell (2005) point to the bipartisan and single-issue nature of sound-bite sabotage in reference to the 2004 elections: With America's young men and women dying in Iraq, North Korea rattling its nuclear saber, insufficient living wage jobs, rising inequality, and declining health care coverage the campaigns both focused on Vietnam. "Incredibly, medals he [Kerry] won under fire became the venue for a renewed Republican attack on the purported military and moral weakness of Democrats. Meanwhile, without a hint of irony, some Democrats attacked Bush for finding a way to avoid combat in a war many of them loathed, and themselves avoided, at the time" (1).

29. Narrowcasting, a private-sector marketing technique now commonly used in campaigns (to sell candidates or policies), refers to tailoring and targeting different messages for different audiences, one spin to mobilize soccer moms and another to mobilize corporate contributors, for instance. Lisa Miller's (2007) recent analysis of Schattschneider provides useful guidance on the importance of this phenomena. She analyzes neighborhood crime debates and finds that, white or black, those residents living closer to crime similarly mobilize "pragmatic concerns about what can be done." She concludes that her renewed attention to the importance of proximity to conflict expansion, displacement, and framing, while recognized by Schattschneider, reveals "that enlarging a conflict's scope can sometimes result in new frames that are actually narrower than the old ones. As the crime problem is broadened to include state-wide or nation-wide constituencies, the social problem origins of criminal violence atrophy and what remains is simply the individual pathology of lawbreakers." Targeted narrowcasting depends on PR experts'

willingness and ability to fake the context, and her findings on proximity, complexity, and conflict expansion make it clear that "as we move away from the context in which complex social problems occur, it becomes difficult to sustain the problem's complexity and simplistic policy frames overtake the more nuanced ones" (20-21).

30. Tim Weiner (2006), "Must We Destroy the CIA to Save It?" reprinted from the *New York Times* in the *Akron Beacon Journal*, emphasis added. Shiller's (2000) widely cited analysis, *Irrational Exuberance*, similarly documents the profound impacts of a distorted information system on the heart and soul of the free market, in the bursting of the dot-com bubble and, perhaps as we write, the real estate bubble. Shiller argues that our information system is distorted, in part by a psychological feedback loop that is perpetuated by favorable media coverage that justifies more favorable coverage, which is part of the dynamic we will unpack with the work of Haltom and McCann (2004) later in this chapter.

31. It might be more accurate to call this an elite or even a commodification bias, since while reporters do privilege official statements as authoritative, our examination of sound-bite sabotage reveals that it is not only public-sector elites who have captured the standing to speak with this type of authority. Increasingly, nonelected interested agents mobilizing branded information, with funding and access advantages, are treated as authoritative.

32. Bennett 1996, ch. 2, 37–77.

33. In the McDonalds coffee case, for instance, interviews with the actual jurors confirm their high levels of initial suspicion in that case (Haltom and McCann 2004, 194).

34. "Indeed, one business executive in a Washington, D.C., public relations and lobbying firm advised that an effective challenge to trial lawyers was to "make Judith Haimes into as notorious a public figure as Willie Horton was in the 1988 presidential campaign" (Haltom and McCann 2004, 4, internal notes deleted).

35. Like Engle (1984), discussed earlier, the common sense that emerges from this saturation effort frames personal injury claims as inappropriate (litigation explosion), but not other legal claims, like contract claims, that are most often brought by the powerful against the power poor.

36. According to Brock (2004), the Manhattan Institute is under the leadership of Roger Hertog, "a very wealthy Wall Street money manager" and co-owner of both *The New Republic* magazine and the *New York Sun* newspaper, a paper "designed to circulate even more right-wing opinion in the Big Apple" (184). Brock explains that conservative leaders such as Newt Gingrich explicitly seek to "neutralize" the media to advance their policy platform, and to do this, at least initially, through a "radical deregulation of the media. The theoretical underpinnings of the maneuvers were laid out in the works of Rupert Murdoch adviser Irwin Stelzer, of AEI and the Hudson Institute; George Gilder, a 'senior fellow' of the Seattle-based Discovery Institute, author of the supply-side economics text *Wealth and Poverty*, and erstwhile *American Spectator* publisher; and Peter Huber, 'senior fellow' of the Manhattan Institute.

Huber [a close advisor to Gingrich] was especially influencial" (302). And Brock documents the extensive, revolving-door and nonmarket-driven synergies between think tanks such as the Manhattan Institute and major network news corporations as well. "The most visible on-air Fox News personalities were political and ideological partisans of a character rarely seen in professional news organizations. David Asman, a daytime anchor, had come from the *Wall Street Journal* editorial page and the Manhattan Institute." Brit Hume came from "the far right *American Spectator*," Tony Snow, the recent Bush White House communications director, came from the *Washington Times* (317). And there are also strong links to book publishing that are a part of this network. "In 2002, *Philanthropy* magazine, published by the right-wing Philanthropy Roundtable, ran a cover story titled 'Eight Books That Changed America,' written by John J. Miller, a writer for the *National Review* and 'Bradley fellow' at the Heritage Foundation. Each of the eight books was substantially underwritten by . . . the same four family foundations that supported the think tank network. According to *Philanthropy*, Myron Magnet's *The Dream and the Nightmare*, a repudiation of the 1960s, 'would not have been written without the Sarah Scaife Foundation, a supporter of the Manhattan Institute's book program in the early 1990s' " (353). The other three foundations referred to are Olin, Bradley, and Coors. The Manhattan Institute was also the infamous home for Charles Murray when he published *Losing Ground*, scholarship that was seriously challenged and yet "soon became the conventional wisdom in Reaganite policy circles," and later, *The Bell Curve*, "which misused statistics to argue that blacks are genetically inferior to whites" (47). The *New York Sun* is described by Brock, who built his career writing for right-wing publications, as a "subsidized . . . employment agency for conservative polemicists, including Peggy Noonan" (184). Similarly, Sun Myung Moon, "who opposes constitutional democracy and calls the United States 'the kingdom of Satan' " has run the *Washington Times* (the paper that President Reagan claimed was his favorite) at enormous losses (over $100 million so far) in order to legitimize extreme conservative views by ensuring they have a place at the center of policy debates (177–78).

37. Edelman notes that changes in the structure and power of the mass media in the past fifty years have invited more systematic attention to its more intentional use by the powerful. "Because more minds can be reached, governments and interest groups try harder to reach them" (1988, 122).

38. Game framing has been increasing dramatically, according to Lawrence, for several reasons. First, PR-style election campaigns that focus strategically on image (displacing other images and often, the argument goes, substance) encourage reporters to attend to every campaign move as the story for the day. Second, reporters seek to reveal strategy "as a defense mechanism against continually being 'spun' or, worse yet, against any perception that they are too easy on the politicians they cover." Third, celebrity journalism further enhances the journalistic bias toward preferring more dramatized angles on the news. Fourth, "treating politics like sports allows journalists to maintain an apparent stance of objectivity." Fifth, game framing allows journalists to

"claim a particular kind of expertise that does not require laborious research into the substance of complex policy debates." Sixth, all of these allow reporters easier ways to meet shorter deadlines in "an industry increasingly focused on the bottom line" (Lawrence 2000, 95).

39. This is a rich understanding of episodic news (often contrasted with thematic news), because episodes are not simply ad hoc or random here. They are (or can be) linked to larger dramas; they can be mobilized as a part of your own or someone else's movie and thus play more powerfully scripted political roles than merely random episodic coverage might suggest.

40. See Lakoff 2004 or Beckett 1997.

41. "Although this argument has become somewhat jaded, it is, as Sidney Verba argues, an important one—particularly in a system in which the economic power of big business is linked with the cultural power of public relations" (Lewis 2001, 26).

42. A recent study of brain activity while puzzling over a political problem found that the tendency to ignore the best available data is a distinctly nonpartisan habit, and, while sound-bite sabotage likely both exacerbates and exploits this dynamic, the study also highlighted one of the most important consequences of calculated information distortion. "None of the circuits involved in conscious reasoning were particularly engaged," according to the study's author. "Essentially, it appears as if partisans twirl the cognitive kaleidoscope until they get the conclusions they want, and then they get massively reinforced for it, with the elimination of negative emotional states and activation of positive ones." According to the *LiveScience* staff writer reporting on the study, the "brain imaging revealed a consistent pattern. Both Republicans and Democrats consistently denied obvious contradictions for their own candidate but detected contradictions in the opposing candidate." See "Democrats and Republicans Both Adept at Ignoring the Facts, Study Finds" (2006) at http://www.livescience.com/othernews/060124_political_decisions.html.

Chapter Four

We recognize that there really is no such thing as a singular academic discourse. Academic discourse is, of course, marked by multiplicity and fluidity. It is always already plural. However, for the purpose of this book, we are referring to the totality of discourses currently comprising academia, which the new media, as a movement, are challenging and expanding. See Elbow (1991), "Reflections on Academic Discourse: How It Relates to Freshman and Colleagues," and Harris (1989), "The Idea of Community in the Study of Writing."

1. See, for example, Kennedy (2005), "The Global Face of Nutrition."

2. While the new media, given their ever-changing natures, are notoriously difficult to define, we define new media as the relatively recent advent of electronic communication systems that have replaced or challenged

static text and pictures. Twenty-some years ago, this label would have been applied to such electronic communication systems as radio, television, cable, and satellite. We still include those systems in our definition of new media, but we now also include the *digital* communication systems that have arisen since the 1990s: the Internet, the World Wide Web, text messaging, blogs, talk radio, podcasts, e-mails, CD-ROMs, DVDs, streaming video, YouTube. com, video games, interactive media, and other forms of computer-enhanced communication. In short, our use of the term refers to a group of electronic-digital communication systems based, in part but not solely, on new information technology.

3. McLuhan and Powers (1989) made a comparable point almost twenty years ago in regard to the effect television has on student cognition and attitude. See their book *The Global Village: Transformations in World Life and Media in the 21st Century*, especially pp. 87–92.

4. See Edelman's *Constructing the Political Spectacle* for a consideration of the role new media and their manipulators play in creating "an impression of pluralist diversity" (1988, 122).

5. See especially Ong's (1962) *The Barbarian Within: And Other Fugitive Essays and Studies*, Postman's (1985) *Amusing Ourselves to Death: Public Discourse in the Age of Show Business*, Hirsch's (1987) *Cultural Literacy: What Every American Needs to Know*, Fisher's (1999) "Apocalypse Yesterday: Writing, Literacy, and the 'Threat' of 'Electronic Technology,' " Leonard's (1997) *Smoke and Mirrors: Violence, Television, and Other American Cultures*, Mittlin's (1999) "Pediatricians Suggest Limits on TV Viewing by Children," McAllister's (1996) *The Commercialization of American Culture: New Advertising, Control and Democracy*, Stephens' (1998) *The Rise of the Image, the Fall of the Word*, and Healy's *Endangered Minds: Why Our Children Don't Think* (1990).

6. See especially Healy (1990), Fisher (1999), Hirsch (1987), Postman (1985), and Stephens (1998).

7. For critiques of Plato's view of writing in the *Phaedrus* and other dialogues, see Leff's (1981) "The Forms of Reality in Plato's *Phaedrus*," Marback's (1994) "Rethinking Plato's Legacy: Neoplatonic Readings of Plato's *Sophist*," Neel's (1988) *Plato, Derrida, and Writing*, Poster's (1993) "Plato's Unwritten Doctrines: A Hermeneutic Problem in Rhetorical Historiography," Quandahl's (1989) "What Is Plato: Inference and Allusion in Plato's *Sophist*," and White's *Rhetoric and Reality in Plato's Phaedrus* (1993).

8. See especially Healy (1990), Fisher (1999), Hirsch (1987), Postman (1985), and Stephens (1998).

9. Except perhaps Neel (1988). See his book *Plato, Derrida, and Writing*.

10. One of the most troubling examples of this doomsday narrative is Heidegger's (1993) essay "The Question Concerning Technology." In this powerful yet frightening work, Heidegger blasts the building of a hydroelectric power plant on the Rhine River. What is disturbing about Heidegger's critique is not his revulsion at the Rhine being turned into "a water-power supplier," into "an object on call for inspection by a tour group ordered there by the vacation industry" (321), but, as Christopher Norris argues, "his undifferentiating

blanket diagnosis of the ills b[r]ought about by modern technology" (1997, 149). Later in the essay, Heidegger will list among the atrocities and monstrosities of modern technology "mechanized agriculture, factory production-lines, the dam on the Rhine River, and the mass slaughter of human beings in the death-camps at Auschwitz and elsewhere" (Norris 1997, 149). To not see the differences between these atrocities, between a damn and death camps, is itself monstrous. See also Norris (1997, n. 56, p. 165) for more on the debate surrounding Heidegger and his critique of technology.

11. While modernism has a long history and is notoriously difficult to define, we define modernism by focusing on what we consider its most salient feature (at least for our book): the coherence of the self as a means to resist the fragmentation of society. While Father Ong's religious faith prevented him from embracing all aspects of modernism, and while he obviously dealt with issues that could and should be seen as postmodern in ethos, Ong's own ethos remained solidly located in the centrality and optimism of a coherent self—and in opposing those forces he thought harmed that self.

12. Critiques of Ong's research into orality and literacy have pointed out its ethnocentrism and its harsh divide of oral-based cultures from print-based cultures based on supposed differences in cognition. See especially Daniell's (1986) "Against the Great Leap Theory of Literacy" and Faigley's (1992) *Fragments of Rationality: Postmodernity and the Subject of Composition*, especially pp. 201–204.

13. See also Havelock's *Origins of Western Literacy* (1976) and *Preface to Plato* (1963).

14. See Ong's *Orality and Literacy: The Technologizing of the Word* (1982, 78–85) and "Writing Is a Technology that Restructures Thought" (1986, 23–50). See also Gronbeck's, Farrell's, and Soukup's (1991) *Media, Consciousness and Culture: Explorations of Walter Ong's Thought*.

15. See Silverstone's article "Television, Rhetoric, and the Return of the Unconscious in Secondary Oral Culture" for a discussion of the concept of "displaced orality" (1991, 148).

16. See especially the works of Baudrillard (1983, 1990, 1993a, b), Berlin (1996), Faigley (1992), Fleckenstein et al. (2002), Fox (1994), Gronbeck et al. (1991), Kress (2003), Lanham (1974, 2006), McComiskey (2000), McLaren and Hammer (1996), Newkirk (1997), Penrod (1997), Selfe (2004), Stafford (1996), and Williams (2002).

17. For other arguments concerning what has been called "The Great Divide" or "The Great Leap" theory of literacy, see Scribner's and Cole's (1981) *The Psychology of Literacy*, Halverson's (1992) "Goody and the Implosion of the Literacy Thesis," and Banya's "Illiteracy, Colonial Legacy, and Education: The Case of Modern Sierra Leone" (1993).

18. See Damasio (1994), *Descartes' Error: Emotion, Reason, and the Human Brain*, especially pp. 96–108.

19. See especially Rosenblatt's (1993) brilliant essay "The Transactional Theory: Against Dualisms."

20. Indeed, Baudrillard believes that simulacra no longer represent what is real but replace it. Understanding images, therefore, "is no longer a question of a false representation of reality (ideology)." It is a question "of concealing the fact that the real is no longer real" (1983, 25).

21. See, for example, Harvey's (1989) *The Condition of Postmodernity: An Enquiry into the Origins of Cultural Change* and Huyssen's (1985) *After the Great Divide: Modernism, Mass Culture, Postmodernism.*

22. See Baudrillard's (1990) *Fatal Strategies*, Jameson's (1991) *Postmodernism, or, The Cultural Logic of Late Capitalism*, Lyotard's (1984) *The Postmodern Condition*, and Vitanza's (1987a) "Critical Sub/Versions of the History of Philosophical Rhetoric" and (1991) "Three Countertheses: Or, A Critical In(ter)vention into Composition Theories and Pedagogies."

23. See Faigley (1992, 211–13).

24. See Hall's (2003) *An Affair of the Mind* for a breakdown of the porn industry's profit margin.

25. For criticisms of Baudrillard's work, see Berlin (1996, 57), Faigley (1992, 211), Svehla (2006, 94), and West (1988, 277).

26. For a discussion on how Foucault's theory of power and repression might point to such resistance, see Muckelbauer's (2000) "On Reading Differently: Through Foucault's Resistance." For a discussion of the impasse of agency in postmodern theory, see Jones's (1996) "Beyond the Postmodern Impasse of Agency: The Resounding Relevance of John Dewey's Tacit Tradition."

27. See Jones's (1996) "Beyond the Postmodern Impasse of Agency" and Newkirk's (1997) *The Performance of Self in Student Writing* (especially pp. 37–54, 84–99) for a Deweyan explanation and defense of agency in light of the postmodern critique.

28. Though the term *postmodernism* is often used as a synonym for poststructuralism and postcolonialism, we recognize that there are key differences among these terms. Yet because of current parlance and the legitimacy of seeing postmodernism, in its broadest sense, as a critique of modernism in which both poststructuralism and postcolonalism participate, we feel comfortable in using quotations from critiques of poststructuralism and postcolonialism to critique the larger phenomenon of postmodernism. For a discussion of the differences between postmodernism and postcolonialism, see Appiah's (1991) "Is the Post-in Postmodernism the Post-in Postcolonial?"

29. Other theorists even more influenced by Marxist theory have been especially critical of what they see as postmodernism's theoretical excess. For example, Ebert (1996) criticizes ludic feminism's immobilizing effect, arguing that such theorists divert attention from the material causes of oppression. Ludic feminism's "poststructuralist assumptions about linguistic play, difference, and the priority of discourse . . . substitute a politics of representation for radical social transformation" (3). Such a substitution, she feels, mystifies the social, material, and economic realities that determine exploitative and hierarchical labor divisions and, consequently, the means for resistance. Similarly, Berlin, while embracing as positive the indeterminacy engendered by

postmodern theory, criticizes radical postmodernism's abandonment of history as resulting in "a fragmented, privatized, and self-absorbed stance incapable of intervening beyond the personal level of experience" (1996, 67).

30. See Frank's (2004) *What's the Matter with Kansas?*

31. Dewey locates the origins of dualistic thinking in the ancient Greeks' search for certainty in a world of great upheaval and suffering. Yet the results of this search created what Dewey considers a strange worldview and the basic problems of Western philosophy. For example, Plato's search for an absolute Truth resulted in a world where that which we cannot see, measure, touch, taste, or test is more Real than the world of our senses and society. For further discussion on this subject see Dewey's (1929b) *The Quest for Certainty*, especially pp. 3–48.

Chapter Five

1. See our earlier discussion in chapter 2 where Schor (2004) analyzes similarly cynical, known, and often intentional impacts of advertising to kids, and chapter 4 on how new media and image-driven communication complicate any analysis of political communication.

2. According to the *Youth Vote Coalition* (http://www.civicyouth.org), voting rates for those between the ages of eighteen and twenty-four have declined 13 to 15 percent since 1972 (the first year that eighteen to twenty-oine-year-olds could vote). More than 50 percent of the under-twenty-five group voted in 1972, less than 40 percent voted in 2000, and 47 percent voted in 2004. In comparison, 66 percent of the over-twenty-five age group voted in 2004. Both Brock and Alterman identify Mortimer Zuckerman as a conservative private-sector leader (real estate mogul and owner of *US News & World Report*), willing and able to use his resource advantages to fake text and context. Brock notes that Zuckerman "repeated fabricated stories about supposedly frivolous lawsuits" (2004, 144), and Alterman describes how Zuckerman would not allow the word "bubble" to be used in his magazine as the dot.com bubble burst, insisting instead that the news advertise an ongoing boom, despite evidence to the contrary (2003, 133).

3. We argue that seeing the spin is critical to democratic citizenship today and includes seeing the techniques constitutive of sound-bite sabotage. See our discussion in chapters 2 and 3 of work by David Brock in particular, as well as Eric Alterman and others, deconstructing the ways in which mainstream news sources provide both liberal and conservative voices, but intentionally conservative sources, such as Fox News, provide strong and interested conservative voices (in terms of our argument here, this means individuals willing and able to mobilize powerful sound bites without constraint by inconvenient data, the norms of professional journalism, or scholarly conventions) to compete with professional journalists cast in the role of the liberal alternative. The result is a spectacle of debate, a phony deliberation, a systematically faked context for analyzing (and understanding) both the issue at hand and the nature of political communication today.

4. The data show increases in attentiveness and activism, which we might use to conclude there has been an increase in civic consciousness, unless civic consciousness, as used here, has been branded to mean blind patriotism, while scholarly analysis and criticism are being branded as just the opinions of "hate America firsters." This is, then, a candidate for a phony framing device for the news, an effort to displace contexts suggested by thoughtful analysis with contexts calculated to sell designer information.

5. As Al Gore (2007) noted in an *Associated Press* release, "Al Gore Claims that Polluters Finance Research to Cast Doubt on Global Warming Theories," the tobacco industry spent millions on misinformation campaigns "to create the appearance that there was disagreement on the science," when there was not. Similarly, in the less well-known (current) energy industry misinformation campaigns to discredit science, data, and serious policy deliberations, Gore notes that we now see "an organized campaign, financed to the tune of about $10 million a year, from some of the largest carbon polluters, to create the impression that there is disagreement in the scientific community. . . . We live in a world where what used to be called propaganda now has a major role to play in shaping public opinion." See also our earlier discussion of Mark Smith's (2000) research for more on this.

6. In a recent Annenberg Election Survey, viewers of Jon Stewart's *The Daily Show* on Comedy Central tested better than viewers of David Letterman's and Jay Leno's late-night television viewers on a six-question politics quiz. While all viewers of these three late-night shows knew "more about the background of presidential candidates and their positions on issues than people who don't watch late-night TV," "Daily Show" viewers "know more about election issues than people who regularly read newspapers or watch television news." Bryan Long (2004) of CNN reports that "Dannagal Goldthwaite Young, a senior research analyst at the Annenberg Public Policy Center of the University of Pennsylvania, said 'Daily Show' viewers came out on top 'even when education, party identification, following politics, watching cable news, receiving campaign information online, age and gender are taken into consideration.' "

7. We are not making a claim against order, or ritual, or traditions themselves here. Deliberation, voting, and education can be constructed as very valuable rituals, but in a democratic society these function most effectively when they are open, open to being contested, and never taken as given, natural, or unchanging. Parody and ridicule are often successfully used to weaken the power of all sorts of rituals—rituals that reinforce hierarchy or privilege and rituals of resistance—in the form of jokes performed by those individuals and institutions with an interest in telling the rest of the story, in highlighting those parts of the story that are obscured by the framing devices targeted for parody or ridicule.

8. See, for example, Krikorian (2004) and Froomkin (2005). In his roast of the president, Colbert highlighted the ongoing insistence by Bush on explaining both his policy positions and his decision-making process as based on his personal belief or conviction, and thus furthering the general sense that faith and evidence are mutually exclusive, and that of the two,

faith is by far the more important in addressing weighty matters. Further, Scarborough's response appears to us to be at odds with the best available data, including the data in the Baumgartner and Jones article that we will discuss later in this chapter.

9. See our discussion of Mill in chapters 1, 3, and 6. See Christie (1977) and Sennett (1970) on the uses of disorder in a democratic society.

10. See our discussion of Mendelberg in chapter 3.

11. See, for example, Arendt (1999), Braithwaite (1989), Honneth (2003), and West (1994), among many others.

12. In addition to Robertson's apology and "clarification," CNN also offered, without explanation, a brief resume of the evangelical preacher/media mogul's other pronouncements from his televised pulpit: "He [Robertson] has suggested in the past that a meteor could strike Florida because of unofficial 'Gay Days' at Disney World and that feminism caused women to kill their children, practice witchcraft and become lesbians" (Robertson, CNN). We find this to be one of the rare examples in the news media of the kind of cynical skewering that would have made Diogenes proud.

13. See, for example, *Hannity & Colmes*.

14. See Freedman's notion of the "false refuge of fairness," found in his *Letters to a Young Journalist* (2006).

15. As we have noted earlier, in choosing the term "sound-bite saboteurs" we in no way mean to imply that the sabotage to which we refer is accomplished through language exclusive of image; this particular example highlights the crucial role of the visual in both sound-bite sabotage and in performances that seek to reveal the spin and strategy of those interested messages.

16. "See, for example, the Kull, Ramsey, and Lewis (2003–2004) article, "Misperceptions, the Media, and the Iraq War," for an in-depth discussion of the PIPA.org study and the polling data released recently by the Pew Research Center for the People and the Press.

17. Here we refer to ideology critique as those undergraduate pedagogies that focus students' attention on "reading" cultural texts and messages accurately, the implicit goal being to defy ideology, avoid hegemony, and create savvy citizens who have thrown off their false consciousness. We argue that this practice *alone* creates the kind of disengaged cynicism that harms democracy, because it encourages passive, isolated subjects. Such pedagogies are often linked to a cultural studies approach to teaching, which is critiqued by Harris (1992) in "The Other Reader," Miller (1996), and Vitanza (1999) in "The Wasteland Grows," among others.

18. See, for example, Freedman (2006), Hardin (2006), Robert Kennedy (2005), and Lakoff (2004).

19. See, for example, Baudrillard (1983), Harris (1992), Miller (1996), and Vitanza (1999).

20. See, for example, Gore's *The Assault on Reason*.

21. These are demonstrably false, in at least two senses. First, not even the Bush administration was making these claims directly, though many criticized

it for intentionally suggesting such claims. Second, the best available evidence from various intelligence reports and analyses, then and since, provides no support for the claims that these are accurate statements.

22. See Robert Kennedy (2005) for an excellent, in-depth discussion of this issue.

23. Among those Americans who believed all three demonstrably false claims to be true, 86 percent supported the invasion. Among those who did not believe any to be true, 23 percent supported the invasion (see Figure R in Kull et al., 2003–2004, 581).

Chapter Six

1. What follows is the public pedagogy for addressing conflicts in democratic deliberations offered by President Obama in a selection from that May 17, 2009, commencement speech.

> The soldier and the lawyer may both love this country with equal passion, and yet reach very different conclusions on the specific steps needed to protect us from harm. The gay activist and the evangelical pastor may both deplore the ravages of HIV/AIDS, but find themselves unable to bridge the cultural divide that might unite their efforts. Those who speak out against stem cell research may be rooted in an admirable conviction about the sacredness of life, but so are the parents of a child with juvenile diabetes who are convinced their son's or daughter's hardships can be relieved. The question, then, is how do we work through these conflicts? Is it possible for us to join hands in common effort? As citizens of a vibrant and varied democracy, how do we engage in vigorous debate . . . without . . . demonizing those with just as strongly held convictions on the other side?
> . . . Open hearts. Open minds. Fair-minded words. It's a way of life. . . . Now, you, Class of 2009, are about to enter the next phase of your life at a time of great uncertainty. You'll be called to help restore a free market that's also fair to all who are willing to work. You'll be called to seek new sources of energy that can save our planet; to give future generations the same chance that you had to receive an extraordinary education. And whether as a person drawn to public service, or simply someone who insists on being an active citizen, you will be exposed to more opinions and ideas broadcast through more means of communication than ever existed before. You'll hear talking heads scream on cable, and you'll read blogs that claim definitive knowledge, and you will watch politicians pretend they know what they're talking about. Occasionally, you may have the great fortune of actually seeing important issues debated by people who do know what they're

talking about, by well-intentioned people with brilliant minds and mastery of the facts. . . .

It's beyond our capacity as human beings to know with certainty. . . . And this doubt should . . . humble us. It should temper our passions, cause us to be wary of too much self-righteousness. It should compel us to remain open and curious and eager to continue the spiritual and moral debate that began for so many of you within the walls of Notre Dame. And within our vast democracy, this doubt should remind us even as we cling to our faith to persuade through reason, through an appeal whenever we can to universal rather than parochial principles, and most of all through an abiding example of good works and charity and kindness and service that moves hearts and minds.

For full text and video of the entire speech go to http://www.huffingtonpost.com/2009/05/17/obama-notre-dame-speech-f_n_204387.html.

2. The phrase "assume or be assumed by" is important to understanding Foucault's argument. The question of agency is always in tension in Foucualt's work. Mechanisms are not simply things we deploy but also things that deploy us. David Bartholomae, influenced by Foucault's poststructuralist thought, eloquently encapsulates this view of disciplinary/discourse power for the classroom. According to Bartholomae, "the student must, by writing, become like us. . . . He must become someone he is not. He must know what we know, talk like we talk; he must locate himself convincingly in a language that is not his own. . . . The struggle of the student writer is not the struggle to bring out that which is within; it is the struggle to carry out those ritual activities that grant one entrance into a closed society (1983, 300).

3. Foucault, of course, rejects such a Descartian split between outer and inner being as itself oppressive. Yet his larger point is that restriction is productive. Power restricts the ways in which a thing can be known or a person can be; however, since there is no innate state of being to maim or stunt, this restriction builds an identity rather than deforms one. Repression is productive. The danger to the individual is that he or she might suffer under and be complicit in making a marginalized identity within a structure. See Foucault's (1990) *The History of Sexuality, Volume I* (especially pp. 10–12) for his discussion of the repressive hypothesis and the role of repression in producing identity.

4. Of course, for Plato knowledge of the Realities allows one to avoid the risk of co-optation. With knowledge of the realities in place, one does not seek a corrupt state's power. One may not be able to avoid the state's wrath in refusing to be co-opted (as Socrates could not), but one's innate self does not have to be tainted if that self is understood. Thus for Plato critical revolution begins and ends with remembering innate being and transcendent knowledge.

5. A power structure's main purpose is to promulgate itself, to grow through its mechanisms of knowledge production—not to adhere to any

specific ideological content. See Foucault's *Discipline and Punish* (especially pp. 257–92) for his argument that the political issues of the penal system are not ideological but mechanical. Specifically, he argues that "If there is an overall political issue around the prison, it is not . . . whether it is to be corrective or not; whether the judges, the psychiatrists or the sociologists are to exercise more power in it than the administrators or the supervisors; it is not even whether we should have prison or something other than prison. At present, the problem lies rather in the steep rise in the use of these mechanisms of normalization and the wide-ranging powers which, through the proliferation of new disciplines, they bring with them" (1979, 306).

   6. Arendt argues that a sober understanding of power and politics leads to the counterintuitive conclusion that the opposite of violence in not nonviolence but politics, a politics without guarantees. "Power and violence are opposites; where the one rules absolutely, the other is absent. Violence appears where power is in jeopardy, but left to its own course it ends in power's disappearance. This implies that it is not correct to think of the opposite of violence as nonviolence; to speak of nonviolent power is actually redundant. Violence can destroy power; it is utterly incapable of creating it" (1999, 11).

   7. See our discussion of Jeffery Smith's work in chapter 3. Baker makes a case for tax and regulatory action against advertisers. Schor makes a similar case for regulation of advertising directed at children.

   8. For a thoughtful competing perspective on anthrax as a moral crisis, see Egan (2002).

   9. While we choose here to focus on elite agency, for reasons articulated throughout this book, we also want to explicitly avoid any suggestion that the analytical framework we are developing precludes a role for grassroots movements. Indeed, we hope our work contributes to students, other scholars, activists, professionals, and critics of the connections among political reform, social change, elite leadership, democratic deliberation, and the positive aspects of new and old media. In our view, however, *sound-bite sabotage* is driven by public- and private-sector elites, and a core element of the problem is that average citizens often lack/are denied access to the corporate-controlled mainstream media production that might enable them to more effectively and directly respond to such sabotage. Furthermore, responses that emerge from, and play out within, other communicative spheres are often distorted by the power of elites to saturate communication channels with their interested messages, thus demanding, we believe, a focus on elite agency—though not alone or independent of public scrutiny—for the sober and serious analysis of how to create and produce and reframe productive approaches to addressing these conflicts. For this reason, we focus on the leadership challenges that the data we provide suggest we must face in order to address sound-bite sabotage, including challenges to our own leadership positions in the classroom and beyond.

   10. While not the central focus of this book, we feel an obligation to show how we have attempted, in our classrooms, to reveal, engage, and

alter the tactics of sound-bite saboteurs. We have included, therefore, as an appendix to our conclusion, examples of media literacy/pop culture exercises that focus on skill development, on sharpening our collective understanding of the sources of bias and distortion in our information systems from interested parties, public and private leaders on both the Left and the Right. It is our hope that by confronting this sabotage, we might enable students and teachers to resist the deleterious effects of sound-bite sabotage and the exploitation of new media.

11. In the intersections of our public and private, academic and communal, and intellectual and political lives, we continue to write and publish and speak in popular, public venues in ways that we hope bridge those at-once distinct and overlapping worlds and work against sound-bite sabotage. We do so through the tools of published narrative, fiction and nonfiction, in popular mainstream media that address the challenges we all face; speaking engagements in our communities that focus on conflict resolution skills; political volunteer work and public speech; public school outreach; and meeting and working with students outside of the particular interests and borders of the university, among others.

Appendix

1. A version of this exercise was first published in Svehla's (2006) "The Supremacy of the Image: Urban Students and the Idea of Secondary Orality." *EAPSU Online: A Journal of Critical and Creative Work* 3 (Fall): 83–107.

2. The actor who played Ali G, Sacha Baron Cohen, would go on to create and star in the 2006 film *Borat: Cultural Learnings of America for Make Benefit Glorious Nation of Kazakhstan*, exactly the kind of transgressive and Diogenestic performance of which we write.

Works Cited

Alterman, Eric. 2003. *What Liberal Media? The Truth About Bias in the News.* New York: Basic Books.

Anderson, Brian. 2005. *South Park Conservatives: The Revolt Against Liberal Media Bias.* Washington, DC: Regnery.

Appiah, Kwarne Anthony. 1991. "Is the Post-in Postmodernism the Post-in Postcolonial?" *Critical Inquiry* 17 (Winter): 336–57.

Arendt, Hanna. 1999. "Excerpt from On Violence." In *Violence and Its Alternatives: an Interdisciplinary Reader,* ed. Manfred Steger and Nancy Lind, 3–11. New York: St. Martin's Press.

Arnold, Matthew. 1993. "Dover Beach." In *The Bedford Introduction to Literature,* 3rd ed., ed. Michael Meyer, 648–49. Boston, MA: Bedford/St. Martin's.

Bachrach, Peter, and Morton Baratz. 1962. "Two Faces of Power." *American Political Science Review* 56 (December): 947–52.

Baker, C. Edwin. 1992. "Advertising and a Democratic Press." *University of Pennsylvania Law Review* 140.6 (June): 2097–2243.

Baker, Thomas. 2005. *The Medical Malpractice Myth.* Chicago, IL: University of Chicago Press.

Bakhtin, Mikhail. 1981. *The Dialogic Imagination: Four Essays.* Edited by Michael Holquist and translated by Caryl Emerson and Michael Holquist. Austin: University of Texas Press.

Banya, Kingsley. 1993. "Illiteracy, Colonial Legacy, and Education: The Case of Modern Sierra Leone." *Comparative Education* 29.2: 159–70.

Barabas, Jason. 2004. "How Deliberation Affects Public Opinions." *American Political Science Review* 98.4 (November): 687–701.

Barber, Benjamin. 2003. *Fear's Empire: War, Terrorism, and Democracy.* New York: Norton.

Barstow, David, and Robin Stein. 2005. "Under Bush, a New Age of Prepackaged Television News." *New York Times,* March 13.

Bartholomae, David. 1983. "Writing Assignments: Where Writing Begins." In *Forum: Essays on Theory and Practice in the Teaching of Writing,* ed. Patricia L. Stock, 300–12. Upper Montclair, NJ: Boynton/Cook.

Baudrillard, Jean. 1983. *Simulations.* Translated by Paul Foss, Paul Patton, and Philip Beitchman. New York: Semiotext(e).

Baudrillard, Jean. 1990. *Fatal Strategies*. Edited by Jim Fleming and translated by Philip Beitchman and W. G. J. Niesluchowski. New York: Semiotext(e).

Baudrillard, Jean. 1993a. *Baudrillard Live: Selected Interviews*. Edited by Mike Gane. New York: Routledge.

Baudrillard, Jean. 1993b. *The Transparency of Evil: Essays on Extreme Phenomena*. Translated by James Benedict. London: Verso.

Baumgartner, Frank, and Bryan Jones. 1993. *Agendas and Instability in American Politics*. Chicago, IL: University of Chicago Press.

Baumgartner, Jody, and Jonathan S. Morris. 2006. "*The Daily Show* Effect: Candidate Evaluations, Efficacy, and American Youth." *American Politics Research* 34.3 (May): 341–67.

Beckett, Katherine. 1997. *Making Crime Pay: Law and Order in Contemporary American Politics*. New York: Oxford University Press.

Bennett, W. Lance. 1996. *News: The Politics of Illusion*. New York: Longman.

Berinsky, Adam. 2005. "The Perverse Consequences of Electoral Reform in the United States." *American Politics Research* 33.4 (July): 471–91.

Berlin, James A. 1996. *Rhetorics, Poetics, and Cultures: Refiguring College English Studies*. Urbana, IL: NCTE.

Bizzell, Patricia. 1990. "Beyond Anti-Foundationalism to Rhetorical Authority: Problems in Defining 'Cultural Literacy.' " *College English* 52.6 (October): 661–75.

Bizzell, Particia, and Bruce Herzberg. 1990. Preface. In *The Rhetorical Tradition: Readings from Classical Times to the Present*, ed. Patricia Bizzell and Bruce Herzberg, v–viii. New York: Bedford/St. Martin's.

Blumstein, Alfred. 1993. "Making Rationality Relevant: The American Society of Criminology 1992 Presidential Address." *Criminology* 31.1 (February): 1–16.

Bogle, John. 2005. *The Battle for the Soul of Capitalism*. New Haven, CT: Yale University Press.

Boisvert, Raymond D. 1988. *John Dewey: Rethinking Our Time*. Albany: State University of New York Press.

Booth, Wayne. 1988. *The Vocation of a Teacher: Rhetorical Occasions, 1967–1988*. Chicago, IL: University of Chicago Press.

Borat: Cultural Learnings of America for Make Benefit Glorious Nation of Kazakhstan. 2006. Dir. Larry Charles. Perf. Sacha Baron Cohen, Pamela Anderson, Ken Davitian. 20th Century Fox.

Borgmann, Albert. 1992. *Crossing the Postmodern Divide*. Chicago, IL: University of Chicago Press.

Boyte, Harry. 1992. "The Critic Critiqued." In *From the Ground Up: Essays on Grassroots and Workplace Democracy*, ed. George Bennello, with commentaries, 209–17. Boston, MA: South End Press.

Boyte, Harry. 1995. "Public Opinion as Public Judgment." In *Public Opinion and the Communication of Consent*, ed. Theodore Salmon and Charles Glasser, 417–36. New York: Guilford.

Braithwaite, John. 1989. *Crime, Shame, and Reintegration*. New York: Cambridge University Press.

Branham, R. Bracht. 1996. "Defacing the Currency: Diogenes' Rhetoric and the *Invention* of Cynicism." In *The Cynics: The Cynic Movement in Antiquity and Its Legacy*, ed. R. Bracht Branham and Marie-Odile Goulet-Cazé, 81–104. Berkeley: University of California Press.

Branham, R. Bracht, and Marie-Odile Goulet-Cazé, eds. 1996. *The Cynics: The Cynic Movement in Antiquity and Its Legacy*. Berkeley: University of California Press.

Brock, David. 2004. *The Republican Noise Machine: Right-Wing Media and How it Corrupts Democracy*. New York: Crown.

Broder, David S. 1994. "War on Cynicism." *Washington Post,* July 6, p. A19.

Brooks, David. 2007. "The Vanishing Neoliberal." *New York Time*s, March 11, p. 14.

Brown, Richard Maxwell. 1969. "Historical Patterns in Violence in America." In *The History of Violence in America*, ed. Hugh Davis Graham and Ted Robert Gurr, 154–226. New York: Bantam.

Cappella, Joseph N., and Kathleen Hall Jamieson. 1997. *Spiral of Cynicism: The Press and the Public Good*. New York: Oxford University Press.

Carter, Jimmy. 2006. *Our Endangered Values: America's Moral Crisis*. New York: Simon and Schuster.

Chaloupka, William. 1999. *Everybody Knows: Cynicism in America*. Minneapolis: University of Minnesota Press.

Chilton, Stephan, Maria Stalzer, and Wyant Cuzzo. 2005. "Habermas's Theory of Communicative Action as a Theoretical Framework for Mediation Practice." *Conflict Resolution Quarterly* 22.3 (Spring): 325–48.

Chiricos, Ted, Kelly Welch, and Marc Gertz. 2004. "Racial Typification of Crime and Support for Punitive Measures." *Criminology* 42.2 (May): 359–90.

Chomsky, Noam. 2000. *Chomsky on Miseducation*. Edited by Donaldo Macedo. Lanham, MD: Rowan & Littlefield.

Chomsky, Noam. 2002. *Media Control: The Spectacular Achievements of Propaganda*. New York: Seven Stories.

Christian, Barbara. 1989. "The Race for Theory." In *Gender and Theory: Dialogues on Feminist Criticism*, ed. Linda S. Kauffman, 225–37. Oxford: Blackwell.

Christie, Nils. 1977. "Conflicts as Property." *The British Journal of Criminology* 17.1 (January): 1–15.

Clear, Todd, Dina Rose, Elin Waring, and Kristen Scully. 2003. "Coercive Mobility and Crime: A Preliminary Examination of Concentrated Incarceration and Social Disorganization." *Justice Quarterly* 20.1 (March): 33–64.

Cocco, Marie. 2006. "A Legacy of Corruption." *Washington Post,* June 9. Rpt. "Congress' Larger Wrong Goes Unpunished." *Akron Beacon Journal* [Akron, OH].

Cohen, Adam. 2007. "Last Term's Winner at the Supreme Court: Judicial Activism." *New York Times,* July 9, p. A16.

Colbert, Stephen. 2006. "You Be the Judge." Transcript of Speech at White House Correspondents Dinner. May 10. http://www.editorandpublisher.com.

Collins, John, and Ross Glover. 2002. *Collateral Language: A User's Guide to America's New War*. New York: New York University Press.

Commager, Henry Steele. 1993. *Commager on Tocqueville*. Columbia: University of Missouri Press.

Conley, Dalton. 2000. "The Racial Wealth Gap: Origins and Implications for Philanthropy in the African-American Community." *Nonprofit & Voluntary Sector Quarterly* 29.4 (December): 530–40.

Damasio, Antonio R. 1994. *Descartes' Error: Emotion, Reason, and the Human Brain*. New York: Putnam.

Danforth, John. 2006. *Faith and Politics: How "Moral Values" Debates Divide America and How to Move Forward together*. New York: Viking Adult.

Daniell, Beth. 1986. "Against the Great Leap Theory of Literacy." *PRE/TEXT* 7.3–4: 181–93.

Danner, Mark. 2007. *Words in a Time of War*. TomDispatch.com. May 13. http://www.markdanner.com/articles/show/130.

Davis, Mike. 1998. *Ecology of Fear: Los Angeles and the Imagination of Disaster*. New York: Vintage.

De Luca, Tom, and John Buell. 2005. *Liars! Cheaters! Evildoers! Demonization and the End of Civil Debate in American Politics*. New York: New York University Press.

"Democrats and Republicans Both Adept at Ignoring the Facts, Study Finds." 2006. January 24. http:www.livescience.com/othernews/060124_political_decisions.html.

Dewey, John. 1917. *Democracy and Education: An Introduction to the Philosophy of Education*. New York: Macmillan.

Dewey, John. 1929a. *Experience and Nature*. 2nd ed. La Salle, IL: Open Court Press.

Dewey, John. 1929b. *The Quest for Certainty: A Study of the Relation of Knowledge and Action*. New York: Minton/Balch.

Dewey, John. 1948. *Reconstruction in Philosophy*. Enlarged ed. Boston, MA: Beacon Press.

Dewey, John. 1964 [1934]. "The Need for a Philosophy of Education." In *John Dewey on Education: Selected Writings*, ed. Reginald Archambault, 1–14. Chicago, IL: University of Chicago Press.

Dewey, John. 1983 [1922]. "Pragmatic America." In *John Dewey: The Middle Works, 1899–1924*, vol. 13, ed. Jo Ann Boydston, 306–16. Carbondale: Southern Illinois University Press.

Dionne, E. J. 2005. "But, of course, no apologies." *Akron Beacon Journal* [Akron, OH], June 19, p. B2.

Dreier, Peter. 2005. How the Media Compound Urban Problems. *Journal of Urban Affairs* 27.2 (June): 193–201.

Drew, Julie. 2001. "Review of *Chomsky on Miseducation*." *JAC* 21.4 (Winter): 922–26.

duCille, Ann. 1994. "Postcolonialism and Afrocentricity: Discourse and Dat Course." In *The Black Columbiad: Defining Moments in African American Literature and Culture*, ed. Werner Sollors and Maria Diedrich, 28–41. Cambridge, MA: Harvard University Press.

Dye, Thomas, and Harmon Zeigler. 2006. *The Irony of Democracy: An Uncommon Introduction to American Politics.* Belmont, CA: Thomson-Wadsworth.

Dyson, Michael Eric. 2001. *Holler if You Hear Me: Searching for Tupac Shakur.* New York: Basic Civitas.

Eagleton, Terry. 1991. *Ideology: An introduction.* London: Verso.

Ebert, Teresa L. 1996. *Ludic Feminism and After: Postmodernism, Desire, and Labor in Late Capitalism.* Ann Arbor: University of Michigan Press.

Edelman, Murray. 1977. *Political Language: Words that Succeed and Policies that Fail.* New York: Academic Press.

Edelman, Murray. 1988. *Constructing the Political Spectacle.* Chicago, IL: University of Chicago Press.

Edelman, Murray. 1995. "The Influence of Rationality Claims on Public Opinion and Policy." In *Public Opinion and the Communication of Consent,* ed. Theodore Glasser and Charles Salmon, 403–17. New York: Guilford.

Edelman, Murray. 2001. *The Politics of Misinformation.* Cambridge: Cambridge University Press.

Egan, R. Danielle. 2002. "Anthrax." In *Collateral Language: A User's Guide to America's New War,* ed. John Collins and Ross Glover, 15–26. New York: New York University Press.

Elbow, Peter. 1991. "Reflections on Academic Discourse: How it Relates to Freshman and Colleagues." *College English* 53.2 (February): 135–55.

Engel, David. 1984. "The Oven Bird's Dong: Insiders, Outsiders and Personal Injuries in an American Community." *Law & Society Review* 18.4: 551–82.

"Enron's awesome cynicism." 2004. Editorial. *New York Times,* June 6. Accessed June 7, 2004. http://www.nytimes.com/2004/06/06/opinion/06SUN4.html.

Fagan, Jeffrey. 1994. "Do Criminal Sanctions Deter Crimes?" In *Drugs and Crime: Evaluating Public Policy Initiatives,* ed. Doris Layton MacKenzie and Craig Uchida, 188–215. Thousand Oaks, CA: Sage.

Fagan, Jeffrey, and Garth Davies. 2000. "Street Stops and Broken Windows: Terry, Race, and Disorder in New York City." *Fordham Urban Law Journal* 28 (December): 457–91.

Faigley, Lester. 1992. *Fragments of Rationality: Postmodernity and the Subject of Composition.* Pittsburgh: University of Pittsburgh Press.

Farsetta, Diane, and Daniel Price. 2006. "Fake TV news: Widespread and Undisclosed." Center for Media and Democracy. April 6. http://www.prwatch.org/fakenews/execsummary.

Ferguson, Ann. 2000. *Bad Boys: Public Schools in the Making of Black Masculinity.* Ann Arbor: University of Michigan Press.

Fiorina, Morris, with Samuel Abrams and Jeremy Pope. 2006. *Culture War? The Myth of a Polarized America.* New York: Pearson Longman.

Fish, Stanley. 2001. "Thoughts on September 11th–October 15, 2001– Condemnation Without Absolutes." *New York Times,* October 15.

Fisher, Lucy. 1999. "Apocalypse Yesterday: Writing, Literacy, and the 'Threat' of 'Electronic Technology.' " In *Cinema-(to)-Graphy: Film and Writing in*

Contemporary Composition Courses, ed. Ellen Bishop, 170–80. Portsmouth, NH: Boynton/Cook.

Fishman, Stephen M., and Lucille McCarthy. 1998. *John Dewey and the Challenge of Classroom Practice*. New York: Teachers College Press.

Fleckenstein, Kristie S., Linda T. Calendrillo, and Demetrice A. Worley, eds. 2002. *Language and Image in the Reading-Writing Classroom: Teaching Vision*. Mahwah, NJ: Lawrence Erlbaum.

Fleisher, Richard, and Jon Bond. 2001. "Evidence of Increasing Polarization among Ordinary Citizens." In *American Political Parties*, ed. Jeffrey Cohen, Richard Fleisher, and Paul Kantor, 55–77. Washington, DC: CQ Press.

Fluery-Steiner, Benjamin. 2002. "Narratives of the Death Sentence: Toward a Theory of Legal Narrativity." *Law & Society Review* 36.3: 549–76.

"Food Industry Fights State Label Rules." 2007. *Akron Beacon Journal* [Akron, OH], August 21, p. A5.

Foucault, Michel. 1972. *The Archeology of Knowledge & the Discourse on Language*. Translated by A. M. Sheridan Smith. New York: Pantheon.

Foucault, Michel. 1979. *Discipline and Punish: The Birth of the Prison*. Translated by Alan Sheridan. New York: Vintage.

Foucault, Michel. 1980. *Power/Knowledge: Selected Interviews and Other Writings 1972–1977*. Edited by Colin Gordon. New York: Pantheon.

Foucault, Michel. 1990. *The History of Sexuality Volume I: An Introduction*. Translated by Robert Hurley. New York: Vintage.

Fox, Roy, ed. 1994. *Images in Language, Media, and Mind*. Urbana, IL: NCTE.

Frank, Thomas. 2004. *What's the Matter with Kansas? How Conservatives Won the Heart of America*. New York: Metropolitan.

Frankfurt, Harry. 2005. *On Bullshit*. Princeton, NJ: Princeton University Press.

Freedman, Paul, Michael Franz, and Kenneth Goldstein. 2004. "Campaign Advertising and Democratic Citizenship." *American Journal of Political Science* 48.4 (October): 723–41.

Freedman, Samuel G. 2006. *Letters to a Young Journalist*. Cambridge, MA: Basic.

Freire, Paulo. 1970. *Pedagogy of the Oppressed*. New York: Continuum.

Friedman, Susan Stanford. 1991. "Post/Poststructuralist Feminist Criticism: The Politics of Recuperation and Negotiation." *New Literary History* 22.2 (Spring): 465–90.

Froomkin, Dan. 2005. "The Gulf Between Rhetoric and Reality." *Washington Post*, September 2. http://www.washingtonpost.com/wpdyn/content/blog/2005/09/02/BL200509201324.html.

Galanter, Marc. 1975. "Why the 'Haves' Come Out Ahead: Speculations on the Limits of Legal Change." *Law & Society Review* 9: 95–160.

Gaventa, John. 1980. *Power and Powerlessness*. Urbana: University of Illinois Press.

Giroux, Henry A. 1994. "Slacking Off: Border Youth and Postmodern Education." *JAC* 14.2 (Winter): 347–66.

Giroux, Henry A. 2001. "Breaking into the Movies: Pedagogy and the Politics of Film." *JAC* 21.3 (Fall): 583–98.

Glassner, Barry. 1999. *The Culture of Fear: Why Americans are Afraid of the Wrong Things.* New York: Basic Books.

Globe editorial. 2007. "Bush's Refusal to Face Reality." January 10. http://www.boston.com/news/nation/washington/articles/2007/01/10/bushs_refusal_to_face_reality/.

Glover, Ross. 2002. "The War on   ." In *Collateral Language: A User's Guide to America's New War,* ed. John Collins and Ross Glover, 207–23. New York: New York University Press.

Goldberg, Jonah. 2007. "Cheney Displays Enviable Style but Opportunism Erodes Goodwill." *The Omaha World Herald* [Omaha, NE], June 30, p. 7B.

Gore Jr., Al. 2005. "Our Democracy Has Been Hollowed Out." Text of prepared speech delivered to the Media Center's *We Media* conference in New York City, October 6. http://www.tompaine.com/print/our_democracy_has_been_hollowed_out.php.

Gore Jr., Al. 2007a. "Al Gore Claims that Polluters Finance Research to Cast Doubt on Global Warming Theories." *Associated Press,* August 7.

Gore Jr., Al. 2007b. *The Assault on Reason.* New York: Penguin.

Gramsci, Antonio. 1971. "The Intellectuals." In *Selections from the Prison Notebooks,* ed. Quintin Hoare and Geoffrey Nowell Smith, 3–23, trans. Quintin Hoare and Geoffrey Nowell Smith. New York: International.

Green, John. 2006. "Tribal Relations." *The Atlantic Monthly* (January–February): 136–42.

Greider, William. 1992. *Who Will Tell the People: The Betrayal of American Democracy.* New York: Simon and Schuster.

Gronbeck, Bruce E., Thomas J. Farrell, and Paul A. Soukup, eds. 1991. *Media, Consciousness and Culture: Explorations of Walter Ong's Thought.* Newbury Park, CA: Sage.

Hall, Laurie. 2003. *An Affair of the Mind.* Wheaton, IL: Tyndale House.

Hall, Stuart, et al. 1978. *Policing the Crisis: Mugging, the State, and Law and Order.* New York: Holmes and Meier.

Haltom, William, and Michael McCann. 2004. *Distorting the Law: Politics, Media, and the Litigation Crisis.* Chicago, IL: University of Chicago Press.

Halverson, John. 1992. "Goody and the Implosion of the Literacy Thesis." *Man-New Series* 27.2 (June): 301–17.

Hancock, Ange-Marie. 2004. *The Politics of Disgust: The Public Identity of the Welfare Queen.* New York: New York University Press.

Hannity & Colmes. 2006. Fox News Network. February 26.

Hardin, Joe. 2006. "Defacing the Currency: Diogenes on *The Daily Show.*" Paper delivered at the Conference on College Composition and Communication, Chicago, March.

Harris, Joseph. 1989. "The Idea of Community in the Study of Writing." *College Composition and Communication* 40.1: 11–22.

Harris, Joseph. 1992. "The Other Reader." *JAC* 12.1 (Winter): 27–37.

Harvey, David. 1989. *The Condition of Postmodernity: An Enquiry into the Origins of Cultural Change*. Oxford: Blackwell.

Havelock, Eric A. 1963. *Preface to Plato*. Cambridge, MA: Belknap Press of Harvard University Press.

Havelock, Eric A. 1976. *Origins of Western Literacy*. Toronto: Ontario Institute of Education.

Havelock, Eric A. 1986. *The Muse Learns to Write: Reflections on Orality and Literacy from Antiquity to the Present*. New Haven, CT: Yale University Press.

Healy, Jane M. 1990. *Endangered Minds: Why Our Children Don't Think*. New York: Simon and Schuster/Touchstone.

Hedges, Chris. 2007. *American Fascists: The Christian Right and the War on America*. New York: Free Press.

Heidegger, Martin. 1993. "The Question Concerning Technology." In *Martin Heidegger: Basic Writings*, 2nd ed., ed. D. F. Krell, 311–41. London: Routledge.

Heineman, Kenneth. 1998. *God is a Conservative: Religion, Politics, and Morality in Contemporary America*. New York: New York University Press.

Herman, Ken. 2005. "White House to Agencies: Ignore GAO's Ruling on 'Illegal' TV News Releases." *Cox News Service*, March 15.

Himmelfarb, Gertrude. 1999. *One Nation, Two Cultures*. New York: Knopf.

Hirsch, E. D. 1987. *Cultural Literacy: What Every American Needs to Know*. Boston, MA: Houghton.

Hofstadter, Richard. 1963. *Anti-Intellectualism in American Life*. New York: Vintage.

Honneth, Axel. 2003. "Personal Identity and Disrespect." In *The New Social Theory Reader*, ed. Steven Seidman and Jeffrey C. Alexander, 39–45. London: Routledge.

Huyssen, Andreas. 1985. *After the Great Divide: Modernism, Mass Culture, Postmodernism*. Bloomington: Indiana University Press.

Huyssen, Andreas. 1987. Foreword. In *Critique of Cynical Reason*, ed. Peter Sloterdijk, ix–xxv, trans. Michael Eldred. Minneapolis: University of Minnesota Press.

Innocenti, Debra. 2002. "The Mind's Eye View: Teaching Students How to Sensualize Language." In Fleckenstein, Calendrillo, and Worley, 59–70.

Iyengar, Shanto, and Donald R. Kinder. 1987. *News that Matters: Television and American Opinion*. Chicago, IL: University of Chicago Press.

James, William. 1948. "Pragmatism's Conception of Truth." In *Essays in Pragmatism*, ed. Alburey Castell, 159–76. New York: Hafner.

Jameson, Fredric. 1991. *Postmodernism, or, The Cultural Logic of Late Capitalism*. Durham, NC: Duke University Press.

Jay, Gregory, and Gerald Graff. 1995. "A Critique of Critical Pedagogy." In *Higher Education Under Fire: Politics, Economics, and the Crisis in the Humanities*, ed. Michael Berube and Cary Nelson, 201–13. New York: Routledge.

Jerit, Jennifer. 2006. "Reform, Rescue, or Run Out of Money? Problem Definition in the Social Security Reform Debate." *Harvard International Journal of Press and Politics* 11.1 (Winter): 9–28.

Johnson, Barbara. 1995. "Writing." In *Critical Terms for Literary Study*, 2nd ed., ed. Frank Lentricchia and Thomas McLaughlin, 39–49. Chicago, IL: University of Chicago Press.

Jones, Donald C. 1996. "Beyond the Postmodern Impasse of Agency: The Resounding Relevance of John Dewey's Tacit Tradition." *JAC* 16.1 (Winter): 81–102.

Juergensemeyer, Mark. 2005. *Gandhi's Way: A Handbook of Conflict Resolution.* Berkeley: University of California Press.

Katzneslon, Ira. 1976. "The Crisis of the Capitalist City: Urban Politics and Social Control." In *Theoretical Perspectives on Urban Politics*, ed. Willis Hawley and Michael Lipsky, 214–29. Englewood Cliffs, NJ: Prentice Hall.

Kennedy, Eileen. 2005. "The Global Face of Nutrition: What Can Governments and Industry Do?" *The Journal of Nutrition* 135: 913–15.

Kennedy Jr., Robert. 2005. *Crimes Against Nature: How George W. Bush and His Corporate Pals are Plundering the Country and Hijacking Our Democracy.* New York: Harper Collins.

Kerbel, Matthew Robert. 1999. *Remote & Controlled: Media Politics in a Cynical Age.* 2nd ed. Boulder, CO: Westview Press.

Kinsely, Michael. 1981. "The Shame of Democrats." *The New Republic* 185.4: 14–16.

Kress, Gunther. 2003. *Literacy in the New Media Age.* New York: Routledge.

Kress, Gunther, and Theo van Leeuwen. 2006. *Reading Images: The Grammar of Visual Design.* 2nd ed. New York: Routledge.

Krikorian, Mark. 2004. "Bush Plan for Illegals Out of Touch with Reality." *Center for Immigration Studies.* January 17. http://www.cis.org/articles/2004/markoped011704.html.

Krueger, Derek. 1996. "The Bawdy and Society: The Shamelessness of Diogenes in Roman Imperial Culture." In Branham and Goulet-Cazé, 222–39.

Krugman, Paul. 2005a. "A Private Obsession." *New York Times* editorial, April 29.

Krugman, Paul. 2005b. "Ailing Health Care." *New York Times* editorial, April 11.

Krugman, Paul. 2005c. "For a Look at Family Values, Try France." *New York Times* editorial, August 2.

Krugman, Paul. 2005d. "The Medical Money Pit." *New York Times* editorial, April 15.

Krugman, Paul. 2005e. "Passing the Buck." *New York Times* editorial, April 22.

Kuhn, Thomas. 1970. *The Structure of Scientific Revolutions.* Chicago, IL: University of Chicago Press.

Kull, Steven, Clay Ramsay, and Evan Lewis. 2003–2004. "Misperceptions, the Media, and the Iraq War." *Political Science Quarterly* 118.4 (Winter: 569–98.

Kupelian, David. 2005. *The Marketing of Evil: How Radicals, Elitists, and Pseudo-Experts Sell us Corruption Disguised as Freedom.* Nashville, TN: WND Books.

Lakoff, George. 2004. *Don't Think of an Elephant!: Know Your Values and Frame the Debate.* White River Junction, VT: Chelsea Green.

Lanham, Richard A. 1974. *Style: An Anti-Textbook.* New Haven, CT: Yale University Press.

Lanham, Richard A. 2006. *The Economics of Attention: Style and Substance in the Age of Information.* Chicago, IL: University of Chicago Press.

Lawrence, Regina. 2000. "Game-Framing the Issues: Tracking the Strategy Frame in Public Policy News." *Political Communication* 17: 93–114.

Leff, Michael. 1981. "The Forms of Reality in Plato's *Phaedrus.*" *Rhetorical Society Quarterly* 11.1 (Winter): 22–23.

Leonard, John. 1997. *Smoke and Mirrors: Violence, Television, and Other American Cultures.* New York: New Press.

Lerner, Michael. 1997. *The Politics of Meaning: Restoring Hope and Possibility in an Age of Cynicism.* Reading, MA: Addison-Wesley.

Lewis, Justin. 2001. *Constructing Public Opinion: How Political Elites Do What They Like and Why We Seem to Go Along with It.* New York: Columbia University Press.

Light, Richard. 2001. *Making the Most of College: Students Speak Their Minds.* Cambridge, MA: Harvard University Press.

Llorente, Marina. 2002. "Civilization versus Barbarism." In *Collateral Language: A User's Guide to America's New War*, ed. John Collins and Ross Glover, 39–51. New York: New York University Press.

Long, Bryan. 2004. " 'Daily Show' Viewers Ace Political Quiz." CNN. September 29. Posted Wednesday 4:17 p.m. EDT (2017 GMT). http://www.cnn.com/2004/SHOWBIZ//TV/09/28/comedy.politics/.

Lyons, William. 1999. *The Politics of Community Policing: Rearranging the Power to Punish.* Ann Arbor: University of Michigan Press.

Lyons, William, and Julie Drew. 2006. *Punishing Schools: Fear and Citizenship in American Education.* Ann Arbor: University of Michigan Press.

Lyotard, Jean Francois. 1984. *The Postmodern Condition: A Report on Knowledge.* Translated by Geoff Benington and Brain Massumi. Minneapolis: University of Minnesota Press.

Madonna. 2001. "Music." *Music.* Maverick. As shown on MTV.

Marback, Richard. 1994. "Rethinking Plato's Legacy: Neoplatonic Readings of Plato's *Sophist.*" *Rhetoric Review* 13: 30–48.

McAllister, Matthew P. 1996. *The Commercialization of American Culture: New Advertising, Control and Democracy.* Thousand Oaks, CA: Sage.

McBride, Keally. 2007. *Punishment and Political Order.* Ann Arbor: University of Michigan Press.

McChesney, Robert. 1997. *Corporate Media and the Threat to Democracy.* New York: Seven Stories Press.

McComiskey, Bruce. 2000. *Teaching Composition as a Social Process.* Logan: Utah State University Press.

McCormick, John. 2006. "Contain the Wealthy and Patrol the Magistrates: Restoring Elite Accountability to Popular Government." *American Political Science Review* 100.2 (May): 147–63.

McGinniss, Joe. 1988. *The Selling of the President*. New York: Penguin.

McLaren, Peter, and Rhonda Hammer. 1996. "Media Knowledges, Warrior Citizenry, and Postmodern Literacies." In *Counternarratives: Cultural Studies and Critical Pedagogies in Postmodern Spaces*, ed. Henry A. Giroux, Colin Lankshear, Peter McLaren, and Michael Peters, 81–115. New York: Routledge.

McLuhan, Marshall, and Bruce R. Powers. 1989. *The Global Village: Transformations in World Life and Media in the 21st Century*. Oxford: Oxford University Press.

McLuhan, Marshall, and Quentin Fiore. 1967. *The Medium is the Message*. New York: Bantam.

Meehan, Albert, and Michael Ponder. 2002. "Race and Place: The Ecology of Racial Profiling African American Motorists." *Justice Quarterly* 19.3 (September): 399–430.

Mendelberg, Tali. 1997. "Executing Hortons: Racial Crime in the 1988 Presidential Campaign." *Public Opinion Quarterly* 61: 134–57.

Mendelberg, Tali. 2001. *The Race Card: Campaign Strategy, Implicit Messages, and the Norm of Equality*. Princeton, NJ: Princeton University Press.

Mill, John Stuart. 1975. "On Liberty." In *John Stuart Mill Three Essays*. New York: Oxford University Press, 5–145.

Miller, Arthur. 2001. "On Politics and the Art of Acting." March 26. http://www.neh.gov/whoweare/miller/lecture.html.

Miller, James. 1994. *The Passion of Michel Foucault*. New York: Anchor.

Miller, Lisa. 2007. "The Representational Biases of Federalism: Scope and Bias in the Political Process, Revisited." *Perspective on Politics* 5.2 (June): 305–21.

Miller, Susan. 1996. "Technologies of Self? Formation." In *Rhetorics, Poetics, and Cultures: Refiguring College English Studies*, ed. James A. Berlin, 207–10. Urbana, IL: NCTE.

Mills, C. Wright. 1956. *The Power Elite*. New York: Oxford University Press.

Milton, John. 1957. *Paradise Lost*. In *John Milton Complete Poems and Major Prose*, ed. Merritt Y. Hughes, 211–469. New York: MacMillian.

Mittlin, Lawrie. 1999. "Pediatricians Suggest Limits on TV Viewing by Children." *New York Times*, August 4.

Morin, Richard. 2006. "Is 'The Daily Show' Bad for Democracy?" *Unconventional Wisdom*. *Washington Post*, June 23, p. A02.

Morning edition. 2007. National Public Radio. April 3.

Moyers, Bill. 2007. "Buying the War." *Bill Moyers Journal*. April 25.

Mouffe, Chantal. 2000. *The Democratic Paradox*. London: Verso.

Mr. Smith Goes to Washington. 1939. Dir. Frank Capra. Perf. James Stewart, Jean Arthur, Claude Rains, Edward Arnold, Guy Kibbee, Charles Lane, and Thomas Mitchell. Columbia Pictures.

Muckelbauer, John. 2000. "On Reading Differently: Through Foucault's Resistance." *College English* 63.1 (September): 71–94.

Murray, Donald. 2003. "Teach Writing as a Process Not Product." In *Cross-Talk in Comp Theory: A Reader*, 2nd ed., ed. Victor Villanueva, 3–6. Urbana, IL: NCTE.

Neel, Jasper. 1988. *Plato, Derrida, and Writing*. Carbondale: Southern Illinois University Press.

Newkirk, Thomas. 1997. *The Performance of Self in Student Writing*. Portsmouth, NH: Heinemann.

Nietzsche, Friedrich. 1937. *The Birth of Tragedy. The Philosophy of Nietzsche*. Translated by Clifton Fadiman. New York: The Modern Library.

Norris, Christopher. 1997. *Against Relativism: Philosophy of Science, Deconstruction and Critical Theory*. Oxford: Blackwell.

Obama, Barack. 2006. *The Audacity of Hope: Thoughts on Reclaiming the American Dream*. New York: Crown.

O'Brien, David. 2005. *Constitutional Law and Politics: Civil Rights and Civil Liberties*. Vol. 2, 6th ed. New York: Norton.

Ong, Walter J. 1962. *The Barbarian Within: And Other Fugitive Essays and Studies*. New York: Macmillan.

Ong, Walter J. 1978. "Literacy and Orality in our Times." *ADE Bulletin* 58 (September): 1–7.

Ong, Walter J. 1982. *Orality and Literacy: The Technologizing of the Word*. London: Methuen.

Ong, Walter J. 1986. "Writing is a Technology that Restructures Thought." In *The Written Word: Literacy in Transition*, ed. Gerd Baumann, 23–50. Oxford: Clarendon.

Paine, Charles. 1999. *The Resistant Writer: Rhetoric as Immunity, 1850 to the Present*. Albany: State University of New York Press.

Patton, Paul. 1995. Introduction. In *The Gulf War Did Not Take Place*, ed. Jean Baudrillard, 1–21, trans. Paul Patton. Bloomington: Indiana University Press.

Payne, Allison, Denise Gottfredson, and Gary Gottfredson. 2003. "Schools as Communities: The Relationships among Communal School Organization, Student Bonding, and School Disorder." *Criminology* 41.3 (August): 749–78.

Pearson, Geoffrey. 1983. *Hooligan: A History of Respectable Fears*. New York: Schocken.

Penrod, Diane. 1997. "Pop Goes the Content: Teaching the Ugly and the Ordinary." In *Miss Grundy Doesn't Teach Here Anymore: Popular Culture and the Composition Classroom*, ed. Diane Penrod, 1–21. Portsmouth, NH: Heinemann.

Phillips, Kevin. 2002. *Wealth and Democracy: A Political History of the American Rich*. New York: Broadway.

Plato. 1990. *Gorgias or On Rhetoric; Reputative*. In *The Rhetorical Tradition: Readings from Classical Times to the Present*, ed. Patricia Bizzell and Bruce Herzberg, 61–112. Boston, MA: Bedford/St. Martin's.

Plato. 1998. *The Apology: Classics of Philosophy*. Edited by Louis P. Pojman. New York: Oxford University Press.

Plato. 2001. *Phaedrus or On the Beautiful; Ethical*. In *The Rhetorical Tradition: Readings from Classical Times to the Present*, 2nd ed., ed. Patricia Bizzell and Bruce Herzberg, 138–68. Boston, MA: Bedford/St. Martin's.

Poster, Carol. 1993. "Plato's Unwritten Doctrines: A Hermeneutic Problem in Rhetorical Historiography." *PRE/TEXT* 14.1–2: 128–38.

Postman, Neil. 1985. *Amusing Ourselves to Death: Public Discourse in the Age of Show Business*. New York: Penguin.

Quandahl, Ellen. 1989. "What is Plato: Inference and Allusion in Plato's *Sophist?*" *Rhetoric Review* 7: 338–51.

Rich, Frank. 2005a. "A High-Tech Lynching in Prime Time." *New York Times*, April 24.

Rich, Frank. 2005b. "Enron, the Model for Bush's Fake News." *New York Times*, reprinted in the *Akron Beacon Journal*, March 21.

Robertson, Pat. 2005. "Robertson apologizes for assassination call." CNN.com. August 25. http://www.cnn.com/2005/US/08/24/robertson.chavez/. Accessed December 14, 2006.

Robertson, Pat. 2006a. "Pat Robertson clarifies his statement regarding Hugo Chavez." *The Official Site of Pat Robertson*. http://www.patrobertson.com/pressreleases/hugochavez.asp. Accessed December 14, 2006.Robertson, Pat. 2006b. Transcript. *The 700 Club*. Christian Broadcast Network. August 22. http://www.mediamatters.org/items/200508220006. Accessed December 14, 2006.

Rosenblatt, Louise. 1993. "The Transactional Theory: Against Dualisms." *College English* 55.4 (April): 377–86.

Saletan, William. 2006. "Master Sunshine: The Overzealous War on Indoor Tanning." http://www.slate.com/default.aspx?id=2141649&nav/tap1. Accessed May 13, 2006.

Salmon, Charles, and Theodore Glasser. 1995. "The Politics of Polling and the Limits of Consent." In *Public Opinion and the Communication of Consent*, ed. Charles Salmon and Theodore Glasser, 437–58. New York: Guilford.

Sampson, Robert, and Dawn Bartusch. 1998. "Legal Cynicism and (Subcultural?) Tolerance of Deviance: The Neighborhood Context of Racial Differences." *Law & Society Review* 32.4: 777–804.

Sarat, Austin, and Thomas Kearns, eds. 1995. *Law's Violence*. Ann Arbor: University of Michigan Press.

Scahill, Jeremy. 2007. *Blackwater: The Rise of the World's Most Powerful Mercenary Army*. New York: Nation.

Scarborough, Joe. 2006. *Scarborough Country*. Hosted by Joe Scarborough. MSNBC. September 12.

Schattschneider, E. E. 1975. *The Semisovereign People: A Realist's View of Democracy in America*. New York: Harcourt Brace.

Scheingold, Stuart. 1984. *The Politics of Law and Order: Street Crime and Public Policy*. New York: Longman.

Schener, Jeffrey. 1999. *The Sound Bite Society: Television and the American Mind.* New York: Four Walls Eight Windows.

Schlosser, Eric. 2002. *Fast Food Nation: The Dark Side of the All-American Meal.* New York: HarperCollins.

Schor, Juliet. 2004. *Born to Buy: The Commercialized Child and the New Consumer Culture.* New York: Scribner.

Scribner, Sylvia, and Michael Cole. 1981. *The Psychology of Literacy.* Cambridge, MA: Harvard University Press.

Selfe, Cynthia L. 2004. "Students Who Teach Us: A Case Study of a New Media Text Designer." In *Writing New Media: Theory and Applications for Expanding the Teaching of Composition,* ed. Anne Frances Wysocki et al., 43–66. Logan: Utah State University Press.

Sennett, Richard. 1970. *The Uses of Disorder: Personal Identity and City Life.* New York: Knopf.

Shiller, Robert. 2000. *Irrational Exuberance.* Princeton, NJ: Princeton University Press.

Shnayerson, Michael. 2007. "A Convenient Untruth." *Vanity Fair* (May): 142–62.

Shogan, Colleen. 2007. "Anti-Intellectualism in the Modern Presidency: A Republican Populism." *Perspectives on Politics* 5.1 (June): 295–303.

Silverstone, Roger. 1991. "Television, Rhetoric, and the Return of the Unconscious in Secondary Oral Culture." In *Media, Consciousness, and Culture: Explorations of Walter Ong's Thought,* ed. Bruce E. Gronbeck, Thomas J. Farrell, and Paul A. Soukup, 147–59. Newbury Park, CA: Sage.

Simon, Jonathan. 2007. *Governing Through Crime: How the War on Crime Transformed American Democracy and Created a Culture of Fear.* New York: Oxford University Press.

Sloterdijk, Peter. 1987. *Critique of Cynical Reason.* Translated by Michael Eldred. Minneapolis: University of Minnesota Press.

Smith, Jeffrey. 2003. *Seeds of Deception: Exposing Industry and Government Lies about the Safety of the Genetically Engineered Foods You're Eating.* Fairfield, IA: Yes! Books.

Smith, Mark. 2000. *American Business and Political Power: Public Opinion, Elections, and Democracy.* Chicago, IL: University of Chicago Press.

Stafford, Barbara Maria. 1996. *Good Looking: Essays on the Virtue of Images.* Cambridge, MA: MIT Press.

Steger, Manfred, and Nancy Lind, eds. 1999. *Violence and Its Alternatives: An Interdisciplinary Reader.* New York: St. Martin's Press.

Stephens, Mitchell. 1998. *The Rise of the Image, the Fall of the Word.* Oxford: University of Oxford Press.

Stone, Clarence. 1989. *Regime Politics: Governing Atlanta, 1946–1988.* Lawrence: University of Kansas Press.

Sunshine, Jason, and Tom Tyler. 2003. "The Role of Procedural Justice and Legitimacy in Shaping Public Support for Policing." *Law & Society Review* 37.3: 513–47.

Svehla, Lance. 2001. "Philosopher-Kings and Teacher-Researchers: The Charge of Anti-Intellectualism in Composition's Theory Wars." *TETYC* 28.4 (May): 383–92.

Svehla, Lance. 2006. "The Supremacy of the Image: Urban Students and the Idea of Secondary Orality." *EAPSU Online: A Journal of Critical and Creative Work* 3 (Fall): 83–107.

Thornton, Patricia, and Thomas Thornton. 2002. "Blowback." In *Collateral Language: A User's Guide to America's New War*, ed. John Collins and Ross Glover, 27–38. New York: New York University Press.

Truss, Lynne. 2006. *Eats, Shoots & Leaves: Why Commas Really Do Make a Difference!* New York: Putnam & Sons.

Tyler, Tom, and Robert Boeckmann. 1997. "Three Strikes and You are Out, But Why? The Psychology of Public Support for Punishing Rule Breakers." *Law and Society Review* 31.2: 200–14.

Vedantam, Shankar. 2007. "The Decoy Effect, or How to Win an Election." *Washington Post*, April 2, p. A03.

Veyne, Paul. 1988. *Did the Greeks Believe Their Myths? An Essay on the Constitutive Imagination*. Chicago, IL: University of Chicago Press.

Vitanza, Victor. 1987a. "Critical Sub/Versions of the History of Philosophical Rhetoric." *Rhetoric Review* 6: 41–65.

Vitanza, Victor. 1987b. " 'Notes' Towards Historiographies of Rhetorics; or the Rhetorics of the Histories of Rhetorics: Traditional, Revisionary, and Sub/Versive." *PRE/TEXT* 8.1–2: 63–125.

Vitanza, Victor. 1991. "Three Countertheses: Or, A Critical In(ter)vention into Composition Theories and Pedagogies." In *Contending with Words: Composition and Rhetoric in a Postmodern Age*, ed. Patricia Harkin and John Schilb, 139–72. New York: MLA.

Vitanza, Victor. 1999. " 'The Wasteland Grows'; Or, What is 'Cultural Studies for Composition' and Why Must We Always Speak Good of It?" *JAC* 19.4 (Fall): 699–703.

Wacquant, Loic. 2001. "Deadly Symbiosis: When Ghetto and Prison Meet and Mesh." *Punishment & Society* 3.1: 95–134.

Weiner, Tim. 2006. "Must We Destroy the CIA to Save It?" *Akron Beacon Journal* [Akron, OH], May 17, p. B2.

Weissman, Steve. 2005. "America's Religious Right—Saints or Subversives?" *Truthout Investigation*, July 26.

West, Cornel. 1988. "Interview with Cornel West." In *Universal Abandon? The Politics of Postmodernism*, ed. Andrew Ross, 269–86. Minneapolis: University of Minnesota Press.

West, Cornel. 1994. *Race Matters*. New York. Vintage.

West, Cornel. 1996. "Diverse New World." In *Left, Right, and Center: Voices from Across the Political Spectrum*, ed. Robert Atwan and Jon Roberts, 46–51. Boston, MA: Bedford/St. Martin's.

White, David A. 1993. *Rhetoric and Reality in Plato's Phaedrus*. Albany: State University of New York Press.

Williams, Bronwyn. 2002. *Tuned In: Television and the Teaching of Writing.* Portsmouth, NH: Heinemann.

Wittgenstien, Ludwig. 1937. *Culture and Values.* Chicago, IL: University of Chicago Press.

Worsham, Lynn. 2002. "Coming to Terms: Theory, Writing, Politics." In *Rhetoric and Composition as Intellectual Work,* ed. Gary A. Olson, 101–14. Carbondale: Southern Illinois University Press.

York, Brian. 2005. *The Vast Left Wing Conspiracy: The Untold Story.* New York: Crown Forum.

Zaller, John. 1992. *The Nature and Origins of Mass Opinion.* New York: Cambridge University Press.

Zipp, John, and Rudy Fenwick. 2006. "Is the Academy a Liberal Hegemony? The Political Orientations and Educational Values of Professors." *Public Opinion Quarterly* 7.3 (Fall): 304–26.

Index